Buying & Owning Property in Central Florida

The essential guide for the sensible buyer!

Garrett Kenny

authorHOUSE®

AuthorHouse™
1663 Liberty Drive
Bloomington, IN 47403
www.authorhouse.com
Phone: 1-800-839-8640

Published by AuthorHouse 12/30/2014

ISBN: 978-1-4969-6160-0 (sc)
ISBN: 978-1-4969-6159-4 (hc)
ISBN: 978-1-4969-6161-7 (e)

Library of Congress Control Number: 2014923001

ACKNOWLEDGEMENTS

I dedicate this book to my wife Angela, my son Aidan and my daughter Brooke: without your love and support I could not have achieved so much. And to Dad, Mum and my sister Levina - I wish you were still here and were able to share all this with us

Important Note

Florida is large and varied. Even Central Florida covers thousands of square miles and contains over a million homes.

Practice and procedure vary from place to place. Sometimes, they can vary even between officials working in the same office in the same town. The differences can be substantial.

Please also remember that the law, practice and procedure changes frequently. This book is up-to-date as of March 2014. It is, therefore, essential that before you take any major decisions or commit yourself to any course of action (particularly one that will be difficult of expensive to undo) you seek reliable local advice.

That advice will, in most cases, come via your Realtor – licensed real estate agent – if it is related to the purchase of your property or, otherwise, from a lawyer practising in the area where you are thinking of buying and specialising in the relevant area of the law.

Thank-yous

Looking back, it seems that thanks are due to so many people for helping me in my life - more than I can include in the short acknowledgment in this book.

So, to all who have played any positive part in my home life, early years, my work and business world, I offer you my thanks and gratitude.

Those I must mention are:

My wife, Angela and children, Aidan and Brooke – thank-you for putting up with my 17-hour work days!

Lorcan Claffey, my Chief Financial Officer and friend of 20 years, who tolerates me every day!

My long-term friend in Ireland, Patrick Mc Carthy, whom I have known since 1978 and was a great influence, especially in my early days

Brendan Mc Donnell, an Irish businessman who backed me financially when I needed to buy my second truck in Ireland and gave me a personal loan because he had faith in me – and was fully repaid!

I would like to offer special thanks to the team at OPP who have not only helped to put this book together, but who have helped me and Feltrim enormously over the last 15 years to get to where we are today. Xavier, Naomi, John, Mina and Martin – thank-you.

My one regret is not being able to bring my Mum and Dad to Florida on vacation, as it was too late in life for them to travel.

Last of all, I thank my sister, Levina, who passed away in 2009, aged 40, for the part she played in my life. Cancer took her away from me.

Disclaimer

This book is intended to be of general interest and to provide some useful orientation for those thinking of buying a property in Central Florida, although it will be just as useful to those buying in other parts of Florida. It is not intended to provide detailed legal or other specialist advice. It can, self-evidently, not take into account any of your personal circumstances and it is, by its very nature, a brief overview of some fairly complicated topics. **It is absolutely no substitute for taking your own legal or other professional advice**. Neither the author nor the publishers accept any responsibility for any action taken or not taken as a result of reading this book.

Whilst we have taken great care whilst writing this book, we do not accept responsibility for any errors in it or omissions from it.

Unless specifically stated, any reference to a person or company is not an endorsement or recommendation of their service.

About The Author

Gary Kenny leads by example. His secret behind being a successful real estate developer and entrepreneur is simple, but effective: he works hard and he plays hard – and he expects his staff to do the same. "I don't ask people to do something I can't do," he says.

What really motivates the down-to-earth Chief Executive Officer of the Florida-based Feltrim Group of Companies is planning, constructing and selling top-quality developments. "I take great pride in planning a project, taking it through to the building stage and then seeing the final product. It gives me a great sense of pride when we deliver a top-class project."

But the reward that the friendly Irish ex-pat gets from building homes of the highest class is more than mere satisfaction; it is also the key to a flourishing business. With more than 25 years' experience in the real estate business behind him, Gary knows that a well-finished product not only achieves a higher sale price, but top-quality developments sell out more quickly than mediocre projects with poor finishes.

Having such a commitment to excellent customer service comes at a high personal cost to himself and his family, and Gary regularly puts in 17-hour days. So why does he do this? The story begins, just like many thousands of others, when Gary – whose full name is Garrett – and his family took a holiday in Florida, in the 1980s. They loved the sunshine state, its amenities, theme parks and relaxed way of life and wanted to spend more holidays there, which eventually led to them buying their first vacation home in 1996.

Now, Gary and his wife, Angela, and children, Aidan (9) and Brooke (6) are based in Florida full-time, but the fulfilment of that dream has never left him and Gary is passionate about helping others find their ideal holiday home or even helping clients emigrate and live in the US permanently, as Feltrim offers "the full service real estate experience, from finding your dream home, through to completion and beyond."

The business leader has a deserved reputation for being down-to-earth and always keeps in mind the maxim, 'I know what I don't know', which is why he works alongside excellent staff, who are just as committed to providing top-quality customer service. "I buy in the knowledge we need or lack. I like to work with a good team around me that can challenge me and the project. I don't like 'yes' men, that just agree with me because I am the boss." If Gary doesn't know the answer to a problem or question, he goes away and researches it himself or finds an expert who can help.

Gary was born in Dublin on 19 March 1962. After leaving school, he went on to work in logistics, warehousing, commercial and residential property development, and sales and marketing. In total, the Feltrim Group has sold real estate worth more than US$600million and he and the Feltrim Group of Companies have won numerous industry awards.

He is a lifelong entrepreneur and has created, established and operated various successful business projects in the USA and abroad, including a trucking business in Ireland, which embraced his love of music and gave him a taste of the 'rock 'n' roll' lifestyle.

"I actually toured with Meat Loaf in the early 90s with my trucking company in Ireland during three weeks of gigs. My first live concert was the Boomtown Rats and Bob Geldof in Ireland, but the best rock and roll band is U2 – great music, a great band and great individuals."

Like many, Gary also enjoys movies and reading – although with such a large work commitment, he does not have much time for either. In fact, he will often buy a book on impulse and not read it until three or four years later! His favourite genre is counter intelligence stories; true-life tales about the FBI, CIA and MI5. He also enjoys reading biographies of business leaders, including Richard Branson, Warren Buffet and Donald Trump.

Gary's love of movies is one way he is able to switch off from work. It all stems from the fact that, as a teenager, he made home movies featuring school friends, including an anti-litter and anti-smoking documentary. At the time, he wanted to work in the movie industry, but there were no real opportunities available. Action films are his favourite and he particularly enjoys watching Bond movies, with their spectacular cars, gadgets – and beautiful women! His favourite actors – whom Gary would love to meet – are Robert De Niro and Al Pacino and his number one actress is Angelina Jolie.

Since his early days, Gary has been a fan of fast cars, and among the first models he owned were a Toyota Celica Sport and Audi Quattro. But the marque he most admires is the ultimate in speed and style, the Ferrari and he is fortunate enough to own one, which is well used. Gary has driven his Ferrari on the racetrack, has passed his advanced driving course in it and has even taken part, with 49 other drivers, in a Ferrari rally across California, from Napa Valley to Monterey.

An important part of the 'playing hard' element of Gary's life is the precious time he spends with family and the 'everyday simple things'. "I enjoy spending time with my wife and kids. We spend weekends doing family stuff, like visiting Disney or playing crazy golf. Aidan enjoys soccer and I enjoy watching him. When he plays, he is very competitive. I enjoy listening to Brooke telling me funny stories about school and watch her drawing pictures of Mommy and Daddy. She comes out with some amazing sentences for a six-year-old! One special time we had together was when I went to Hawaii for my fiftieth birthday and stayed at the Disney Aulani Resort. It was really fantastic!"

Gary is acutely aware that he has a lot to be thankful for – including his family, colleagues and friends. These include Lorcan Claffey "my Chief Financial Officer at Feltrim and friend of twenty years, who tolerates me every day." His long-term friend in Ireland, Patrick McCarthy, whom he has known since 1978, and has been a strong influence, particularly in the early days, and Gary is also grateful to Irish businessman Brendan McDonnell, who backed him financially when he needed to buy his 2CD truck in Ireland. "I didn't have the money, so he gave me a personal loan because he had faith in me – and he was fully repaid."

With all he has to be thankful for, Gary also has had a few sorrows in his life. Two specific regrets are never being able to bring his Mum and Dad on vacation to Florida, as they were too old to travel, and the passing away of his sister, who looked after his business interests in Ireland. She sadly died in 2009 at the age of 40. "Cancer took her away from me and I still miss her so much."

Gary's life in underlined by the simple belief: "treat others as you expect people to treat you. Follow that, and you can't go far wrong," he says.

FELTRIM,
WE STRIVE TO EXCEED YOUR EXPECTATIONS

BY OFFERING COMPREHENSIVE, INNOVATIVE, QUALITY-INFUSED PRODUCTS
AND SERVICES, COUPLED WITH THE HIGHEST LEVEL OF CUSTOMER CARE

- Established in Florida for 18 years. All our properties are in central Florida
- Foreclosed properties start from $56,000
- "One stop shop" developer and full rental & maintenance management all in-house

Contact us today:

garrett@feltrim.com
001 407 922 2806
www.c21teamfeltrim.com

Contents

Foreword

Why did I want to write this book?

I started living in Central Florida in 1996 and moved here permanently in 2001. I have since built up a very successful business developing, selling and managing property in Central Florida

> *1,100 people per day move to Central Florida*

Based in Orlando, my two companies are Feltrim Developments and C21 Team Feltrim. The development company has successfully built over 600 residential units both for the local owner-occupier and the international investor and holiday homebuyer. Feltrim Developments has also been responsible for a variety of commercial developments including retail and office units. We currently have about 650 commercial and residential properties under management and also manage six HOAs – Home Owners' Associations.

Century21 Team Feltrim has three sales offices in the Orlando area employing about 50 Realtors and licensed sales agents.

I work in the business with my wife Angela. We share a passion for Central Florida and we are so confident about its future that we have invested a large part of our family's wealth in real estate in the area.

The more I look at the books and guides available to those who want to join us here in Florida – whether as the owners of a holiday home or an investment property or as people coming to settle in the sun - the more I have become depressed about the poor quality of the materials available.

I know how many things can appear worrying to someone not familiar with the way things are done here and I know just how many things I know today that I really wish I had been aware of when I first came to Florida.

So I decided to put pen to paper.

I hope you find this book easy to understand, interesting and – above all – useful.

My aims are simple:

- to give you a short, readable and practical outline to buying property in Central Florida;
- to help you understand and solve the problems involved
- to save you time, stress and money.

In short, I will deal with the "must knows".

I will also explain the significance and importance of some of the choices you will have to make. This is not always obvious!

In addition, I will link you to sources with fuller information.

What you will NOT find in this book are discussions about the best restaurants in the area or descriptions of the various attractions in Orlando. If you are buying this book, you will be happy to get that information from other (and better) sources.

Finally, although I have worked in the Florida real estate industry for over 15 years, this book is only a general guide and does not constitute legal or other advice.

If you are thinking of buying a property or doing business in another country **ALWAYS** take professional advice.

Introduction

In this book I focus on buying property (real estate – I use the words interchangeably) in Central Florida but almost everything in it applies equally to any purchase anywhere in Florida.

I focus on Central Florida because this is my "patch". I know the area within 15 miles of Disney like the back of my hand and the area within 25 miles of Disney very well.

Central Florida is not an official region or geographical area and so it doesn't have an exact definition. Most people would agree that its centre is the Orlando area and that it roughly stretches as far as Daytona in the North East, Cape Canaveral in the South East and Tampa in the West.

If you are working in the real estate industry, it is incredibly important to know the area where you are based really well. That includes having a comprehensive knowledge of every neighbourhood, every developer, every project, all of the community facilities, the political background etc. If you are choosing a real estate company to work with, it is just as important that you choose a company with that level of knowledge. I am constantly surprised by people selling property in my area who know very little about it – in the case of some of the overseas companies, the person may only have visited the area two or three times.

Let's get one thing clear right at the beginning. Buying a property in Central Florida is as safe as – or safer than - buying a property anywhere else in the world. The combination of the rigorous training of lawyers and estate agents (Realtors™) and the strength and independence of the US legal system make it a safe haven for investors of all nationalities.

On reading a book such as this – which must explain the potential pitfalls if it is to serve any useful purpose – it can seem a frightening or dangerous experience. But if you go about the purchase in the right way, it is not dangerous and should not be frightening. The same or similar dangers arise when buying a house in your own country. You do not worry about those dangers because you are familiar with them and, more importantly, because you are shielded against contact with most of them by your professional advisers. The same should be true when buying in Florida. Read this book to understand the background and why some of the problems exist. Ask the professionals to advise you about any issues that worry you and leave them to avoid the landmines!

Terminology

There are a few preliminary points to deal with in order to save time later.

Sex

I am told this is always a good way to start a book or, in this case, a section of a book. I am, of course, talking about nothing more vulgar than the unfortunate lack, in the English language, of a simple but neutral way of describing a person. The generic "he" can cause offence. "S/he" seems contrived and, in any case, the method cannot be extended to the "his/hers" choice. The use of "they" for the singular is confusing. And in a world where printing costs, and the writer's fees, are determined by the thousand words, repeatedly saying "he, she or they" or "his, her or their" is expensive as well as tedious for the reader. So I will generally use "he" or "him". Sorry!

Estate Agents

Estate agents are referred to by several different names, some of them polite. In the UK, estate agents; in Ireland, auctioneers; in the US, Realtors (though, strictly speaking, only a person who is a member of the Realtor™ franchise can call himself a Realtor) or property brokers. For the purposes of this book I am going to treat them as being all the same and refer to them, collectively, as Realtors. Sorry again!

Money

Many people have difficulty in understanding funny foreign money so I will generally give prices in US dollars ($) with an approximate conversion into £ sterling (£), euro (€), Renminbi (¥) and Rubles (RUB). Exchange rates, of course, vary wildly over time and in a few years the figures given will probably be treated with either nostalgia or amusement.

At the time of writing March 2014:

- $1 = approximately £0.61, €0.73, ¥6.22 and RUB-36.32
- £1 = approximately €1.20, $1.-65, ¥-10.27 and RUB-59.88
- €1 = approximately £0.84, $1.38, ¥8.59 and RUB50.08
- ¥1 = approximately £0.097, $0.16, €0.12 and RUB5.83
- RUB = approximately £0.017, $0.028, €0.02 and ¥0.17

Prices

Prices quoted are usually only rough estimates.

Useful Addresses & Telephone Numbers

At the end of each chapter I include a list of useful addresses and telephone numbers. Any organisations referred to in the chapter should (with a bit of luck!) be on the list.

Law

Legal systems vary greatly around the world and, quite often, they use similar words to mean very different things. Therefore, whenever possible, I will explain the relevant US legal terms by reference to the words used to explain the same concept in other legal systems

Initial Research

If you're going to spend a lot of money on a house, you should do some research first. Obvious? Yes, but surprisingly few people follow this advice. Some will get away with it. I know several people who have bought homes in Florida 'on a whim' and who have ended up buying a property that they really love: a property that might even have made them some money. I know many more who would admit that they made a mistake. Some have bought the wrong property in the wrong place. Some have paid too much for the house. Some have paid more than they can really afford. Some have just structured the purchase in a way that is going to cost them a great deal of completely unnecessary tax.

So, right at the beginning of this book, let us be clear. Going to look at a property should be the last stage of your journey, not the first.

Even smart, professional people can get this wrong. An accountant from Ireland was on vacation in Florida and, on a day out, saw and bought an investment apartment. The seller had promised that the property would pay him a rental income of $250 per night. He signed the contract without checking out this or anything else about his purchase. Such an income was just impossible. To pay him $250, the rental agency would have to be generating nearly $500 in order to allow for the commission paid to the travel agent and the costs associated with the letting. The property was just not worth this amount. Sure enough, 4 or 5 months later the buyer came to see me to ask whether we would take over the management of this property. Not only had he not received his $250 per night, he had not been paid anything at all: an expensive mistake that could have been avoided completely if he had carried out a bit of research before buying.

Some people think that all this is just making the whole thing too complicated. They will research the fuel consumption, performance and likely depreciation of the car they're going to buy, but not the suitability or performance of the expensive property investment that they're about to make. If you share this view, I suggest you skip to the next chapter. Just don't blame me when it goes wrong.

I am not suggesting that you need to investigate all of the things set out in this chapter. Some will not concern you. Others you will already know. However, the process of thinking about the purchase of your home is not only useful, but also a part of what should be the great adventure of buying it. So, with that in mind, here are a few of the things that you might want to think about.

Understand the System

The system of buying and selling property in Florida is, not surprisingly, different from the system of buying property wherever you might live. On balance, it will probably be neither better nor worse – just different It may have many superficial similarities, which can lull you into a false sense of familiarity and over confidence. *The most important thing to remember is that buying a home in Florida is just as safe as buying a property back*

home – providing that you take the right professional advice and precautions when doing so. If you do not take such advice there are many expensive traps for the unwary.

Select an Area

You cannot scour the whole of Florida, or even the whole of Central Florida, looking for a property. It is just too big. Those who do not narrow down the scope of their search fairly early on tend to go round and round in ever decreasing circles and never buy a property. No area is perfect. It is all a question of personal preference. Yet there is, behind it all, a logical process of selection that, if used sensibly, can help you choose an area – or, more likely, eliminate others.

Fix a Budget

Fix a budget for the operation. What is the maximum that you are prepared to spend to end up with a house ready to live in? Include the cost of purchase, any essential repairs or improvements and the taxes and fees payable.

If you are buying a new property or one that does not need major repair this is fairly simple.

If you are buying a house in need of repair, fixing a budget is clearly more difficult. You will always underestimate the cost of the repairs. No job ever finishes exactly on budget! Buyers, however, create a rod for their own backs by their unrealistic costings. Often the extent of repairs needed goes far beyond what is obvious. It is just as expensive to repair a roof or rewire in Florida as it is back home. Remember that Florida has a challenging climate, with temperatures going into the 90s sometimes combined with 100% humidity. This is a recipe for decay of wooden structures, however well protected they may be. ***If you are buying a property that needs major work, do not commit yourself until you have had an inspection (UK survey) and builders estimates for the work shown to be necessary.*** If you are told that there is no time for this and that you will lose the property if you can't sign today/this week/before Easter, walk away or insist on putting a condition in the contract making the sale subject to a satisfactory outcome to these enquiries.

When thinking about the costs of the purchase, a rough rule of thumb is to allow 2% of the price for fees and taxes, if you are not taking out a mortgage and 4% if you are. Either way, if you intend to use a lawyer (which, as we shall see, is usually not the practise in ordinary purchase transactions), you should add an extra 1% for their fees. You should get some change out of these amounts, but they are a good planning aid.

Sellers' Market

At this point it is probably worth pointing out that the property market in Central Florida is currently turning into a sellers' market.

After 5 years of crisis and dramatic falls in the price of real estate, the market is recovering. The April Case-Schiller survey of property prices – probably the most well-known and respected measure of the US property market – showed that prices in the US as a whole rose 9.3% in the preceding year. Prices in the Orlando area have risen well above that rate. They are still well short of 2006 levels, but the combination of low mortgage rates, better availability of mortgage finance, greater consumer confidence and the feeling that prices will continue to rise is bringing many people back into the market. When you couple this with a shortage of stock (because many people are unwilling or unable to sell at prices so much lower than what they paid for the property) a sellers' market is created. This is a market where the sellers feel that they can push for higher prices and dictate, for example, the speed with which the transaction will have to take place.

Orlando Prices – an Example
2 bedroom, 2 bathroom
condominium apartment in the
popular Tuscana development in
the Davenport area of the city.
Price in 2006: $350,000
Price in 2009: $65,000
Price in 2012: $100,000
Price in March 2014: $125,000.
Note that this price is still well
below the cost of construction
of the property – always a
good sign of a bargain.

Why Are You Buying?

Most extraordinary of all is the fact that so few people ask themselves this very basic question. Are they buying a holiday home? Are they buying a place for future retirement? Are they buying the property as an investment? Is it, perhaps, a holiday home that you want to pay its way or, at least, come close to covering its running costs? If you are not clear about these most basic issues you cannot expect the adventure to end well. I have lost count of the number of times that a couple have had a minor 'matrimonial' in my office when it turns out that the husband thinks they are buying an investment and the wife thinks they're buying a holiday home. Or, of course, the other way round.

I tell them to go away and discuss it over dinner. They are usually back the following morning with a clearer idea of what they want to do.

Buying a Property as an Investment

Why are you buying?

If you're buying property as a pure investment then you will want to buy a property that is going to generate new income or a capital gain: -or preferably both. You will want the results of your due diligence to indicate, pretty clearly, that this is going to happen.

If you're buying a property that you want to use as a holiday home, but let for part of the time to cover all or part of its running costs, then your analysis of its potential as an investment may be a little less rigorous, but the analysis should still be done. In this case, you may attach more importance to how well the property suits your requirements as a holiday home and accept the limitations that flow from that. For example, if you want a property located in the middle of the countryside, you have to accept that such a property will not be as productive a letting proposition as a property located in the city or by the sea. However, even if this is your plan, it might be as well to think about the extent to which you're prepared to make compromises in your holiday preferences if those compromises are going to improve the financial performance of the investment. Would you be prepared to buy a property located a little nearer to where there is popular demand? Would you be prepared to buy a property that is a more attractive letting proposition? Would you be prepared to buy a property with less inherent running costs (for example, with smaller grounds or without a swimming pool)?

If you are looking to combine a holiday home with something that will make you a little money, you can help yourself a great deal by only using the property in the low season – in Orlando, the first two weeks in September, the first two weeks in October, the first two weeks in November and the first two weeks in January. You can also help by finding your own tenants to supplement the efforts of your management company, especially during this low season period. Getting your neighbours, family and friends to visit at this time will create extra income at very little extra cost and so significantly improve your bottom line.

What is your attitude to risk and reward?

Every investment carries some risk. Some carry a great deal more risk than others.

One of the most common misapprehensions amongst the people that I see is that they misunderstand the nature of risk and reward. They assume, because it seems intuitive to do so, that the greater the risk, the greater the reward. This is simply not true. There are many property investments that carry truly astronomical amounts of risk and yet come nowhere close to providing the potential for reward, appropriate to the level of risk that you are taking. Conversely, there are many property investments where the risk factor is relatively low and yet the likely rewards surprisingly high.

For most people, this second type of property will be the better bet.

As an aside, I believe that Central Florida is a great investment destination as well as a great destination for a holiday home, for the same basic reason: Disney.

When you see the thriving city of Orlando today – with well over 2 million people living in the area and an average of 1 million visitors per week – it is hard to imagine that, only 40 years ago, Orlando was a small, sleepy farming town of less than 300,000 people.

When Disney started buying land in the 1970s, they paid $100 per acre. Today, if you could buy an acre near the theme parks, it would cost you over $125,000.

The Walt Disney World Resort has been so successful it has attracted many other theme parks to the area, making Orlando "The Theme Park Capital of the World". It is these theme parks that attract millions of visitors. Not just parents with children, but conferences (Orlando is now the largest conference centre in the US) and sporting events. These visitors create a huge demand for rental accommodation and many prefer to stay in houses and condos. The huge amount of economic activity also draws in many people from other parts of the US, keen to work in this booming economy and all of this drives demand for property.

But I digress.

I encourage potential buyers (and, if they are a couple, they should do this separately) to rate themselves on a scale of 1 to 10. A person with a score of 1 is truly risk averse: the sort of person who throws out a can of food on the very day it reaches its 'sell by' date. A person with a score of 10 is happy to go bungee jumping. Often, you will find that the two people in a couple have very different scores. In these cases, it is not simply a question of working out the average. It is a question of working out the level of risk with which both will be comfortable.

What is your attitude to diversification?

Some investors are content to have all their eggs in one basket. For some, the one property that they're buying will be their only investment of any size. Such concentration of your funds is probably not a good idea and it is certainly not something that would be recommended by most investment professionals. Yet some investors have only limited funds and really like the idea of investing in real estate. In this case, limited or no diversification might be the price they have to pay and that they are prepared to pay. However, even these investors would be well advised to think about the possibility of a co-ownership scheme (program), with a share in several properties rather than the outright ownership of only one property.

Other investors are absolutely insistent on diversification of their investment portfolio. Some have rigid percentages from which they will not deviate. Often, those percentages will change as the years go by, to reflect their changing investment objectives and financial situation.

One of the figures may be the percentage of their total assets that they wish to see invested in real estate. A second might be the percentage that they wish to see invested in overseas real estate. Another could be the maximum amount, or the maximum percentage, of the overseas real estate pot that they would wish to see placed in any one investment, or in any one country, or in any one type of property. This might sound a little complicated and, quite clearly, a certain amount of flexibility is probably a good idea, but the basic principle is sensible.

For the investor in overseas real estate who wants to build a diversified portfolio of international real estate, it is beyond the scope of this book to address all the necessary issues such as: How to choose real estate assets in different parts of the world that mesh together and form a sensible, balanced whole, taking into account the investment prospects in different parts of the world, the currency prospects in those countries and the relative merits of the different categories of real estate (residential, commercial, land etc.) that are available

If building a diversified property portfolio, it can make a lot of sense to take some professional advice. This can help you filter the masses of information that is available and choose the most beneficial combinations of countries, areas and types of property. Doing the research necessary to make the best decision takes far more time than most people are prepared to invest and there are simply too many choices and too much information for most people to process. Professional advice need not be expensive.

Even if you are buying just one investment property, it is worth discussing your needs with a good Realtor who really understands the area. Just like in your own country, some places and some types of property will rent better than others. Choosing the property that best meets your requirements can make a huge difference to the performance of your investment.

I remember one client who wanted to buy a beautiful lake front property in a glitzy development. She was paying well over a million dollars. It was the wrong property in the wrong place and, to make matters worse, the developer also had problems. I advised her not to buy it and her attorney also advised her not to buy it, but she went ahead. A neighbouring property is now on sale for $100,000. Fortunately, she is wealthy but nobody wants to write off a million dollars because of a bad investment decision.

On a more positive note, after the crash of 2007/8, there were some spectacular bargains to be had in the area, provided you had cash to pay for them. By knowing the area, I was able to guide a client to a $60,000 property (previously being sold for over $300,000) which has since doubled in value and which is producing a return on investment of nearly 15%.

These bargains attracted serious investors and investment funds from all over the world. One fund alone – a hedge fund – bought 6,000 units. That is 6,000 homes and apartments in the Central Florida area.

Now the days when you could find this type of bargain are more or less over. The market has turned and prices are rising. Yet you can still buy at prices well under half of what you would have had to pay at the peak of the market and, more importantly, at prices less than the cost of the construction of the building – i.e. the cost of the land, the concrete, the timber and the tile, without any element of profit for the builder or developer. In a market where there is strong demand, this is always a key indicator of a bargain. If you cannot build the same product for the money and there is demand for it, prices must, eventually, rise to more than the cost of construction.

What is your attitude to liquidity?

An investment in real estate is, by its nature, an illiquid investment. In other words, it cannot be sold quickly if you need the cash.

Many people are not too worried by this. Provided they have other investments in cash, or which they can turn to cash quite quickly, they are prepared to accept the illiquidity as the price they have to pay for the other attributes of real estate investments that appeal to them.

Yet, even within the category of real estate investments, there are some that are much more illiquid than others. An apartment in the centre of London, Paris or Miami might sell quite quickly, even in bad times, whereas a rural property 10 miles from the nearest road might take years to sell if there is a low in the property market.

If you can accept the basic fact of illiquidity, but need to limit that illiquidity as far as possible, then you must factor this into your choice of property. Do this by choosing a property in an area where there is a long history of strong demand. For example, in the Windermere area of Orlando prices fell during the crisis but properties still sold quite quickly, because it was a sought after area, in beautiful surrounding and with the best schools in town.

What is your investment strategy?

If you are thinking of buying a property as an investment you have, clearly, included real estate in your investment strategy, but that does not bring the matter to an end. There are many different strategies within the category of real estate investment.

Investing for income

Some people are investing for income. They might be retired and using the income to add to their pension. They might like the idea of the property increasing in value, but that is not their primary aim. They want income. They want secure income and they want an income that is likely to be strong in the future.

They will need to buy the most appropriate property at the lowest possible price.

They will then need to decide what to do with it. Should they rent it out short term or long term?

In many areas of Central Florida there are zoning restrictions that dictate that you cannot rent out the property on short term lettings. Short term lettings are tenancies of less than 6 months.

Many investors prefer to buy in areas where you are permitted to rent either long or short term. They believe this gives them more flexibility and, of course, it allows them to use the properties themselves for their own vacations between lettings.

Now, if you are not interested in using the property yourself, it is worth noting that properties in areas zoned only for long term letting can be cheaper than similar properties in areas where you can let for just a few weeks at a time to holidaymakers.

This means that you can get a better yield on the money that you are investing.

Add to this the fact that, in my experience, the average property let on a long term basis is likely to generate an annual return a couple of percentage points higher than the same property let on a short term basis. Thus it is not surprising that many people investing for rental yield will look at long term renting in areas where this is the only type of renting permitted. This will not be the right solution every time, but it is probably your starting point when it comes to making a plan.

To find the best property you will need to use the services of a good Realtor. There are lots around, not just my company!

It is also worth pointing out that, whether you are letting short or long term, you will need the services of good property managers. Some companies divide this role into two parts – the property manager (who looks after the fabric of the building) and the rental manager (who looks after finding tenants and servicing their needs). I prefer to combine these two roles as I think it is more efficient and, therefore, cheaper. Whichever way you choose to do it, you need to make sure you use good companies and get a good deal. Some short term rental companies will charge 40% of the rent received for their work in finding and servicing the tenants. Others will charge 25% which, on the face of it, is a much better deal. Just be sure, however, that they give a good service. 40% of 50 weeks rented out at $1,000 per week (net to you $30,000) is better than 25% of 40 weeks rented out at $800 per week (net to you $25,800).

How do you choose a good rental company? Personal recommendation and talking to them. I return to this subject later.

Investing for growth

Other property buyers are not concerned about income. They perhaps have plenty. They want a place where their investment can grow in value to the greatest extent possible. In other words, they're looking for capital growth.

As is always the case, some will be looking for a bit of both.

Short sales and repossessions

In recent years, a lot of people were in financial difficulty and found it impossible to repay their mortgages.

In these cases, the banks had two options. They could either repossess the property – in Florida, as in many part of the world, a slow and expensive process – or they could agree to a "short sale".

A short sale is where the bank allows the owner to sell the property for less than the amount owed to them under the mortgage and then swallows the loss, or at least a large part of it. In other words the bank writes off all or part of the debt. This hurts the banks but it can hurt them a lot less than going to the time, trouble and expense of repossessing the property and then selling it for even less that they would have got on a short sale.

On the face of it then, these look like a great deal for anyone looking to pay the smallest possible amount of money for a property. This works whether you are investing for income or investing for capital growth.

However, not surprisingly, this is not as simple as it first seems. A lot of repossessed properties and short sale properties are not in great locations and many can be in a bad state of repair – some damaged by the owners forced to leave them. Now, of course, there can be some in great locations and in good repair but – especially if you are a foreign buyer living thousands of miles away – you will need the assistance of a good Realtor to locate the bargains on your behalf.

An additional problem with short sales is that, even when the bank has given agreement to the sale in principle, they have to agree the actual terms of the sale and – for various reasons – this can lead (at best) to long delays or (at worst) to the sale falling through.

There is a place in your investment strategy for these properties but you cannot rely on them.

I write more about short sales later in this chapter.

It is also worth mentioning, in passing, the possibility of buying repossessed properties at judicial auctions. For a foreign based buyer, this is usually a bad idea. Unless you are prepared to buy blind – a very dangerous strategy – the cost of checking out these properties and then bidding tends to outweigh the financial advantages. You could check out 100, find 10 that interest you and fail at auction to buy any at a price acceptable to you.

Despite the improving economy, for the time being at least there are still a lot of short sales around and the number will probably increase further as banks turn away from foreclosure when dealing with bad debts. According to a conference I attended recently, the banks think this will continue until at least the end of 2014. The good news: is that the banks are getting faster and more efficient in dealing with short sales and they are prepared to accept more reasonable offers.

Long or short term?

Some will be looking to invest for the long term. For example, the pensioner or the pension fund. They want to buy a property that will perform now and that is likely to perform equally well in 10 or 20 years' time. They do not want to go to the expense and trouble of having to sell their property and buy another (or even another category of investment) in a few years' time. They have often done their maths and worked out that the costs of acquisition and sale are substantial and can dramatically reduce the net performance of their investment.

Others are happy to buy and then sell at a profit. Some will wish to do so very quickly. In other words, they will be looking for a real bargain which they can sell on without delay - possibly not even getting to the stage where they take legal title to it. Of this group, some will wish to rent out the property for the period between the time when they buy it and the time when they sell it, whereas others will wish to keep it in pristine new condition until resale.

Selling quickly before you take title – often known a flipping – was a very popular strategy and, many would say, a major contributory factor in the financial crash. Opportunities for a quick turnaround still exist – strategies such as buy ugly and cheap, make pretty and sell dear – but pure flipping will seldom work today.

Buy to improve

Others will want to buy and then improve the property before selling it on.

If you are locally resident and a handyman or if you are a good project manager with a thorough understanding of the local property market, this can be a very successful investment strategy.

Buying 'off plan'

What about buying 'off plan'? This means buying property before it has been fully built and, in many cases, before construction has even started. In thriving markets, such purchases can produce large rewards. It is not uncommon for the launch price to be 40% or 50% less than the price at the time when the properties have been fully built. This is for a number of reasons. Developers need the money to launch the project and, very often, they cannot raise the bank finance needed to do this. They therefore sell their first few properties at very heavily discounted prices in order to generate the necessary funds. Developers (and their banks) also like to see confirmed sales as this makes other sales easier and raising finance less challenging.

The obvious, but often underestimated, danger is that the project never raises the necessary finance and never gets built which means that you might lose the money you have invested. In some countries, there are protective mechanisms to secure the money you have paid in these cases, but in none of them do those mechanisms work with 100% reliability. As a result of bitter experience, many people have decided to steer well clear of off plan developments.

If you are looking to invest in an off plan development, you should be looking, very carefully at the precise terms of the protection being offered to you. If the development is not completed and title delivered to you, is it absolutely guaranteed that you will get your money back? Who is giving the guarantee? Do you trust them? Do they have the financial capacity to repay you if something goes seriously wrong?

If you are thinking of buying off plan, you need to make sure that any monies you pay are held safely in escrow. In other words, it is held safely by an independent third party. The money will then be released to the builder by the escrow agent at various stages of the construction – your sales contract will highlight at what different stages these funds are to be transferred to the builder.

It is important to ensure that the escrow agent is an independent agent. If you pay it across to an entity controlled by the developer then, whatever your legal rights, it can be difficult to get your money back.

It is best if the escrow is held by an independent title company.

Investment funds

Some investors are put off by the idea of owning bricks and mortar. They dislike the potential cost of buying and selling yet they like the concept of investment in real estate. As a result, they look at investment funds. There are many of these around the world and of many types. The same two great risks attach to all of them. How good was the choice of the property upon which the fund was based? How expensive is the fund's management? In many cases, the choice of property might leave a lot to be desired and, in just as many cases, the administrative charges associated with the fund might seem very high.

However, some property investment funds and REITs (Real Estate Investment Trusts) have a proven track record of performing well over many years and can be well worth a look, as an alternative to buying your own property.

Development

There is money to be made in property development and so some investors try to cut out the middleman by becoming developers themselves. In my experience, few succeed – at least in their first development. They find that it is a lot more complicated than they thought and that there are a lot more hidden costs than they expected. Most lose money. Property development, certainly internationally, is not a game for amateurs or the faint hearted.

"Professionals" can also come unstuck. One of my best salesmen saw what we were doing and thought he'd have a go himself. He paid several hundred thousand dollars for a great piece of land. It was a disaster. The development never happened, the bank foreclosed and he lost his shirt.

Even we have come unstuck in some development projects. We always insist on a substantial contingencies allowance in the budget of any project on which we are working, but this may not prove enough. Recently, the county changed the rules about the fire safety sprinklers required in one of our projects and the change cost us $1.5 million. We could handle this, but for a smaller developer it could have pushed the project into bankruptcy.

Think carefully before going down the developer route – and take the best advice you can find. Even if you follow the best advice, be aware that there will always be unexpected expenditure and build in a big contingency to cover the risk.

Other Strategies

There are a number of other strategies and they can be combined in any number of the mixes. The important thing is to think through your personal objectives and how you want to achieve them.

What about below market value' (BMV)?

Some properties are marketed as being 'below market value'. Sometimes this is true and they can present spectacular bargains. On other occasions, such claims are nothing more than an unethical marketing ploy. Do not take them at face value.

Why would somebody be selling at less than market value? There are many reasons. It may be that they have bought a number of units in a development and secured a substantial discount doing so. If they can sell quickly, they can afford to pass them on as individual units, at much less than the price of such an individual unit in the marketplace. On other occasions, the sale might be by somebody who is in serious financial difficulty, or whose personal circumstances mean that he wants to get rid of the property quickly. For example, his employment might have come to an end and he is now leaving the country, or he is in the process of getting a divorce and he and his wife need to turn their house into cash and buy two smaller properties before one of them kills the other.

If you want to buy in the BMV market, make sure that you are dealing with a good and reputable seller or agent and crosscheck the value claimed for the property. The importance of this cannot be overstressed. You need to make sure that your own realtor goes through the values of several suggested comparable properties (comps) with you and satisfies you that the "bargain" is genuine.

What about Distressed Property?

In the last few years there has been a lot of talk about "distressed property".

Distressed Property is property that is being sold because the seller is in difficulty. The seller could be a private individual who has bought a property that he can no longer afford -- either a holiday home or his primary residence -- or it could be a developer who is unable to clear the units in his development and is in trouble with his bank. I have touched on the issue of distressed property in the section on properties that are below market value, but it's important to understand that, whilst distressed property is often being sold at below market value, this is not always the case and it is certainly not always the case that below market value property is distressed property. They are first cousins, not identical twins.

There is a whole range of distress. At the lower level, you find the person who is merely anxious to sell and is, therefore, prepared to lower the price a little in order to do so. At the top of the range, you find the person whose house will be repossessed in a few weeks' time if he does not sell it and who knows that any equity he has built up will simply disappear into the pocket of the banks when the property is repossessed. He will be a far more motivated seller and prepared to take a much bigger hit on the price of the property. Sadly, somebody's misfortune is always somebody else's opportunity.

Developers often find themselves in a slightly different position. Sometimes, just like private individuals, they know that, if they do not sell the units very quickly, the bank will repossessed them or put the company into administration. However, on many other occasions the position is not quite that dire. The developer may have sold 90% of the project and covered his costs, but he is not capable of selling the last few units which would generate a profit. Without the profit, he cannot go on to his next development and so the inability to sell may be losing him not just the profit on those units, but the potential profit on the whole new development. This will usually be much higher. Add to this the fact that he may have sales staff on site who are costing him every single day and you can see that he will be motivated to dispose of these last troublesome units at significant discounts. In some cases, the developer may not want to give cash discounts because he feels that this would be breaking faith with his earlier buyers, whose properties could be seen as being thereby devalued, but in these cases he may well be prepared to give you substantial, alternative incentives. A complete furniture pack, a new car, a two-week cruise etc. However, as the recession has got deeper, so more and more developers are prepared simply to cut the price of the last units in their development.

Distressed sales offer a major opportunity to buyers. In many places, there has been a substantial oversupply of property and the cost of both new and resale units might have fallen by 40%, 50% or even 60% compared to the peak -- which was typically in around 2007.

There is much less distressed property around today than there was a couple of years ago, but it is still there and it can still offer a bargain.

But the mere fact that the property has fallen substantially in price does not, of itself, make it a good buy. Some are lousy properties in lousy areas. Most will remain lousy properties in lousy areas. However cheap they are, they are too expensive and a bad buy.

How does the property of interest to you rate in comparison to other similar properties in the area? Fortunately, this information is normally fairly easy to obtain. There are a range of Internet sites to help you. But that takes time and you have to ask yourself whether you are sufficiently familiar with the various areas and types of property to identify the properties with true potential.

Better to speak to a Realtor. They know their patch and they can help you understand which of these "bargains" are real bargains and which are just trouble waiting to happen.

The good news is that, as things work in Florida, Realtors have access to every property on the market, whichever Realtor is selling it; so by consulting a Realtor you are not restricting yourself to just the properties on his books. Better still, he or she will have access to the very latest information about the price and availability of a particular property; many websites lag well behind the market, as they are not updated sufficiently often.

Your consultation will be free of charge.

Of course, before consulting a Realtor, using the Internet to visit other estate agents' sites can also give you a good preliminary sense of market values and, of course, going round agents offices and looking in their windows also works. This will help you get the best out of your meeting with your Realtor.

There is another test of value which I find very useful. If the house is

What is Basel III?
BASEL III (named after Basel in Switzerland, the home of international banking) is a global regulatory standard on the adequacy of the capital held by banks. It deals with stress testing banks and assessing their market liquidity risk. It was agreed by the members of the Basel Committee on Banking Supervision during 2010-11. This is the third generation of the Basel Accords, which date back to 1988. It was developed in response to the deficiencies in financial regulation revealed by the late-2000s financial crisis. The key changes to capital requirements came into force in 2013.

on sale at less than the cost of construction -- that is to say, the cost of the bricks, mortar, timber and labour used to build it -- this is a good indication of value. Barring a complete collapse in the economy and wages, nobody is going to be able to come and build another property for the price you are paying. The cost of construction is also usually fairly easy to establish by local enquiry.

Whilst talking of distressed sales, I must also make mention of "short sales". Short sales are sales of property that is under threat of repossession by a bank, but where the bank permits the owner to sell the property and to sell it at a price less than the amount outstanding on the mortgage. They agree to write off the balance. Many banks will do this. They do it for a number of reasons. In some cases, dealing with the property in this way can avoid it appearing as a distressed loan in their accounts and, as a result, can avoid the need for them to write off the loan and weaken their balance sheet. This is becoming more and more important as banks all over the world have to strengthen their balance sheets by introducing more capital. The introduction of the new Basel III rules for international banking (which increase the amount of capital required by banks) makes this problem even more pressing. Another reason why the bank might agree to a short sell is that they realise that there are giving nothing away. If they repossess the property, they will probably not sell at a higher price yet they will incur the substantial cost and delays associated with the repossession, plus the estate agents costs and other charges associated with the sale. In theory, they might have been able to recover any loss from the seller, but, if the seller has no money, this is likely to be a non-existent remedy.

Remember that distressed property is not the solution to all ills. Many of the properties on sale may have been poorly maintained because the owner was in financial difficulty.

Many may be in poor locations. Remember the second golden rule of property investment: a property is only a bargain if you can later sell it at a profit.

If you are thinking of buying any type of distressed property, the advice is simple. Make sure that you are dealing with a good and reputable seller or agent and check that the price really does represent good value.

> *A property is only a bargain if you can later sell it at a profit*

What is your timescale?

This will greatly affect the property that you're going to buy.
Are you looking to make money over five years, 10 years or 20 years? As a general rule, real estate investments do not work well for timescales of less than five years, although there have been some exceptions.

What's going to happen to the currency?

When you buy a property in another country it is quite likely that, in that country, they will use a different currency. This adds another level of opportunity and another level of risk to the transaction.

Currency exchange rates can fluctuate dramatically, sometimes over a relatively short time frame.

If this works in your favour it can be hugely beneficial. If you buy a property that goes up in value by 30%, that is good news. If, during the same period, the currency has also risen in value against your own – say by 20% – this is a huge added bonus. On the other hand, of course, if the currency has fallen in value against your own, then when you come to sell your property and convert funds back into your own currency you will not make nearly as much money and, in the worst-case, you could even lose money.

I have had this experience myself – in both directions.

This may be obvious but what can you do about it?

Nobody can predict with any accuracy and in detail what is going to happen to the value of any two currencies over the next few years but a little bit of study can help you understand whether it is likely that currency A is going to rise or fall against currency B.

There are a number of things that you can do. A good starting point is to look at the history of currency values. These can be found at many points on the Internet. I normally use SMART CURRENCY because I find its website at http://www.smartcurrencyexchange.com easy to understand and the information contained on this easy to follow, with simple graphs.

You will find some sample currency exchange rates on Page 19 of this book.

You can also look at the basic economic background of the two countries concerned. For example, in 2013, most people would probably think that (at least in the medium or long term) the Chinese currency or the Brazilian currency is likely to rise against the US dollar. Of course, there is no guarantee of this and there is certainly no guarantee that they will do so over any given period of time, but it does seem a pretty safe long-term bet. When making these judgements, as well as using your own intellect and instinct, you can also speak to various currency brokers or read their forecasts.

How are you going to pay for the property?

There are many choices. See the section 'Do you want finance?'

From the point of view of the investor, the decision is not always a simple question of whether or not you need the money. In some cases, tax considerations can make it attractive to have mortgage finance, even though you are well able to pay in cash.

Of course, all of this depends upon your personal circumstances. In particular, it depends upon the country in which you live and how they treat mortgage finance costs when assessing income derived from a property.

It is worth pointing out – and I will return to this later – when buying in Florida, various taxes are payable to the State of Florida. These include document stamp taxes. Although there are a few exceptions, if you buy a property in one name (say your own name) and later decide that would work better for tax purposes if you put the property into (say) the name of your daughter, you could end up having to pay these taxes twice. These can amount to thousands of dollars (0.7% of the value). In addition, you would then be likely to have to rearrange any associated mortgage at further cost and paying further taxes.

In other words, make your plan before you buy the property.

Generally, this means seeing your licensed estate agent (Realtor), lawyer, accountant or financial advisor as early as possible in the process of buying a property – ideally, at the time when you have decided that buying a property might be a good idea and long before you have identified a particular house to buy.

This is a recurring theme. Plan first. Look at property second.

Do you want to let (rent out) the property?

Most people who buy residential property as an investment want to rent it out. The question is, who are they going to rent it to?

There are two main tactics.

The first is to rent it out on a short term let, typically to people taking their holidays. The rent per week will usually be much higher than you would obtain on a long-term let and you will be able to use the property yourself for the periods when it is not let. However, there are drawbacks. The administration is more complicated. The property management is more expensive, because of the number of handovers required. There may be more wear and tear on the property. There may well be longer periods when nobody is paying you any rent.

The alternative is to let the property on long term rental. This will be less attractive if you wish to use the property, in part, as a holiday home but it can be a much less stressful method of generating rental income.

As always, you might fall lucky and get the best of both worlds. If you are in a place with a university, look for the opportunity to rent to academic staff, particularly visiting academic staff, who are likely to want to rent only for the academic year, leaving you with the three summer months to use the property yourself.

WILLIAM G HICKS PA

 WILLIAM HICKS HAS DEDICATED HIMSELF TO THE PRACTICE OF IMMIGRATION LAW.

WE TRULY UNDERSTAND THE NEED TO CHOOSE A STONG LEGAL TEAM AND TO HAVE THE REQUIRED EXPERT SUPPORT TO NAVIGATE THE US IMMIGRATION VISA PROCESS

 7380 SAND LAKE ROAD, SUITE 500, ORLANDO FL 32819

 +1 407 718 8046

info@myusaimmigrationattorney.com

WWW.MYUSAIMMIGRATIONATTORNEY.COM

Rental Potential

Be realistic in assessing rental potential.

The most important thing to understand is that there are thousands of properties which, commercially speaking, are almost impossible to let. A rustic house in a rural backwater may find a few tenants during the year, but this will not be enough to generate a sensible commercial return on your investment. If you are interested in such a house, you will probably have accepted this and view any rental income as a bonus that may help to defray some of the expenses of ownership.

Assessing rental potential is a skill that takes time to acquire. There are, however some good indicators of property that is likely to let well.

The way you furnish the property will have a considerable impact upon its rental potential. The wrong furniture can lose you 30% of your lettings. People want to rent something furnished to their tastes. As everyone has different tastes, this can make your furnishing choices tricky. Neutral – but not too bland – tends to work best. So does furnishing with local furniture, not stuff brought from your home.

Cheap furniture is a bad idea and usually ends up costing you a lot more in the long run.

When it comes to assessing the rental potential of a property you are thinking of buying, the most important tip is to speak to your real estate advisor. They should be able to give you a very accurate estimate of the rental potential of any particular property in their area – both as it stands and if you were to improve it to a particular standard.

They can also advise you as to the most appropriate style of furnishings and, often, where best to buy them.

See the section on renting out your property.

How are you going to manage the property?

This vital point tends to be at the bottom of most people's agenda, but it should be right at the top. In fact, in many cases, the availability of good property management could dictate where you buy or, at least, eliminate certain candidate countries or areas.

Put simply, in some places Property Management is hugely expensive, totally unreliable and corrupt. You will be promised the earth and delivered nothing. Needless to say, it's a good idea to avoid these places!

One question that always arises is whether you need a management company, or whether you can do it yourself with the assistance of a few local tradesmen and a cleaner. I believe you can NOT do it yourself at least unless, or until, you have had quite a lot of experience and seen the pattern of how things work in this particular place.

What you might think about doing -- indeed, what you should think about doing -- is to supplement the efforts of the local agent by finding tenants of your own from amongst your family and friends, or even by advertising in your local supermarket, newspaper, or on your own website.

Fortunately, there are other places where it is relatively simple to select a good and reliable management company able to manage your property cost effectively and to save you many sleepless nights.

So how do you choose a property management company?

There are three simple rules.

- Always ask for recommendations. These could be from your estate agent, from your other professional advisers, or from somebody you know who lives in the area.
- Take up references from the firms that have been recommended to you. Preferably, ask other foreign buyers what they think of the service that they have received. Phone them. Are they genuine customers? Are they happy? If you have any doubts, go elsewhere.
- Inspection. Insist on inspecting a couple of properties that they are currently managing. If they're dirty, go elsewhere. If you don't, you will have claims for compensation from dissatisfied tenants. Also inspect their premises, their website and their information pack. Are these people you would choose if you were looking to rent a property?

Once you have found your preferred management company, monitor them. There is an overwhelming temptation, when you are thousands of miles away, for management companies to pocket the rental money and not tell you about every letting. Needless to say, good and reputable agents will not do this, but some companies do -- even in the most regulated environments.

How do you monitor them? Tell them, even if it is a downright lie, that you have friends who have properties in the same area and that, whenever any of you is in the area, you check on each other's properties to make sure that they are in good condition and to see whether they have been let. More importantly and better, make sure there is a phone in the house and phone it, religiously, every week. Note the results. If the call is answered, you expect to see some rental income for that week.

I was involved in helping a client whose property was being looked after by a local property management company. They were not giving him proper accounts and they were often late with their payments. The rental levels also seemed very low – in this part of Florida we can achieve over 70% occupancy. I was so suspicious that I drove past the place a few times in the evening to check whether there were any lights on and whether rentals were being declared for the days that I saw lights. In the end, I asked to see the telephone bill saying that the client needed it for tax purposes. There were a lot of 0800 calls. A quick check showed that they were to local pizza companies – on days when the property was not supposedly rented out!

I don't like to see people being ripped off. This experience made me decide to offer a proper, professional, rental management service as part of our operations.

Now, of course, to make this all work you need a proper written contract with the management company, providing for detailed disclosure of income and expenses and the right to remove the company for non-performance, or inadequate performance of their obligations. Oh, and remember to insert a clause that states that if you find the tenants yourself, the management company gets a much lower fee, since they are merely managing the property whilst those tenants are there. This will leave them to charge their normal and much higher percentage when they both find the tenant and manage the property.

Rental management companies and property management companies charge vastly different amounts for what looks like the same service. On closer examination, this is not always the case. When comparing quotes, make sure you are comparing like with like. Exactly what is included in each quote and what could be charged as extras?

As a very rough guide, you should expect to pay between 25% and 40% for an all-inclusive Property Management service dealing with short term lets. Often, you get what you pay for. As I have already said, a good company charging you 40% is better than a bad company charging you 25%. Having said that, we are a good company and we normally charge 25% (June 2013).

What is your exit strategy?

How are you going to turn this investment into a profit?

It's worth remembering at this point the old adage that, in property investment, you make your money when you buy the property, not when you sell it. In other words, if you pay too much, or buy the wrong property, you are not likely to do well with the investment, however long you keep the property, or however well the market does. If the market does well, the property can still turn out to be a reasonable investment but it will never catch up on what you lost by paying too much in the beginning.

Despite the obvious truth of this adage you can still spoil a good investment by selling at the wrong time or for too little money.

At both ends of the sausage machine, it is a good idea to get advice from a good real estate professional.

Do you have a clear strategy for bringing the investment to an end? What is going to trigger the sale of the property? Is it going to be the expiry of a certain number of years (an easy option if there are a number of you investing in the project and you want certainty) or is it going to be when the property makes a certain amount of potential capital gains or, dare I say it, loses a certain percentage of its value?

If you are buying a property with a view to selling on at a profit, exactly who is likely to want to buy the property from you at the time when you want to sell it? Is there a clearly defined target market? What evidence is there that this exists? What evidence is there that they will pay you the mark-up that you wish for?

Buying a Property as a Place to Live

Immigration

If you want to live in a place on a permanent basis, or even if you wish to visit on a regular basis as a tourist, it is important that you have the legal right to do so.

For this reason, the whole question of visas and immigration rights can be of major concern. This is particularly so if you come from countries from which immigration or tourism is a problem. For buyers from those countries, for example China, the whole question of whether they can obtain the necessary visas to visit, study or stay in their target country will determine whether they will buy there.

If visas and immigration are going to be important to you, it is best to check the position before you start looking at properties and as part of your due diligence process.

Only use certified and registered specialist immigration attorneys or advisors and always get references – and check them – before you engage their services.

See the chapter on visas and immigration.

Practical Issues

When buying a property as a holiday home, or as a place to live permanently, there are some very basic practical issues that are all too easily overlooked in the excitement of finding a beautiful home.

Access

How you going to get there? Where will you fly from and to? How long will it take? What will it cost?

If you buy in a place like Orlando, which has a major international airport, life will be easier than if you buy in a place two or three hours' drive away from the nearest international airport. There are many such places in Florida. It is not just the drive time, it is the fact that you are going to have to waste the best part of an hour picking up your hire car and **then** drive for two or three hours – all at the end of a very long flight.

Of course, if you're going to be living in a place permanently, you may not be too worried about a lengthy journey from your former home, but do remember that you're likely to want family and friends to visit and that they will be worried about these issues.

Once you have arrived in the country, how long will it take to get from the airport to your property? There is a lot of research that indicates that, if the travel distance from the airport at either end of your journey is more than about an hour, you will lose 25% of your potential visitors. More than 1½ hours and you lose 50%. Granted, your family is likely to be a little more dedicated if they are their visiting, but even they will have their limitations. Nobody wants to face a long drive after a long and tedious flight.

Is there any public transport? You may be quite content to travel everywhere by car, but there will be times when access to public transport is either highly advantageous or essential. Remember that the years will pass by and there may come a time when you are less comfortable about driving. What happens if you break a leg? What happens when your car is in for repair? What happens if you simply want to go to a good party? In Central Florida, there is little emphasis on public transport – everyone has a car – but it is coming, slowly. A new metro rail system is being built in Orlando over the next couple of years. Until then, public transport is likely to be a taxi!

Even if you are comfortable with being totally reliant upon your car, if there is no public transport you will become an unpaid taxi driver whenever your children or grandchildren visit, especially if they are under 25 and so unable to hire a car.

Facilities

What facilities exist in the area?

Is there a hospital? Does it have a department that deals with your particular medical condition? Is there a local doctor? Are there any language issues?

Will you have access to all the things that you like to do? Horse riding? Bridge? Cricket (OK, probably only if you are English, Indian or Australian)? Good restaurants? Do you visit the theatre or opera? What is available? Are you of a particular religious persuasion and is there a suitable church/synagogue/mosque nearby? Are you a golfer? If so, just one or two golf courses in the vicinity is unlikely to satisfy you for long. Are you thinking of retiring to the area? If so you will need a major shopping centre within an hour or so by car. Are you sociable? Is this an area where you will find "your kind of (English speaking?) people"? Do you expect your teenage children to visit? If so, is there anything for them in the area? The shopping mall might not cut it!

Is there a local shop within walking distance – or, at least, only a short and easy drive away? Surprisingly, this facility is the amenity that is most valued by my clients who have bought a property. It does not need to be a big shop: just a shop that sells milk and bread and beer. It was not on their list of things to look out for, but it is something that they really value if they have it. Therefore, perhaps it might be added to your tick list.

Shops within residential communities are quite rare but these integrated facilities are, slowly, becoming a little more common.

Cost of Living

What is the cost of living? What matters is not the official cost of living but the cost of living in the way in which you live. Especially if you're going to be living in the area on a long-term basis, it is worth going to the local shops to check this out. Look out, in particular, for the cost of items such as cigarettes and alcohol. Depending on where you come from, these can often turn out to be a nasty surprise. Look out also for the big-ticket items such as energy costs and medical insurance.

Just as important as the present cost of living is the question of what the cost of living is likely to be in a few years' time. Is the cost of living stable or is it rising sharply? Many people have moved to a place only to find, 10 years later, that it is no longer cheap and that they can no longer afford to live there.

Of course, an important part of this calculation – if you come from abroad and have a pension or other income paid in foreign currency – is what is likely to happen to exchange rates over the next few years. I have already dealt with this issue.

Type of Property

Your choice of the type of property to buy will, of course, depend upon your personal preferences and requirements. Yet the choice might not be quite that simple.

Why are you buying property? Is it a holiday home, a place to be occupied for several months or a place in which you intend to live permanently, either now or at some time in the future?

If it is a holiday home, something small and easy to maintain has lots of advantages. Many properties are designed specifically for use as holiday homes. You may find, for example, that they have little storage space because this is not needed if you're only going to be there for two or three weeks. For holiday use, there is a lot to be said for something that you can simply lock up and leave without having to worry about arrangements for cleaning the pool, or doing the gardening.

If you're looking for a more permanent residence you are likely to have different priorities. Room sizes will need to be bigger. You will need more storage space. You may need a more sophisticated heating and air conditioning system. You will probably want a garage and a decent sized garden.

It is worth, at the outset, thinking through your requirements and listing them.

Space

Whether you're buying a holiday home, or a place in which to live permanently, there is one thing you should never forget. Countless people have told me that their biggest regret is that they did not buy something larger. You have no idea how many family and friends you have until you buy a nice house in Florida! The world and his dog will want to visit and you will not have the space to accommodate them. Your simple plan of one bedroom for you, one bedroom for guests and one bedroom for junk won't work, because your guests will overlap. So, if you have a bit of spare cash, think of buying a property one size bigger than you first anticipated.

It is for this reason that really large houses are popular in Florida and, strangely, can rent very well. A lot of people come to Florida for multigenerational holidays. The grandparents can invite their 4 children and 8 grandchildren. This leads to a demand for 6 and 8 bedroom properties which, if you allow for a couple of people sleeping on couches in the living area, can house up to 20 people. These properties are also popular with golf parties, groups coming for weddings or sporting groups.

Such is the demand for these larger properties that, in my next development, I am making special arrangements for a few homes containing two or three master suites – bedrooms, bathrooms and a small living area for each suite.

Furniture

Do you want to take your furniture with you? For most people it does not make any sense. See the chapter on "Settling in".

Remember that, if you are going to rent your property out on a long term basis, you are likely to want to rent it with no furniture, as such tenants prefer to use their own furniture and will pay more for the privilege. This, incidentally, also tends to spoil any plans that you had to use your long term rental property for a month or two between tenants.

If you are renting on a short time basis you will, hardly surprising, need to provide furniture. Modern tenants expect high quality furniture and good quality furniture will help maximise your rental income.

Cheap furniture is expensive. It breaks or wears out and costs you more in the long term.

Cars

Are you going to want to own a car? If so, you will need somewhere secure to park it -- especially if it is a holiday home and the car will be left unattended for long periods of time.

One trick I have discovered is that you can take out a car insurance policy which has vacation insurance cover. This allows you to call the company on the day when you leave the country and they will then reduce the cover on your car so that it is protected against fire and theft but not for any involvement in an accident. Just remember to put it back on full cover when you come back to the country! As the risk and cost of claims is very low whilst your car is parked, your insurance charges can go down quite a lot.

Talking about insurance, the rules over here are likely to be quite different from the rules where you live, so using a good insurance broker who is familiar with foreign clients can save you a lot of trouble and money.

Surprisingly often the cost of insuring, taxing and maintaining your local car plus airport parking and the depreciation of its value can amount to as much – or more – than renting a new, clean car on each visit. Renting also means you can choose the type of car you need for that particular visit. If granny is coming, rent an up market car with lots of legroom and easy rear seat access! If it's your girlfriend, who can resist a Mustang or a Corvette? Look to cheap, local car hire companies *as well as* the big names, who sometimes have surprisingly good deals available.

For most people buying a holiday home, it makes a lot more sense to rent a car whilst they're there. You don't have to worry about repairs, maintenance, insurance and so on and you can return it when it gets dirty!

Pets

Are you going to be taking your pets?

If so, you need to consult a vet in your own country a long time before you intend to travel – at least 6 months.

Your ability to bring your pets with you and the medical certificates they will need will depend upon the type of pet and where you are coming from.

The Country

As part of your initial due diligence you should find out a bit about the country. You should also find out a little about the state or area where you're thinking of buying. Some of the things you find out could well surprise you, particularly if you have been visiting for many years, at the same time of the year.

There is a mass of information available on the Internet.

Don't forget to look closely at the climate. Many people buying in Florida are motivated, in large measure, by the thought of a better climate. What is "better" depends on your personal perspective.

Sometimes the figures can come as a nasty shock. This is, again, particularly so if you've visited the place many times, but at the same time of year. You may be completely unprepared, for example, for the peak summer temperature. See Appendix 3 for climate details.

Remember that temperature & rainfall charts do not tell the whole story. Wind, lack of shelter, altitude and other factors can greatly influence your perception of the climate, which is what really matters. A place where it rains for 200 days per year will seem wetter than a place with the same amount of rainfall, but where it only rains for 60 days. Figures can also conceal substantial daily variations.

Where To Buy?

The decision as to where to buy is equally important, both for investors and people wishing to buy a home for their own use, but the factors to take into account will be rather different. I have dealt with these in the two sections above.

Get to know the place

The way that is most fun – and undoubtedly the best – is to travel extensively and to get to know the areas both in summer and in winter. The need to know them in both seasons cannot be over emphasised. Some summer resorts close down almost completely in the winter months. The climate, which was so agreeable in June, can be absolutely awful in January. Or the other way round. The place that was a tranquil twenty minute drive from town in May might well involve a two hour nose to tail ordeal in August.

Very few people –including me – know the whole of Florida well. It is so huge that it is unreasonable to expect someone buying a holiday or even a retirement home to do so. In a sense it is unnecessary. If you like a particular place and would like a home there, does it matter that somewhere else there might be a place you like just as much or even better? Most people, therefore, select the area to live from the areas they already know plus, perhaps, another couple that they have read about and decide to visit before making their final decision. A fair substitute for an initial visit is a bit of reading. General guides can give you a reasonable feel for what a place will be like. Follow that up with some more specific reading about the areas that interest you, television programmes etc. and you will be ready for a productive exploratory visit. The Internet, libraries, and the Tourist Board are also good sources of information.

Most people know within a few minutes of arriving in a town whether it is somewhere they would like to live. A two-week self-drive holiday, using inexpensive small hotels, can therefore cover a lot of ground. Take a large-scale map or motoring atlas. Be a vandal. Write your comments about the places you visit on the page. Otherwise you will never remember which was which. Buy some postcards to remind you of the scenery or, these days and especially if you are a gadget man, take a video or digital camera. This is much better, but remember to keep a record of which place is which! Pick up a copy of the local paper for each area. You will often find these in roadside stands or in supermarkets. It will give you some idea of what is happening in the area and also supply details of local estate agents and property prices. Visit the local tourist office, if there is one, for more information about the area and an idea of what goes on throughout the year. Look in estate agents window and make a note – again on the map – of the sort of prices you will have to pay for property of the type that interests you. ***But don't go inside.*** Make it an absolute rule **that you will not look at any properties**. If you do you will be caught in the classic trap of focusing on bricks and mortar rather than the area. What matters most is the area where you are going to live. There are nice houses in every area.

Provided the initial look at prices doesn't make you faint, if you like the town mark it with a big ✓and move on to the next place. If it is not for you, mark the map with a big ✗and, likewise, move on.

Once you have short-listed your two or three most likely places, try to visit them in both summer and winter. Spend a little time there. Make contact with estate agents and look at property to your heart's content. Sadly, many people will simply not have the time to follow this advice, but this doesn't mean it is bad advice!

Generally, when going to see property you will be accompanied by the Realtor. This will either be your Realtor – the person you have appointed to help you find a property – or the seller's Realtor.

Under the system in the US, it is a really good idea for you to appoint a Realtor to help you find a property. This person – known as a Buyer's Agent – has the professional and legal responsibility to look after your interests and not the interests of the seller. They will help you find and filter properties and, if you choose a good one, give you huge amounts of helpful, practical advice. Better still, they are paid for by the seller!

If you are dealing with a private seller (i.e. someone who is not using an agent) and you do not have your own Buyer's Agent, when you do finally go looking at property, take a mobile phone. If you don't have one, buy one. Property can be nearly impossible to find and it can save much gnashing of teeth if you can phone and ask for directions. It is also courteous to telephone if you are delayed en route. Thinking about it, this is another very good reason for using a Buyer's Agent – though, in the case of a sale by owner, you will need to pay them a fee for the work they do.

The choice is yours

One thing applies to all buyers but, particularly, to the person buying for their own use. Remember that rules are there to be broken. In the end, the choice of location and type of property is down to personal preference. You are probably buying a home in Central Florida because you have been reasonably successful in life. One of the rewards of such success should be the ability to do as you please. It is too easy to forget, as you become immersed in the detailed planning for the purchase, that this whole exercise is supposed to be *fun*. If you want to throw reason to the wind and buy the house of your dreams, there is nothing wrong with doing so – provided you understand that this is what you are doing. After all, who really ***needs*** a villa overlooking the sea or with a jetty onto a lake?

I can remember a couple who bought the most ridiculously inappropriate house. He had only one leg and she had MS. They fell in love with the house divided over five floors and with no elevator. There were three sets of stairs between the kitchen and the pool. Their family was horrified and thought that their parents had finally lost their marbles. The clients bought the property and loved every moment of living in it for the five years before they both died, within a few weeks of each other.

What Price to Pay?

Whether you are buying a holiday home or buying an investment property, you do not want to pay too much for it.

The first stage of working out how much you will have to pay is deciding what type of property you want to buy. Sometimes, the most sensible and effective cost-saving measure is to buy a property that caters to your needs, but does no more. It is very tempting, when you're being shown round a beautiful house with a beautiful view by a very persuasive estate agent and after a lovely, long amber liquid lunch, to say "The hell with it! It is only another $50,000. Let's have it."

See the chapter "Inspections (Surveys) & Appraisals (Valuations)" on how to guard against this risk.

Who should own the property?

Whether you're buying a property for investment or buying it as a place in which to live or spend your holidays, the choice of the best form of legal ownership for the property is of huge (and hugely underestimated) importance. See the next chapter "Who Should own the Property".

What about owning the property through your pension fund?

For many people this can be a very attractive and highly advantageous way of owning property abroad. See the next chapter "Who Should own the Property".

Should you have an appraisal (valuation) or an inspection (survey)?

See the chapter "Surveys (Inspections) and Valuations (Appraisals}" for consideration of this topic.

Do You Want Finance?

Whether you are buying as an investment, or as a place to live, the choice of whether to take some finance on your purchase is important and not quite as straightforward as it might at first seem.

See the chapter "Finance" for more details.

Choosing Advisers

At various places in this chapter I have referred to the need for advisers or, at the very least, the desirability of taking advice at certain points. How do you find such advisers? How do you choose between them? How do you decide which one to appoint?

This is not easy.

The same general principle applies to each category of adviser. If possible, get personal recommendations from people who have used their service and been happy. If this is not possible, ask for a recommendation from one of your existing advisers (for example, your Realtor) with whom you are happy.

Once you have a recommendation, check out their website and download or ask for their client information pack. Is it clearly written? Do you understand what they are talking about? If you do not, it is probably better to look elsewhere. Unfortunately, some professionals – though very clever – are very poor at communication and dealing with them is likely to cause you unnecessary complication and stress.

Once you have the information pack, check to see that the service meets your requirements and that you are happy with the price.

Then ask to speak to the person concerned. Does he or she sound like a person you can work with? Are they clear about your requirements? Can they satisfy those requirements within the price quoted?

If you decide to appoint the service provider, make sure that all of the key requirements are put in writing. This does not need to be a long document, but five minutes spent now can save hours of arguing and aggravation later.

Realtor

See the chapter "Finding the Right Property" for guidance on how to choose an estate agent.

Appraisers (Valuers)

Only use approved appraisers. They have to abide by a code of ethics and can be disciplined, suspended or struck off if they do not.

Your estate agent may well be able to recommend a qualified appraiser or, if he cannot, try the American Society of Appraisers: www.appraisers.org. They list their members in each area.

Surveyors (Property Inspectors/Home Inspectors)

"The home inspection industry is plagued by incompetent inspectors. Most states do not require licensing. Anyone can call themselves a home inspector. Therefore, it is important to screen an inspector before hiring him. It is well worth the effort to find a seasoned professional"

It is not me saying this. It is Home Inspections USA.

See the chapter "Surveys and Appraisals" for more details.

Mortgage Brokers

You do not need a mortgage broker. If you prefer, you can deal directly with a bank.

Having said that, it is probably a good idea to have one.

A broker can review the market and get you the best possible deal. Two out of three Americans use a mortgage broker to purchase a home They do this because mortgage brokers offer home buyers more options and a wider selection of loan products.

For a foreigner, it is probably even more advisable to use a broker – but one who is experienced in working with foreign buyers. Their needs are different. The range of products available for them is smaller. The possibility for delay and wasted time is greater as the bank employees involved will also, probably, be unsure of what is required.

Although there will be a cost associated with using a broker, he or she will probably save you far more than they cost – certainly in grief, probably in cash.

If you want to use a broker then, once again, you should seek a recommendation.

You have two main choices - a broker based in the place where you are buying or (if there is one) a broker based where you live. The broker near the property is likely to have a wider range of options available.

If you want to use a broker near where the property is located, your estate agent probably works with one that he can recommend. It is pretty safe to accept his recommendation. You both have the same objective. Both of you want a broker who is going to be able to find the necessary finance and to find it as quickly as possible.

If you are going to use a local broker, use a trained and certified broker. The National Association of Mortgage Brokers (NAMB - www.namb.org) is, it says, "a not-for-profit organization committed to promoting the highest degree of professionalism for its members and providing ethical and professional standards against which mortgage brokers can be measured".

NAMB has developed a certification program and a code of conduct. NAMB certification is gained only once the candidate has met certain requirements of experience and knowledge to practice mortgage brokering and has passed a written examination.

If you prefer to use a broker in your own country, you should remember that arranging overseas mortgages may not be a regulated activity and so you will have little or no protection if the broker does anything wrong. You should check the position in the country where you live.

Financial Advisers

If you need financial advice concerning any of the issues raised in this book, you will need to choose your advisors very carefully. Very few have the skills and knowledge necessary to understand the implications of cross-border transactions. This is not really surprising. There are relatively few of them and the advice they are giving almost always complicated, involving the law and tax systems of a least two and sometimes three or four different countries.

In most European and many other countries, the provision of financial advice is strictly regulated. Giving regulated advice without being properly qualified is a criminal offence. It is, therefore, essential that you choose somebody who not only has the correct skills, but also the correct paperwork confirming his entitlement to give advice in the country where you are located.

Lawyers

Strangely, in the US, few people use a lawyer to help deal with their purchase of property. Strangely, that is, to people who come from countries where the use of a lawyer is almost universal.

There are two main reasons for this. First, the US Realtor is fully qualified and deals with much of the work that, in other countries, would be dealt with by a lawyer. Second, the US system of title transfer uses title insurance companies who investigate and guarantee the title to your property, in effect doing much of the work that a lawyer or notary might do in other places.

There are still circumstances where consulting a lawyer makes sense;. For example, if your financial circumstances are complex, or you intend to buy the property through your family trust or pension fund. Equally, it makes sense to consult a lawyer at the outset if you want to move to the US and need immigration advice; sometimes the way you choose to own your property can help or hinder the immigration process.

Generally, however, people rely upon the combined efforts of their Realtor and the title insurance company.

Should you visit the property before you buy?

Yes.

Except in the most unusual circumstances, it is insane not to see a property before you buy it. If you're buying "off plan", you need to see the area where the property is to be built.

Even if you're buying a property purely as an investment, it is better to see the property and the area in which it is located. Doing so has saved quite a number of people from some pretty dangerous deals.

The exceptions? Perhaps if you are buying off plan property in an area that you know well. Perhaps if you're buying an investment property and you already know and trust the judgement of the person recommending it to you. Perhaps if you're buying a property in a building you already know.

In every other case, go and see what you're buying.

Summary

You may have noticed that this chapter is the longest in the book -- and by some margin. That is because it is the most important. It is lack of preparation and lack of due diligence that causes 80% of all the problems experienced by people buying property abroad.

Useful Names & Addresses

Team Feltrim: http://www.c21teamfeltrim.com (my company). The website has useful background information and featured international property

The primary steps to getting Florida residential property: http://www.britstoflorida.com/buying_infla.html

Mid Florida Investment Properties: http://www.floridahomeflipping.com/become-an-investor/central-florida-homes/

Trulia Mid Florida homes for sale: http://www.trulia.com/for_sale/2271_nh

Foreign National Investors in Florida Real Estate: http://www.linkedin.com/groups/Foreign-National-Investors-in-Florida-3667650

Orlando Villas Forums: http://www.orlando-guide.info/forums/

USA Canada Real Estate Investors talk group: http://www.linkedin.com/groups/USA-Canada-Real-Estate-Investors-4040151

Canadian Real Estate Referral Network: http://www.linkedin.com/groups/Canadian-Real-Estate-Referral-Network-2180887

News, advice, listings and tools for real estate: https://twitter.com/MSNRealEstate

Real Estate Blogs Florida: http://boldrealestategroup.com/blog/

American Society of Appraisers: http://www.appraisers.org

Online Real Estate: http://www.realtor.com/

IRS: http://www.irs.gov

Real Estate Lawyer: http://www.bakerdonelson.com/martha-a-hartley

Smart Currency: http://www.smartcurrencyexchange.com

EB5 Select: http://www.eb5select.com

Associations

AIPP (Association of International Property Professionals) http://www.aipp.org.uk

The Chinese American Real Estate Association: http://www.carea.org

The Canadian Real Estate Association (CREA) is one of Canada's largest single-industry trade Associations: http://www.crea.ca

Central Florida Realty Investors: http://cfri.net

Journals

Property Wire: http://www.propertywire.com

Christie's International Real Estate: http://www.christiesrealestate.com/eng

Property Week: http://www.propertyweek.com

OPP Connect: http://www.opp-connect.com

Shows and Exhibitions

Middle East's largest annual Real Estate Event: http://www.cityscapeglobal.com

APITS (A Place In The Sun): http://www.aplaceinthesun.com

DOMEXPO International Real Estate Exhibition: http://www.domexpo.ru/eng

Canada Real Estate Forums: http://www.realestateforums.com/landing/index.php

MIPIM: http://www.mipim.com

Social Media

Florida Home Owners Forum: http://www.top-forums.com/

Canada Buy South International Real Estate Referral Network: http://www.linkedin.com/groups/Canada-Buy-South-International-Real-4857213

General Florida forum with real estate section: http://www.city-data.com/forum/orlando/

Orlando Real Estate Investing & Landlord's Meetup Group: http://www.meetup.com/realestate-215/

Who Should Own the Property?

The importance of this question is one of the most important and yet difficult things to get across to buyers.

Why Is This Important?

It is something to which most buyers give little thought. Yet making the right decision about the best form of legal ownership can save you absolutely huge amounts of totally unnecessary taxes, both during your lifetime and on your death. We are talking tens of thousands of dollars on a perfectly ordinary home. It can also save you an enormous amount of trouble, stress and aggravation. In the end, that is even more important than the money.

It is also important to understand that the ways in which you can save this money may be far from obvious. Indeed, sometimes the ways to save money can be exactly the opposite of the ways in which you might save money on a similar deal back home. For example, in some countries buying a home in the name of a corporation can be a really good idea from a tax-saving point of view, but in Florida it would (usually) be a big mistake.

Only someone who thoroughly understands the Florida legal and tax systems and the way in which they interact with the systems where you live can give you this advice. This might be an experienced Realtor, but is likely to be a specialist Florida tax lawyer or tax advisor.

What Are You Trying To Achieve

Strategies for the ownership of your property abroad are intended to achieve five objectives.

1. To save you tax

    Put at its very simplest, choosing the most appropriate form of legal ownership for the property can save you huge amounts of tax, both during your lifetime and on your death. This is all perfectly legitimate. You are not asked to do anything underhand. All that you're doing is making sure that your wealth is not taxed twice and that you have arranged your affairs in the most tax efficient way possible.

2. To ensure that your wealth is inherited, on your death, by the people you wish to inherit.

    To those of us brought up in an Anglo-Saxon environment and within the common law, this seems a strange concern. We are used to a world in which we can (within very broad limits) leave our property to whom we wish, on our death. We can leave it to our wife or children. We can leave it to our mistress. We can leave it to charity.

Only in exceptional circumstances can our choice be challenged.

This is not the case in other parts of the world, or under other legal systems. I will return to this in more detail later.

3. To minimise cost and delay associated with the transfer of property, particularly on death

    In many places, the administrative steps needed to transfer the ownership of the property, particularly on death, are time-consuming and expensive. If these can be avoided this is an advantage.

4. To protect assets

    We live in an increasingly litigious world. We always used to say that it was only in America where anybody would sue you for anything, but, sadly, that is now also true in many other countries.

    The sensible arrangement of your affairs can help protect your assets from attack. This is, perhaps, particularly important if you're thinking of retiring abroad.

5. To afford privacy to those who want it.

How does this work?

There is no 'one size fits all' answer to the question of who should be the owner of your property. Everything depends upon your personal circumstances and your long-term wishes. I strongly recommend that, once you've decided to buy a house, you seek the guidance of your Realtor, lawyers or accountants before making a final decision about ownership. If, in your case, it's not really going to make any difference, they will be able to tell you this quickly and at little cost. If they can save you $200,000 you will be very happy.

All I can do in this book is point out to you some of the basic principles behind the choice of ownership and why the choice is important.

The most important factors determining how the choice will affect you are your nationality and the place where you are 'tax resident'. See the chapter on Taxes for an explanation of the meaning of 'tax resident'. For present purposes, let's assume that it means the country where you usually live.

Changing the way in which you legally owned the property can affect you in three main ways.

First, in some countries you do not have the freedom to leave your property as you wish when you die. Some categories of relatives (typically your children) have certain fixed rights that it is either difficult or impossible to circumvent. This means, for example, that even if you might want to leave your property to your wife (or, even more problematically, the person you live with) you will simply not be able to do so. Your children will automatically inherit. If this is a problem from which you are going to suffer it is an even more important reason for choosing the right form of ownership, than the mere saving of some tax.

Second, in some countries the tax system works so that the way in which property is distributed on death dramatically changes the amount of tax payable on the value of the property. For example, if you left the property to someone who was not your wife or child (such as the person you live with) the tax rate could be horrendous whereas leaving the property in a slightly different way could reduce the tax payable by 75% or more.

Third, the choice of the way in which you own the property can affect the amount of tax that you have to pay on any income or gain in value made by the property during your lifetime. Sometimes the difference can be huge.

There are various strategies available to you when it comes to deciding who should be the owner of the property. The correct one will depend upon your personal circumstances. Remember that, when we talk about saving tax, you are concerned not only with your tax position in the state where you buy the property, but also the tax position in the country where you live.

Let me give a couple of simple examples. They are only examples. Depending upon where you live and where the property is located, they may work beautifully, or not at all.

1. Imagine that you live in the country where gifts on death, even between husband and wife, are not tax-free. Imagine that the law permits (as in the UK) a gift from husband to wife during their lifetime and for that gift to be tax-free provided that the person making the gift survives for seven years.

   If the husband and wife wished to buy a property overseas, they could do so in their joint names or they could do so in one name only.

   If the wife is rather younger than the husband, it could well make sense for the property to be bought in the wife's name alone. That might involve a gift from husband to wife but that gift would be tax-free provided that the husband survives for seven years.

   However, as far as the authorities in the country where the property is located are concerned, that property is, and always has been, the property of the wife. On the husband's death, there will be no transfer of ownership and so no tax.

2. Imagine that you live in a country where you pay income tax at 50% on your earnings, but where your wife only pays 20%. If you put the property into both names and then rent it out, part of the income will be taxed at the higher rate

and part at the lower rate. On the other hand, if you put the property only in the wife's name, all the income would be taxed at the lower rate.

These examples are both far too simple, in that they do not take into account the potential obligations in both the country where the property is located and the country where you are based for tax purposes. But they do, I hope, indicate that some very simple and undramatic changes to your plans can save you significant amounts of money.

Things can get a little complicated.

Just to give you a flavour: one system of estate and gift taxation applies to U.S. citizens and to foreign citizens domiciled in the United States, and a separate system applies to foreign citizens who are not domiciled in the United States. An individual is domiciled in the United States if he or she actually resides here and has the intention to remain in the United States indefinitely.

U.S. Citizens and U.S. Domiciled Foreign Citizens

A U.S. citizen, or U.S.-domiciled foreign citizen, is subject to gift tax on the fair market value of all gifts made during his lifetime, unless an exclusion exists. What are the exclusions? Most notably, (for 2012) a donor is permitted to make tax-free gifts of up to $13,000 annually to each donee. Married couples, generally, can treat such gifts as if each spouse made half of the gift, thereby doubling the amount that can pass tax-free annually to any one donee. The ability to split the gifts is available only if both spouses are U.S. citizens, or U.S.-domiciled foreign citizens. Gifts to the individual's spouse qualify for special treatment. All gifts made to a spouse who is a U.S. citizen are exempt from gift tax. In contrast, for 2012, annual gifts of up to $139,000 to a spouse who is not a U.S. citizen are exempt from gift tax.

Upon the death of a U.S. citizen or U.S.-domiciled foreign individual, his or her taxable estate is subject to estate tax. The taxable estate includes the fair market value of all of a decedent's assets, wherever located, less certain deductions. Deductions are permitted for funeral and administration expenses, creditors' claims, charitable bequests, casualty losses, and other expenses.

During the individual's lifetime, current taxable gifts are added to all prior taxable gifts and a tentative tax is computed, using the gift and estate tax rate table. The tentative tax is then reduced by any prior gift taxes paid and by the applicable credit amount. At death, the taxable estate is added to all prior taxable gifts and the same tax calculation method is applied. The tax rate on taxable transfers in excess of $5,000,000, in 2012, is 35%.

The most important estate tax deduction is the marital deduction, which generally permits all transfers of property to the deceased's spouse to be excluded from taxation, but only if the spouse is a U.S. citizen.

Generally, no marital deduction is allowable for property passing outright to a spouse who is not a U.S. citizen. Relief, however, may be available under certain estate tax treaties. In addition, if the surviving spouse becomes a U.S. citizen before the federal estate tax return of the deceased is filed, property passing to the spouse can qualify for the marital deduction, if the spouse was a U.S. resident at all times after the deceased's death and before becoming a U.S. citizen.

The marital deduction, however, is available for property passing to a qualified domestic trust (QDOT) for the benefit of a spouse who is not a U.S. citizen.

A QDOT must satisfy the following conditions:

The trust instrument must require that at least one trustee is a U.S. citizen or domestic corporation, and that no distribution from the trust may be made without the approval of this trustee;

The trust must meet the requirements in the Treasury regulations to ensure the collection of the estate tax on a subsequent taxable event; and

The executor must make an election to have the QDOT provisions apply. (Your tax adviser should be consulted to determine that the requisite conditions are satisfied.)

Property passing from the deceased to the surviving spouse outside of the probate estate will qualify for QDOT treatment, if transferred to the QDOT by the due date of the deceased's estate tax return. A special rule (estate tax credit rule) is provided to coordinate the estate tax treatment of property passing to a non-U.S. citizen, with the treatment of property passing to a U.S. citizen (which is eligible for the marital deduction). If the property passes to a non-U.S. citizen, who later becomes a U.S. citizen or domiciliary and is later subject to U.S. estate tax, a credit will be permitted to the estate of the second spouse for estate tax paid by the first spouse on such property. This rule, which applies regardless of whether a QDOT is used, results in only one level of taxation on the property transferred to a spouse.

Non-domiciled Foreign Citizens

Most gifts made by non-domiciled foreign citizens ("NDFC") are exempt from U.S. gift taxes. However, these individuals are subject to U.S. gift tax on gifts of real property and on tangible personal property located within the United States. Gifts of intangible property are generally not subject to the gift tax even if the intangibles are U.S. assets (e.g., U.S. stocks and bonds). Gifts by a NDFC to his or her spouse are treated the same as gifts by U.S. citizens. Thus, gifts qualify for the unlimited marital deduction if the spouse is a U.S. citizen and for the $139,000 annual exclusion if the spouse is not a U.S. citizen. The $13,000 annual exclusion (for 2012) per donee is allowed, but gift-splitting between spouses is not available. The gift tax rates for NDFCs are generally the same as for gifts made by U.S. citizens and U.S.-domiciled foreign citizens, except that the applicable credit amount (discussed above) is not available.

of a NDFC is limited to certain tangible and intangible property situated
tes. For example, stocks and bonds of U.S. corporations or real property
ited States are included in the U.S. estate of a NDFC. However, deposits
h of a U.S. or foreign bank, deposits with a foreign branch of a U.S. bank,
igations (the interest income on which is not taxable to non-resident
aliens), and proceeds from a life insurance policy on the life of a deceased NDFC are not
considered to be property situated in the United States and, therefore, are not included in
the NDFC's gross estate.

The estate tax rates that apply to the estates of NDFCs are the same rates applicable to
the estates of U.S. citizens and U.S.-domiciled foreign citizens. A special unified credit is
provided for NDFCs that will exempt the first $60,000 of the U.S. taxable estate from U.S.
estate tax. Foreign citizens domiciled in certain countries that have estate tax treaties with
the United States are allowed to claim a pro-rate portion of the credit allowed to a U.S.
citizen. The United States has negotiated a number of treaties with respect to estate and gift
taxes of foreign citizens. Their provisions should also be reviewed to obtain any available
benefits.

I set all this out just to point out how complex the law can be and to stress, once again,
that a book such as this can do no more than skim the surface. We hope to be able to flag
up some of the issues. You then need to take proper professional advice, in this case from a
specialist accountant or tax attorney, to decide your best course of action.

The good news is that this complexity can save you a fortune, if you take advantage of the
rules. Of course, the flip side is that, if you don't make best use of the rules, you will be
losing out on a fortune.

So, having said that, let's take a quick look at the options.

Your Options

Sole ownership

In some cases it could be sensible to put the property in the name of one person only. If
your husband runs a high-risk business, of if he is 90 and you are 22, this could make
sense. On the other hand, if the wife runs a company that is about to go bust and she
herself is likely to go bankrupt, then it might be much more sensible to put the property
into the husband's name alone in order to avoid it falling into the hands of her creditors.

But this is seldom a good idea from the point of view of tax or inheritance planning.

Co-ownership

If two people are buying together, they will normally buy in both their names. This seems
natural and, in most cases, it reflects reality.

Indeed, whenever people purchase real property together, unless some other structure is put in place and put in place properly, they are considered co-owners of the property.

There are three main types of co-ownership: (1) tenancy in common; (2) joint tenancy; and (3) tenancy by the entirety. Each type of co-ownership has distinct requirements necessary for it to be created and each provides different rights and obligations for the property owners.

Understanding the types of co-ownership will help you to better determine what type of co-ownership is best for you. Since each type of co-ownership has different rights and obligations, choosing the wrong type of co-ownership may be a costly mistake. Your Realtor or lawyers should be consulted to ensure that the best type of co-ownership is selected.

Tenants in Common -- When the type of co-ownership is not specifically stated, by default, a tenancy in common is likely to exist. Each tenant in common has a separate fractional interest in the entire property. Although each tenant in common has a separate interest in the property, each may possess and use the whole property. Tenants in common may hold unequal interest in the property, but the interest held by each tenant in common is a fractional interest in the entire property (e.g. Bob owns a 25% interest in the property and Ann owns a 75% interest). Each tenant in common may freely transfer his/her interest in the property.

Tenants in common do not have the right of survivorship. Therefore, upon the death of one tenant in common, his/her interest passes via a will or through the laws of intestacy to another person or persons who will then become a tenant in common with the surviving co-owner(s). Note that this is the reverse of the UK position, where the default is a joint tenancy.

Joint Tenancy -- The most attractive feature of joint tenancy is the right of survivorship. Upon the death of one joint tenant, his or her interest immediately passes to the surviving joint tenant(s) and not to the deceased's estate. Joint tenants hold a single unified interest in the entire property. Each joint tenant must have equal shares in the property (e.g. Bob and Ann each hold a 50% interest). Each joint tenant may occupy the entire property, subject only to the rights of the other joint tenant(s).

Unlike tenants in common, joint tenancy has several requirements that must be met in order to be properly created. These vary from state to state, but the law generally requires that, in order for a joint tenancy to be created, specific language must be included in the deed of transfer. Such language includes that the grantees take the land: "jointly"; "as joint tenants"; "in joint tenancy"; "to them and the survivor of them"; or using other language in the instrument that it was clearly intended to create an estate in joint tenancy. However, even if such language is contained in the conveying instrument, a joint tenancy may not exist. There are four additional common law requirements (or "unities") necessary in order to create a joint tenancy. The four unities are: (1) Unity of time. The interests of the joint tenants must vest at the same time; (2) Unity of possession. The joint tenants must have undivided interests in the whole property, not divided interests in separate parts; (3) Unity of title. The Joint tenants must derive their interest by the same instrument (e.g. a deed or will); and (4) Unity of interest. Each joint tenant must have estates of the same type and same duration (e.g. some type of freehold estate). All four unities must exist. If one unity is missing at any time during the joint tenancy, the type of co-ownership automatically changes to a tenancy in common. A joint tenancy may be created by a will or deed, but may never be created by intestacy because there has to be an instrument expressing joint tenancy. A joint tenancy is freely transferable.

You can later change your mind and alter the form of tenancy. This can be by agreement between all of co-owners or by court order. This process is called partition.

A partition is a judicial separation of property held in joint ownership by one or more individual. Partition is used when at least one co-owner wants to terminate the property co-ownership, regardless of the desires of the other co-owners. Since each co-owner has a fractional portion of the entire property, partition is necessary to properly divide the property (or its sale proceeds). Under partition, the court will either physically divide the property, or order it to be sold and the proceeds distributed according to the per cent interest held by each co-owner. Selling the property and dividing the proceeds is called "partition by sale" and is used by the courts whenever a geographic division of the property is not feasible. The partition process involves all co-owners.

Note, however, that changing the structure in this way is to be avoided if possible, or unless you have had clear advice that it is OK to proceed. It can have adverse tax consequences where the property is located, at home or both.

Tenancy by the Entirety -- This type of co-ownership is exclusively available between husband and wife. Similar to joint tenancy, tenancy by the entirety provides the right of survivorship. To exist, tenancy by the entirety requires that the four unities of joint tenancy exist plus a fifth: unity of marriage between the two co-owners. However, even if all five unities exist, the type of co-ownership may still be joint tenancy if the conveying instrument indicates such. Unlike joint tenancy, tenancy by the entirety does not allow one spouse to convey his/her interest to a third party. However, one spouse may convey his/her interest to the other spouse. A tenancy by the entirety may only be terminated by divorce, death, or mutual agreement by both spouses. A terminated tenancy by the entirety becomes a tenancy in common.

Although the type of co-ownership need not necessarily be specified in the offer to purchase, or the purchase and sale agreement, it must be contained in the deed giving ownership of the real property to the co-owners.

I must repeat that it is very important to seek clear advice from your Realtor or lawyer about the form of ownership that will suit you best, both with regard to the consequences in the US and the consequences in the country where you live.

You can later change your mind and alter the form of tenancy. This can be by agreement between all of co-owners or by court order. This process is called partition and is explained above.

Partition is available to all but tenants by the entirety. Partition is also not available if all co-owners agree to prohibit partitions. Courts will honor this agreement for a reasonable period of time.

Adding your children to the title

If you decide to buy together as tenants in common then, in certain cases, it can make sense to split the ownership other than 50/50. If, for example, you have three children and your wife has two, then to secure each of those children an equal share on your death you might think about buying 60% in your name and 40% in your wife's name.

But what about going further? If you give your children the money to buy part of the property and so put them on the title now, you may save quite a lot of inheritance tax. On your death you will only own (say) one fifth of the property rather than one half. Only that part will be taxable. It may be such a small value as to result in a tax free inheritance. Of course, if you give them the money to buy the whole of the property then, on your death, there will be nothing to pass by inheritance and so no inheritance tax. The property is already theirs.

These plans only work sensibly if your children are over 18. Of course, there are drawbacks. For example, if they fall out with you, they can insist on the sale of the property and receiving their share.

Putting the property in the name of your children only

If you put the property only in the name of your children (possibly reserving for yourself a life estate – see below) then the property is theirs. On your death there will be little or no inheritance tax and there will be no need to incur the legal expenses involved in dealing with an inheritance. This sounds attractive. Remember, however, that you have lost control. It is no longer your property. If your children divorce their husband/wife will be able to claim a share. If they die before you without children of their own, you will end up inheriting the property back from them and having to pay inheritance tax for the privilege of doing so.

A life estate is the right to use the property for a lifetime. So, on your death, your rights would be extinguished, **but** your second wife or partner, who still has a life estate, would still be able to use the property. Only on their death would the property pass in full to the people to whom you gave it years earlier. This device can not only protect your right to use the property, but also save large amounts of inheritance tax, particularly if you are young, the property is valuable and you survive for many years. As ever, there are also drawbacks, not least being the fact that after the gift you no longer own the property. If you wish to sell, you need the agreement of the "owners", who will be entitled to their share of the proceeds of sale and who would have to agree to buy you a new house.

If you wish to do this, you must structure the gift carefully. Otherwise it could be taxable *at once*.

A trust or foundation

Some people and in some circumstances will choose to own the house through a trust, possibly linked to a corporate vehicle. There would be two main reasons for doing this. If you come from a country where the rules concerning the inheritance of real estate are different from and more restrictive than the rules concerning the inheritance of personal property (sometimes known as movable property) then the ownership of shares in a corporation might be freely transferable to whoever you wish on your death, whereas the ownership of the real estate itself might be subject to the rules of forced inheritance, so forcing the property to be passed to your children. The second reason is that many people, for purely innocent reasons, prefer the anonymity or increased privacy presented by owning the property through a trust. If you are a pop star or a famous sports person, you might not want your name to appear on public record as the owner of a particular house.

The Americans love trusts and foundations. Trust law is complicated and outside the scope of this little book but the use of these structures can be hugely beneficial. Just remember two things: that US tax laws were drafted by tax attorneys to keep all the other tax attorneys in business and that if you can think of a rich and famous American family then you know a family that has a trust or a foundation! The Kennedys. The Rockefellers. Elvis.

US limited company

For some people owning a property via a limited company can look like a very attractive option. You own the shares in a company, not a house. There are various types of company.

This seldom works well in the US and it can also have adverse tax consequences where you live. It can be complicated and give rise to lots of on-going paperwork.

Buying through a company gives rise to a host of potential problems as well as benefits. The plan needs to be studied closely by your advisers, so that you can decide whether it makes sense in the short, medium **and** long term.

Company based in the country where you live

It is rare for a purchase through a company based where you live to make sense for a holiday home or single investment property. This is despite the fact that the ability to pay for the property with the company's money, without drawing it out of the company and possibly having to pay local tax on the withdrawal, is attractive. Once again you need expert advice from someone familiar with the law of both countries.

A US LLC

An LLC (limited liability company) is a flexible form of legal structure sometimes used to own a property in the US – and, indeed, for many other purposes. It blends some of the legal elements of partnership and some of corporate structures.

An LLC is not a corporation; it is a legal form of company that provides limited liability to its owners in the vast majority of United States jurisdictions, including Florida.

LLCs do not need to be organized for profit.

For U.S. federal income tax purposes, an LLC is treated by default as a "pass-through entity". This means that it is not required to file tax returns or pay tax on its profits. Instead, the money made is treated as being the income of the owners of the LLC and taxed in their hands.

Another useful feature is that, for real estate companies, each separate property can be owned by its own, individual LLC, thereby shielding not only the owners from personal liability if anything goes wrong, but also their other properties from cross-liability.

For these and a number of other reasons, again depending entirely upon your personal circumstances, ownership through an LLC can be a good idea; for others it would be an expensive waste of time.

If you are interested in exploring the possibilities offered by an LLC, take advice as soon as possible. The advice will usually come from a lawyer or accountant experienced in this field.

Your Realtor will be able to have a preliminary discussion with you about whether an LLC might work for you and then, if appropriate, refer you to a suitable adviser.

What about owning through your pension fund?

Owning your property through your pension fund can be a very good idea.

For the UK buyer, the vehicles usually used as a Self Invested Personal Pension (SIPP) or the Small Self Administered Scheme (SSAS).

Other countries offer similar structures.

Detailed examination of these complicated pension products is beyond the scope of this book that you should understand that investing in property through your pension can be highly beneficial, for two main reasons. The first is that, just as with every other payment made from a pension fund, you will usually have received tax relief on the amount that you paid into the fund and so the tax man will, in effect, be providing part of the money that you are using to buy the property. The second advantage is that all of the income from your investment and any capital gains made by it will be free of UK tax. The amount in the fund will also be free of UK inheritance tax. Note that there will not be any freedom from any taxes in the country where the property is located, so you need to give careful thought to be ownership structure adopted when buying through a pension fund.

Of course, no such benefits ever come without a price tag. In the case of buying property through your pension fund, the two main disadvantages are that there are limits on the types of property that you can own (purely residential property is normally not acceptable) and you can have no personal use of the property.

I have used the UK as an example, but similar opportunities to own via a pension fund exist for buyers from other countries.

If this option is interest to you, you need to take professional advice at a very early stage. It is your fund that will be buying the property, not you. It is therefore your fund that will have to sign the contract. They will not be able to do so until the money is in place and they have decided on the most sensible ownership structure in which to hold the property. All this can take a little time. It needs to be sorted out before you go looking at houses.

Summary

In each and every one of these ownership scenarios there are lots of 'ifs and buts'. Sometimes they won't work. Sometimes they will only work if you take additional steps beyond the mere structure of the title of the property. Sometimes they might work, but present other dangers which you think of as being more worrying than the tax that might otherwise have to be paid. For example, if you choose to give the property to your children and even assuming that the law in your country would treat that as a valid gift, removing the property from your estate for tax purposes, the property then becomes their property. If they get divorced, half of it may go to their spouses. If they fall out with you, they can stop you from using it. If they die before you, you might inherit it back from them and have to pay inheritance tax for the privilege of doing so.

This is complicated. It can also save you a huge amount of trouble and money. Take some advice before making your final decision as to who should own the property.

Until then, there is usually no problem if you see a property that you would like to buy. In your preliminary contract, you can simply say that you wish to reserve the property and then decide to buy not in your name but in the name of some other person. However, on occasions, even this can present some problems and so it is much better to clarify the question of who should be the owner of the property calmly and without pressure of time whilst you are doing your research and before you have gone shopping.

Just remember that you need to get this right first time round. If you buy the property (say) in your own name and later decide that it would have been better to put it in the name of (say) your children, you can end up having to pay all of the taxes and expenses when you bought the property for a second time PLUS you might have to pay taxes in the US, in your own country or in both on the value of the gift you have made to (in this case) your children.

How To Choose

For each Buyer of a home in the US, one of the options set out above will suit him perfectly. Another might just about make sense. The rest would be an expensive waste of money.

The trouble is, it is not obvious which is the right choice! You need *in every case* to take advice. If your case is simple, so will be the advice. If it is complex, the time and money spent will be repaid many times over.

Decide what you would like to do. Then take advice as to what works best.

Don't get caught up with complicated solutions to simple problems, unless it is going to save you a lot of money and you are prepared to put up with the costs and restrictions associated with your choice.

Remember that, very often, you will be paying out good money today in order to save money many years in the future and there is no guarantee that, by the time the situation arises, the rules will not have changed. So listen carefully to the advice and use your own common sense to work out whether the steps recommended are really worthwhile. Taking advantage of a loophole in the law is one thing; loopholes can be closed. Taking advantage of a basic principle of US law which has been there for hundreds of years and which is highly unlikely to be changed any time soon is something entirely different and, usually, much more secure.

Useful Names & Addresses

Real estate lawyer: http://www.bakerdonelson.com/martha-a-hartley/

IRS: http://www.irs.gov

Finding the Right Property

Realtors & Other Licenced Property Professionals

Over 95% of foreigners buying a property in Central Florida will do so via a Realtor™ or other property professional. As I explained in the introduction, in this book I am using the terms Realtor, estate agent and property sales agent interchangeably, although this is not strictly correct as Realtors can only use that title if they are signed up to the association of Realtors™ and agree to abide by their rules.

Local Realtors, estate agents etc.

Choosing the right estate agent for an international purchase should be quite different from choosing an agent with whom to work in your own country. The services they offer are likely to be very different from those to which you are accustomed and the whole position concerning professional standards and regulation is also likely to be different.

Real estate brokers also often operate (with the appropriate licences) as appraisers, property management companies and property letting agents.

There are four key points that you need to understand.

1. Do they operate a multiple listing service (MLS)?

    If you come from a country, such as the UK, France or China, where such a service does not exist, or at least does not exist in a comprehensive form, you will probably not realise the significance of this question, but the existence of an MLS really does transform the way in which the whole real estate market works.

    An MLS does two things. It is a mechanism by which participating estate agents share access to sellers and buyers. The estate agent, who has been instructed to sell the property ("the listing agent"), places the details of the property in the MLS and offers to share commission with the estate agent who introduces the buyer. Behind this conceptually simple arrangement is a marketing database, permitting all participating agents to access all of the properties in the system. Its purpose is to provide accurate and structured data about properties for sale, instantly accessible (via their estate agents) to anyone in the market to buy a property.

2. What services do they offer?

    Are they working for the seller – a seller's agent?

    Is the seller's agent's responsibility simply to sell the property for the best price they can achieve?

Are they offering to work for you as your agent -- a buyer's agent or a buyer's broker -- in such a way that you are their client and it is to you that they owe their legal responsibility?

Are they offering a "dual agency" – under which their brokerage/agency represents both parties? Dual agency agreements are no longer permitted in Florida.

These agents have legal responsibilities to both parties. This can create great legal problems in terms of disputes arising out of conflicts of interest.

Are they a "transaction broker", sitting between the two parties to put the deal together but owing no specific fiduciary duties to either and -- if they are – what are their responsibilities? This is illegal in many states, but the default position in Florida.

Do they offer any additional services such as property management or rental management once you have bought the property?

It is important to be clear about this at the beginning of your relationship.

3.   Are they regulated – and by whom?

This is a little complicated but it is important.

Remember that the role of the US Realtor (or equivalent) may be different from the role of the estate agent in the country where you live.

Real estate sales are regulated by Florida law.

In order to be involved in negotiating the sale or purchase of real estate in Florida, a person must be a "Licensed Real Estate Professional".

These Licensed Real Estate Professionals can be brokers, who have passed a higher level of exams and have the right to own and run offices and to supervise other professionals. Other professionals include real estate agents (sometimes called sales agents) – who are qualified but only authorised to deal with sales under the supervision of a broker.

Compare this with the situation on some other countries. For example, in the UK there is no qualification. A person can be a plumber today and, without any qualifications or experience, set up an estate agency tomorrow.

They cannot do this in the US. In the US, in order to practice as an estate agent (whether under the name of a Realtor or otherwise) they must be professionally qualified and hold a licence to practice. From that point onwards they will be heavily regulated.

This regulation is very important for your protection.

Brokers or sales agents may or may not be part of the Realtor's organisation. If they choose to be a member, they must abide by its stringent code of conduct in addition to any other rules.

4. What will they cost you?

    If you work only with the seller's agent/broker, you will pay nothing.

    If you work with your own buyer's agent/broker, you will usually pay nothing. The position will be explained clearly in a document supplied to you by the agent concerned.

    If you work with a transaction broker, the seller pays his fees by way of a share of the sales commission.

Your options

Using a Seller's Agent

The job of most Licensed Real Estate Professionals is, of course, to find buyers for properties entrusted to them by a seller. But there the similarity ends.

Whichever type of seller's agent you visit and wherever they are based, please remember that they are being paid by the seller to sell the property. They are not being paid by you to look after your interests. However helpful and professional they may be, if you do not sign a contract to buy then they do not receive their commission and their children starve. They therefore have their own interests to look after, which broadly coincide with those of the sellers, but which might not coincide with yours.

It is for this reason that we recommend that you should always appoint your own Buyers Agent. He or she is looking after you. See below.

Despite this, the seller's estate agent (listing agent) can be a mine of useful information, knowledge about the area and practical help. The large majority is genuinely enthusiastic about property in the US and about you joining their community. Take advantage of what they have to offer, form a rapport with them, buy a property through them….but get everything checked by your own buyer's agent and, of course, your legal adviser - just as you would at home.

Using a Buyer's Agent

A great difference between the local US estate agent or broker and the one you are likely to have worked with at home is that, in the US, you may well retain your own agent to help you locate property and negotiate with the seller and his agent.

These buyer's agents are responsible to you, not the seller – though they will usually be paid by receiving a percentage of the seller's agent's commission and so (usually) do not cost you anything.

One particularly nice thing about the American system is that any participating Realtor will have access to every listed property in his area and some will be able to access everything in the whole country. That is a lot of property! Over 2.4 million homes on sale.

Therefore, if you decide to use a buyer's agent, the most important thing is to find somebody who gives you confidence and that you feel you can work with.

Much of the work that Team Feltrim does is as the buyer's agent. Like all other Realtors, we have to make it very clear to you whether we are working with you as a buyer's agent, a seller's agent or as an independent broker (see below).

Using a Dual Agency

This is to be avoided. They work for both buyer and seller and have legal responsibilities to both. A recipe for disaster.

This is now illegal in Florida. If you are offered a dual agency, appoint your own buyer's broker!

Using a Transaction Broker

The transaction broker tries to put together the deal between the buyer and seller, without owing a full fiduciary responsibility to either. He or she is, legally, neutral. They do not "represent" either party. They have a limited duty of confidentiality to both parties, but must disclose the things specifically required by law. They are obliged to work honestly and fairly and to exercise due care and skill in their work.

This is the most common form of brokerage in Florida.

Whichever you use!

In order to protect his often substantial commission, the agent will usually ask you to sign a document before he takes you to see any property. This is a statement setting out your mutual obligations and, most importantly, the basis upon which you are working with the agent and how he is being paid. See the sample at Appendix 7.

This document also proves that it was he who has introduced you to the property, so avoiding later arguments about who should be paid the commission due.

This is perfectly normal.

What are Realtors™?

Most estate agents in the US have signed up to be members of the National Association of Realtors: Realtors™. All 1.2 million of them! Realtors™ is North America's largest trade association. It is also its own regulatory body and operates the main multiple listing service: MLS. Small wonder so many have joined.

> *"When representing a buyer, seller, landlord, tenant, or other client as an agent, REALTORS® pledge themselves to protect and promote the interests of their client. This obligation to the client is primary, but it does not relieve REALTORS® of their obligation to treat all parties honestly..."*

Realtor is a frequently-used word in many countries to describe any person or company involved in the real estate trade, regardless of their NAR status or American residence. However, in the United States, the National Association of Realtors obtained registrations for the words "REALTOR" and "REALTORS" as collective trademarks, so only members of the NAR can call lawfully themselves realtors.

The general responsibility of your Realtor™

The position of the Realtor is clearly set out in the NRA code of ethics.

In typical American fashion, the code starts with a ringing preamble:

"Under all is the land. Upon its wise utilization and widely allocated ownership depend the survival and growth of free institutions and of our civilization. REALTORS® should recognize that the interests of the nation and its citizens require the highest and best use of the land and the widest distribution of land ownership. They require the creation of adequate housing, the building of functioning cities, the development of productive industries and farms, and the preservation of a healthful environment.

Such interests impose obligations beyond those of ordinary commerce. They impose grave social responsibility and a patriotic duty to which REALTORS' should dedicate themselves, and for which they should be diligent in preparing themselves. REALTORS', therefore, are zealous to maintain and improve the standards of their calling and share with their fellow REALTORS' a common responsibility for its integrity and honor."

What will your Realtor cost you?

Standard of Practice 1-13 deals with the question of fees:

"When entering into buyer/tenant agreements, REALTORS® must advise potential clients of:

- the REALTOR®'s company policies regarding cooperation;
- the amount of compensation to be paid by the client;
- the potential for additional or offsetting compensation from other brokers, from the seller or landlord, or from other parties;
- any potential for the buyer/tenant representative to act as a disclosed dual agent, e.g. listing broker, subagent, landlord's agent, etc., and
- the possibility that sellers or sellers' representatives may not treat the existence, terms, or conditions of offers as confidential unless confidentiality is required by law, regulation, or by any confidentiality agreement between the parties."

Summary

Each of these– seller's agent, buyer's agent and independent broker - has different legal consequences.

As you might imagine, the detailed rules are quite complicated, but the most important thing to understand is that a seller's agent is working for the benefit of the seller and not for the benefit of the buyer, whereas a buyer's agent is looking after the interest of the buyer, not the seller. None of them can actively mislead the other parties in the transaction and all have to abide by certain minimum standards.

For most buyers – especially for those who come from overseas – we recommend the use of a buyer's agent, especially one who is familiar with dealing with people who come from your country.

You will find that this makes life very much easier and it is reassuring to know that your Realtor is working only for you. As I have already explained, the buyer's agent is almost always paid by way of commission paid by the seller, so using one does not cost you anything.

To my way of thinking – having experienced the US system and the systems in some other countries – this system (and the MLS that makes it possible) is a thoroughly good idea and something that should be copied in other countries.

Despite the rather dubious reputation enjoyed by estate agents all over the world, if you have to deal with an estate agent, there is no better or safer place to do so than in the US.

Despite the fact that you could, in theory, use an agent anywhere in the country, you are probably best off starting to look for property by using an estate agent in the immediate vicinity of the place where you are looking. Local newspapers will give you an indication of which agents are advertising, and so active, in your area. You can also get names off the internet (under *realtors*). See the chapter "Research" for guidance as to how to choose the best agent.

How do we work at Team Feltrim?

By dealing with a reputable real estate company, you should enjoy the same level of service whether the person dealing with you is a broker or a sales agent.

At Team Feltrim, our brokers are also Realtors and we have also joined the Century21 franchise, which means that we are inspected by them and have to follow their code of conduct, in addition to the Realtor's code of conduct. This gives our clients the maximum level of protection possible.

At Team Feltrim we also have realtors and licensed sales agents speaking several languages and experienced in dealing with people of many nationalities. Recent buyers have come from Argentina, Brazil, Canada, China, Colombia, Ireland, Scandinavia, Singapore, Spain, the UK and – of course – the US.

Estate agents based in the country where you live

In addition to estate agents based in the US, there are a number of people based in other countries who sell property in the US. Most popular areas are covered.

On the face of it, it might appear more convenient to use someone based near to where you live. Apart from anything else, they are in your time zone. However, such agents will usually lack the detailed knowledge of the local market that is so important for the successful conclusion of a transaction and they can often simply get in the way by being another link in the chain of communication.

A few US agents maintain branch offices in other countries. You might find this helpful.

Although, under the law in the country where they are based, they might be entitled to call themselves estate agents, it is important to note that, in many cases, they are not licensed to work as estate agents/brokers in the US.

They very often work in association with one or more US agents, often covering a wider area than a single local agent would cover. They advertise or market the properties through exhibitions etc. and then act as an intermediary between the potential buyer and the US estate agent. Because they deal with 'foreign' buyers all the time, they should be able to anticipate some of the common problems that can arise and smooth the progress of the transaction.

Generally they should share the commission of the US agent – who is very pleased that he can expand his potential buyer base through the introduction of foreign buyers. Thus, their services should cost you nothing extra.

Unfortunately, it is not as simple as that. Some are operating illegally. Some charge substantial amounts of extra commission for their services and often they do not disclose that commission to the buyer. There is nothing wrong with paying someone who is doing a useful job, but you should be told that you are expected to do so. You can then decide whether the convenience of dealing with someone in Britain is worth the extra cost. Always ask for confirmation that the price you will be paying is exactly the same as you would have paid in the US or, if there is an extra charge, the amount of the charge.

However, many of these non-US based sellers are highly experienced and very reputable. Before deciding which to use, ask about their level of experience and check whether they are legally permitted to undertake this work. It is more difficult to assess whether they are reputable. A good starting point is to see whether they are members of AIPP (the Association of Overseas Property Professionals – www.aipp.org.uk – Tel: +44 203 207 9095). This is an international, non-profit organisation that agents and developers can join if they are experienced in the field, are prepared to be scrutinised and willing to abide by its code of conduct.

Other Ways

Of course, using an agent is not the only way of finding property, though (especially for a foreign buyer) it is usually the best.

DIY sales

In the US, especially in big cities and rural areas, far more property is sold "person to person" than in the UK. These are known as 'For Sale by Owner' or FSBO deals. There are a variety of different sources of information about such properties for sale. See www.forsalebyowner.com for materials and listings.

By all means have a look at such sites but, for most foreign buyers, it will be far better to deal with an estate agent.

Of course, one of the most popular reasons why homeowners choose to sell their house without the assistance of an agent is to avoid paying an agent's commission In the US the agent's fee typically makes up 6% of the selling price of the property.

When a homeowner decides to sell his home without a real estate agent and a buyer who is not working with an agent wants to buy the home, the seller pays no commission because no real estate agents are involved.

But this does not mean that you cannot use an agent if you find a FSBO property that you really want to buy. If a buyer who is represented by an estate agent is interested in a FSBO home, that buyer's agent may request the owner pay him commission, or finder's fee, for bringing the buyer. The seller may agree to pay the fee or he may refuse. Clearly, the seller is not legally obliged to pay any commission.

If the seller will not pay any commission, the buyer's agent is usually paid by the buyer.

According to a press release by the National Association of Realtors (NAR), in 2009 11% of US real estate transactions were FSBO. This was down from 13% in 2008 and a peak of 20% in 1987. However, some believe those statistics may be misleading and suggest that the true size of the U.S. FSBO market is closer to 22%.

Local newspapers

Individuals place advertisements in the "For Sale" section of the local paper.

Specialist local property press

In most areas, there are specialist free magazines, which exist primarily to carry advertisements from estate agents selling property. Some have just a local coverage, others a regional or even national coverage.

There is also a more specialist property press. See www.world-newspapers.com/real-estate.html

Internet

There is a huge amount of property available for private sale on the internet. In May 2013 a Google search for "real estate for sale Florida" generated 347 million results! Be extra careful when buying over the internet.

Property shows

Some of the international property shows have a section where private individuals can post details of property for sale. Contact the show organisers for details.

Auctions

Property in the US can be bought at auction, just as in the UK.

Some auctions are voluntary. Others are run by court order, after foreclosure on a mortgage, or by the government disposing of property that it has seized.

See www.auctioncompanyofamerica.com, http://usa-foreclosure.com or www.usa.gov/shopping/shopping.shtml for a sample of what is available.

Prices can be very attractive. A few years ago, at the height of the last recession, there were incredible bargains with prices, perhaps, 30% of "value". Now auctions usually offer less spectacular bargains, but can still be attractive. This is because, particularly in many judicial auctions, the process is intended first and foremost to recover someone's debt. Once that and the considerable costs have been covered, there is little reason to press for a higher price, even though the owner will ultimately receive the excess.

Buying a property at auction is not simple for someone who does not live in the area and it is vitally important that you have taken all the normal preparatory steps – including seeing a lawyer – before you embark on the process.

The procedure leading up to the auction is basically the same whether the auction is a judicial auction or a voluntary auction.

First, you must know that the auction is taking place. They are usually advertised 6 to 8 weeks in advance. This will be in specialist press and on the internet.

Second, you must find out what is in the auction. Brief details of the property to be sold are published. These details of the property will mean nothing to you. The place could be derelict or next door to a nuclear power station – or both. You will need to inspect the property and decide whether it is of interest. This is a time consuming and potentially costly process. Remember that you could have to inspect twenty properties to find three you might like and then you might be outbid on all three. An alternative to personal inspection is to get someone to do it for you. This is not as satisfactory, but a local estate agent will, for a fee, go to look at the property and give you a description of it. If you're lucky, he might post or email you some photographs. His fee, typically about $300 if the property is close to his office, will probably be less than the cost of travel. Some people buy blind. This is for real poker players.

Third, you will need to check out the legal situation of the property before the date of the auction. Most of the steps needed in an ordinary purchase will be required (see below).

Fourth, many properties on sale by auction are not in the best of condition. You will therefore need to get estimates as to the likely cost of repairs or improvements, so as to make sure that the price you bid is not so high as to make the project non-viable.

Fifth, you will have to appoint your Realtor or advisor to act on your behalf at the auction. You would be brave or foolish not to be represented. The lawyer will explain precisely what will need to be done for this particular auction. You will have to tell him the maximum price you want to offer and pay him the bidding deposit. Your will also have to give him your personal details for the contract.

You do not need to attend the auction – your representative will be able to do so for you. He will probably require a power of attorney for that purpose. He will, of course, charge you for this work. Get an estimate.

Even though you do not need to be present, an auction (especially a judicial auction) is a most interesting event, so you might want to go along.

Although the prices at auction can be very attractive, you must bear in mind that you will face additional costs over and above those on a normal purchase. These are likely to raise the overall costs.

It may also possible to buy a US property at auction in the country where you live. This is very rare. The auction acts simply as a preliminary sale of the property. The sale will need to be formalised in the usual way (see below).

Notaries

Notaries in the US perform a very different role from their role in Europe. Basically, they just witness the signature of certain types of documents.

They do not advise buyers or sellers about the transferring of the ownership of property.

They do not prepare the contracts and other documents needed to sell a property.

They do not sell property.

If you come from a country where the notary plays a key role in the transfer of ownership of property, you need to understand that the US system is totally different; the notary is, essentially, irrelevant to it and he will do nothing to protect your interests.

The Need To Visit

It is probably worth repeating: do not buy a property without seeing it!

Renting instead of Buying

If you are moving permanently to the US there is sometimes a lot to be said for temporarily renting a place in the area where you are thinking of living. It is best to do this for a full year before deciding whether to live there. In Florida, standard leases are for 12 months. Shorter leases are subject to sales tax, so more complicated and expensive. If you decide you like the area, allow time within your 12 month rental to find and buy your new home,

Alternatively, try a series of short term (maximum one month) rentals in an area zoned for such rentals. This could be a good idea if you are pretty clear about where you want to buy and what you are looking for, as the process of buying, especially if you are buying without a mortgage, can be quite quick.

Try to rent something similar to what you are thinking of buying and do not rent unseen - take a short holiday to find your rental property.

If you rent, you are less likely to commit yourself to a purchase in an area you turn out not to like. It also avoids the expensive process of having to sell the property and buy another, either in the US or back home. The overall cost of moving within the US is likely to be about 10% of the price of your new property, being the fees on the purchase of the new property and the estate agents' fee for selling the old one. A move back home would (depending on the value of the property bought) be likely to cost about 8% - 3% sales expenses and 5% purchase expenses in England or wherever you live.

There are drawbacks to renting:

1. In the past, property prices in many areas have risen rapidly. Delaying 18 months would probably have cost you about 15%-20% in increased property cost This is a lot more than your money would have made if invested, so the delay would have cost you money. This is not the case any longer but many are predicting modest price rises in the near future.

2. The rent you pay out is dead money. This would probably be about 5% of the value of a property per annum.

3. You want to get on with your life, especially if you have just retired.

4. Moving is stressful. You will have to do it twice rather than once.

5. Moving into temporary accommodation can produce a lack of attachment to the area, which can mean that you don't commit to it and give it a fair try. You are always looking back over your shoulder rather than forward to your new life.

6. It can be hard to find good accommodation available on an 18 month let.

If you are thinking of a holiday home, it can also make sense to rent rather than buy. The biggest drawback to owning a property overseas is that you feel compelled to take all your holidays there. You are paying for it so you should use it! If you invested the money spent on the holiday home in real estate chosen only for its investment potential, it could generate a good income, which would pay for a holiday anywhere in the world. Of course, renting is never as satisfying as owning your own home. You do not know the quality of what you will find on arrival. You won't be able to leave your clothes there and so travel light. You won't have friends there and so feel part of the community. You won't be able to offer the use of the property to family and friends. You may even find that your investment of the cash saved has performed less well than the house you wanted to buy.

Useful Names & Addresses

Team Feltrim: www.c21teamfeltrim.com (My company)

The primary steps to getting Florida residential property: http://www.britstoflorida.com/buying_infla.html

Mid Florida Investment Properties: http://www.floridahomeflipping.com/become-an-investor/central-florida-homes/

Online real estate: http://www.realtor.com/

Real Estate Blogs Florida: http://boldrealestategroup.com/blog/

Inspections (Surveys) & Appraisals (Valuations)

Once you've chosen the house you want to buy, you need to make sure that the price is a fair price and that it doesn't contain any nasty hidden secrets. At this point, there are several choices open to you. Much depends upon your relationship with your estate agent.

Inspections (Surveys)

What is an Inspection?

In the context of a purchase in the US, a home inspection is a limited, non-invasive examination of the condition of a home. Home inspections are usually conducted by a home inspector who has the training and certifications to perform such inspections. The inspector prepares and delivers to the client a written report of findings. The home inspector describes the condition of the home at the time of inspection but does not guarantee future condition, efficiency, or life expectancy of systems or components.

An inspector will check the roof, basement, heating system, water heater, air-conditioning system, structure, plumbing, electrical, and many other aspects of buildings, looking for improper building practices, those items that require extensive repairs, items that are general maintenance issues, as well as some fire and safety issues. However, please note that a home inspection is not technically exhaustive and does not imply that every defect will be discovered.

Things that will be excluded from the inspection (unless otherwise agreed) will include: code or zoning violations, permit research, property measurements or surveys, boundaries, easements or right of way, conditions of title, proximity to environmental hazards, noise interference, soil or geological conditions, well water systems or water quality, underground sewer lines and/or waste disposal systems, buried piping, cisterns, underground water tanks and sprinkler.

A complete list of standards and procedures for home inspections can be found at the National Association of Home /inspectors – www.nahi.org. A general inspection standard for all types of buildings can be found at the National Academy of Building Inspection Engineers - www.nabie.org.

Why Have an Inspection (Survey)?

Whatever property you are thinking of buying, you should consider having it inspected **before** you commit yourself to the purchase. It costs just as much and causes just as much disruption to repair property in the US as it does back home, so you don't want any surprises.

In fact – foolishly – very few buyers of property in the US do this.

For new or nearly new property, you should have the benefit of some construction guarantees. Your estate agent will tell you what is available in any given case.

For older property (and, arguably, for younger property too) you should consider a survey.

If you decide on a survey there are a number of options available to you.

Choosing an Inspector (Surveyor)

How do you decide which inspector should inspect your property?

Once again, the best way is by recommendation from someone you trust. Who referred you to the inspector? The best referral is from someone you personally know and trust, and who was satisfied with the inspector's performance. Although many real-estate professionals refer quality home inspectors, there is a possible conflict of interest with this type of referral. If you were not reliably referred to the inspector, then ask for references from past clients, preferably from several years past.

Is the inspector experienced? A full-time inspector who performs 250 or more inspections per year and has many years' experience is most desirable.

Which inspector will the inspection company send? When dealing with an inspection company the reputations of both the company and the inspector who is assigned to your home are important. Request that an experienced inspector be assigned rather than a new one.

Is the inspector covered by errors and omissions insurance and general liability insurance? It is to your advantage that your inspector has this coverage. Do not be afraid to ask for a copy of the policies.

How long does the inspection take? Ask how long the inspection will take and how many other inspections will be performed on the same day as yours. If the inspection takes less than 2 hours, find another inspector. Performing a thorough inspection is very tiring, so arrange to be the first or second one of the day.

How much does the inspection cost? Several hundred dollars. This is a small price to pay to get the best protection you can, for perhaps the biggest purchase of your life.

What type of report do you get and when do you get it? You may want to ask this question since there are several answers. An inspection should include a signed report that describes what was inspected and the condition of each inspected item. Some inspectors use a checklist type of form with stock responses. Other inspectors simply provide a written description of the conditions found. A modern alternative to these are computer-generated reports. The best of these are generated by advanced home inspection software systems and include comments specific to each home. An important question to ask is, "When do I get the report?" The checklist type and the handwritten type are usually delivered to you on-site. Computer-generated reports are also available on-site from a few inspectors who bring a portable computer to the job. Otherwise, the inspector mails the report. You may want to know up front how long you can expect to wait for it.

Is the inspector affiliated with any organizations? There are many local, state, and national organizations that an inspector can join, as well as many franchises that an inspector can purchase. However, membership in any organization does not guarantee a quality inspector. In the end, the individual inspector's experience and knowledge will determine the quality of the inspection.

Types of Inspection (Surveys)

What type of inspection do you need? Since, in some states, inspectors are not licensed, there are a number of choices and it is worthwhile giving them a little thought.

Real Estate Broker

It may be possible to arrange for another local estate agent to give the property a quick "once over", to comment on the price asked and any obvious problem areas. This is far short of a survey. This is not a good idea and few agents will be prepared to offer this service.

Independent Professional Inspector (Surveyor)

Your estate agent can put you in touch with the right people. In most rural areas, there will be limited choice. If you prefer, you can select "blind" from a list of local members supplied by one of the many organisations to which inspectors are affiliated.

You will find that the report is different from the sort of report you would get from a surveyor 'back home'. Many people find it a little "thin", with too much focus on issues that are not their primary concern. It may take several forms, from a simple tick list to a full-bloodied computer generated but very detailed report. Make sure you know what type of report you will be receiving.

Builder

If you are going to do a virtual demolition and rebuild, then it might make more sense to get a builder to do a report on the property. A reputable and experienced builder will also be able to comment (unofficially) on whether he thinks the price is reasonable for the property in its existing state. Make sure you ask for a written quotation for any building work proposed. As in any country it is as well to get several quotes, though this can be tricky.

Bank or Lender's Inspection

This is no substitute for a proper survey. Most lenders do not ask for one and, where they do, it is normally fairly peremptory, limited to a check on whether it is imminently about to fall over and whether it is worth the money the bank is lending you.

<u>*Arranging a Inspection (Survey)*</u>

This can be done via your buyer's estate agent or, if you are using one, your lawyer.

<u>*What is 'Normal'?*</u>

Please be aware that, as in every country, the completed inspection report can look a bit frightening. This is particularly so if you are buying an older property. It is made worse by the difference in terminology used in the United States. You may want to discuss the report with your buyer's agent.

New Home Inspection

Before committing to buying a new house, you will want to make sure that you have an experienced and reputable home contractor or inspector walk through the home and do a thorough inspection.

This inspection can find flaws in a home that you, as a lay-person, may not be able to find by yourself.

If you are looking at a house that is currently being constructed, it is also a good idea to have the inspector walk through the unfinished home at a few key points in its construction process to ensure that the build quality is good.

If you are able to have your inspector walk through the home during the construction process, you should ask the developer to allow your inspector to view the home at these key points:

- Near the beginning, when the foundation is poured,
- After the framing of the house is completed, and
- After the home has been finished

At these points, the inspector should be able to view and inspect important portions of the home, like the electrical system, heating, plumbing, roofing, insulation, and the walls.

Appraisals (Valuations)

<u>*What is an appraisal?*</u>

An appraisal determines the value of a property. In the US this is usually worked out on the property's market value, generally calculated on a Highest & Best Use basis.

If you are using an estate agent who is working on your behalf to protect your interests -- a "buyer's agent" -- then that agent should be advising you of the value of the property and, if it is overpriced, the amount you should be offering for it.

They do this by way of "comps" – comparables. In the old days, this required a lot of local knowledge by the agent concerned and a large Rolodex file (do you remember them?). These days it is all done by clever computer software and, in fact, there is a lot of information on the internet as to the price at which individual homes have sold.

Where a good Realtor comes into his own and where he can help you as a buyer's agent is by being able to advise you about which properties that have been sold in the recent past are truly equivalent to yours and why. This still requires local knowledge.

In some cases your Realtor might recommend that you have a formal appraisal of the value of the property. If you are going to take out a mortgage, your lender will almost certainly require one. If you're buying via your pension fund, it is quite common for the pension fund trustees to insist upon an independent valuation.

Of course, an appraisal will cost you a certain amount of money. Fees are negotiable but tend to be pretty consistent within an area.

It is important to understand that an appraisal is merely attributing a value to the property. It is not a report on the state or condition of the property. That is an inspection (survey).

What both the appraisal and the inspection have in common is that, if they do not come up as you expect, they are a good basis to try to agree a reduction in the price with the seller. If the appraisal suggests that the property is worth $200,000 and the asking price is $250,000, you may well want to go back to the seller to try to agree a lower figure. It is better if you do this before you have signed a contract, but this is very often not possible and so the contract will commonly contain a condition (contingency) giving you (say) 30 days in which to carry out any due diligence enquiries – which could include an appraisal or an inspection. If the due diligence is not satisfactory, you can pull out of the deal and get your money back, provided you do so during the period stated in the contract.

If you are going to have an appraisal (or an inspection) it is therefore important that you either insert a special condition in the contract saying that if the property does not appraise at the sale price you can cancel the deal, or that you have a general due diligence condition allowing you to do the same thing. Many sellers do not like special appraisal contingencies.

This assumes that you have a Realtor acting as your buyer's agent, or that you know enough about the market to insist on and arrange these things yourself. On the other hand, if you have just walked into the office of estate agent who has been retained by the seller to sell the property, then you cannot expect that agent to tell you that the property is overpriced. His job is to maximise the amount that his client (the seller) receives from the sale of the property.

This is a really important distinction and one that is overlooked by most buyers, as it may not be a distinction that operates in their own country.

See the section on 'choosing advisers' in the chapter "Research" for more details.

Even if you are being advised by an agent who has recognised that he is your agent and looking after your interests, it is a good idea to get a second opinion about the value of the property you are thinking of buying. First of all, no agent - however experienced -- is going to judge the price correctly every single time. Secondly, although he is working for you, in most cases the buyer's agent is paid for by the seller and does not get paid unless the seller is agreed and goes through.

Fortunately, there are a number of simple and free ways to check the value of the property, just to confirm that what your agent feels is correct.

First, there are the obvious ways. If you're buying a relatively normal property – for example, not a short sale- you will be able to walk around the various estate agents offices in the town and see the prices of similar properties for sale. There will probably also be local newspapers or local property papers displaying details of lots of property for sale and these, too, are an invaluable source of information.

Useful Names & Addresses

We now live in an Internet world and there is also plenty of opportunity to check the prices of similar properties on the Internet. In particular, I recommend that you take a look at:

www.zillow.com: look, in particular, at the Recently Sold properties.

www.realtors.com: millions of properties

www.trulia.com: prices displayed as a map

Please bear in mind that, to differing extents, these sites are sometimes out of date.

If you want more than this, you will need an appraisal (valuation).

Finance

Whether you are buying as an investment or as a place to live, the choice of whether to take some finance for your purchase is important and not quite as straightforward as it might at first seem.

Some people just don't want a mortgage. They have just spent 30 years paying off their old one! Others need one if the transaction is to proceed. Some people see tax and other advantages in taking a mortgage, even if they could afford to pay cash.

A few years ago, almost everybody wanted a mortgage.

If the property is viewed simply as an investment, a mortgage allows you to increase your benefit from the capital growth of the property by "leveraging" the investment. If you buy a house for $200,000 and it increases in value by $50,000 that is a 25% return on your investment. If you had only put in $50,000 of your own money and borrowed the other $150,000 then the increase in value represents a return of 100% on your investment. If the rate of increase in the value of the property is more than the mortgage rate, you have won. In the past, property in most popular areas has gone up in value by much more than the mortgage rate. Recently, even a lot of well-chosen property has not. The key questions are whether that will continue and, if so, for how long.

At the moment, as in many other parts of the world, obtaining mortgage finance is much more difficult than it used to be. As a foreign buyer, you will seldom be able to obtain mortgage finance of more than 65% of the price you are paying or the appraised value of the property, whichever is lower, and the lender is likely to look quite closely at your financial services before agreeing even this amount of funding.

However, it is gradually getting a little easier – but don't expect it to go back to the crazy days of 100+% mortgages any time soon.

Your Realtor will be able to advise you about what is available and on what terms.

In addition, at the present time, whilst it is relatively simple to obtain a mortgage loan to buy an ordinary house, it is almost impossible to obtain a loan to buy a condo – an apartment or a house that shares common facilities and where you only own the interior of your property in your own name and own the walls, roofs, pools, parking areas etc. jointly with the other owners in the condominium.

In practice, in 2012 and 2013, most foreign buyers and many American buyers have been buying without mortgage finance. They have been using their savings, or, in the case of some foreign buyers, they have been taking out an additional mortgage loan on their primary home.

How Do You Want To Pay for the Property?

You have lots of choices.

Cash?

Of course, you may have lots of cash and be happy to pay in cash. At this point, it is worth clarifying something very important. When we talk about buying in cash we mean buying without a mortgage. We do not mean taking a suitcase of cash from the country where you live and handing it over to the seller. You may have heard stories of this happening and, indeed, in some places it did happen some years ago, but do not even think about doing it today. There are legal limits to the amounts of cash you can take out of the country without either declaring it or obtaining approval.

If you ignore those limits, at the very best you risk your money being impounded by the customs authorities in your own country and then having to jump through hoops to get it back and, probably, having to pay a substantial fine or penalty. In the worst case, the authorities will simply keep the money.

If you get the money out of your own country, it is likely to be detected when you reach your destination and to be seized there. It will then be even more complicated and expensive to sort the problem out, even assuming it can be sorted out at all.

Don't do it.

Deferred Payment (Seller Financing)?

Because of the more difficult mortgage availability, some developers and private sellers are prepared to provide developer finance to people buying in their developments. This is worth exploring, particularly as the rates can be very low.

If you're thinking of taking developer or seller finance, it is important to make sure that you will obtain legal title to the property when you make the balance of your payment, leaving the developer only with a mortgage over your property to protect the remaining amount due to him.

Some developers try to retain legal title to the property until you have made the final payment. This exposes you to the considerable risk that another person, to whom the developer owes money, could put a legal charge upon the property (which, legally speaking, still belongs to the developer) to protect their debt. In some cases this is illegal and in every case it is to be avoided, if at all possible.

There are two basic methods of seller financing:

Mortgage

The first method occurs when the seller takes back a mortgage on the home. The buyer signs a promise to repay the loan AND either a mortgage or deed of trust. In Florida only the mortgage is used. Both of these would allow the seller to foreclose on the buyer should the buyer default on the payments under the purchase agreement.

The seller then transfers the deed to the buyer. Therefore, the buyer has title and can sell the house or refinance it, just like if he or she had obtained a mortgage from a bank or commercial lender (as long as the buyer keeps current on the payments described in the purchase agreement).

Rent to own

The second method is like a "rent to own" contract.

The seller keeps the title until the buyer pays off the loan. After the loan is paid off, the seller transfers title to the buyer through a deed. This type of purchase agreement is called different names such as "contract for deed," "contract of sale," "land sale contract," or "instalment sales contract". Because the title is not transferred to the buyer until later, the buyer does not have the power to sell or refinance the property, until after he or she pays off the loan and title is transferred. Because of this limited power, this second method is less popular than the first.

The former method is infinitely preferable.

Mortgage?

On the Property You Are Buying?

Many people think that mortgages are no longer available. They think that the banking crisis has brought an end to all of that and, in particular, an end to mortgages for foreigners.

This is not correct. It is no longer as simple as it used to be to obtain mortgage finance and the percentage of the loan to value is likely to be lower than it used to be, but mortgages are still available to the right person for the right property.

Depending upon your personal circumstances and your tax position, they can also be financially beneficial -- even if you don't actually need the money. However, this is less of the case than it used to be, because of general tightening of the tax codes in most countries and a lessened ability to claim tax relief on the cost of servicing a mortgage to buy a foreign property. It is worth checking your own personal position. Remember, once again, that you are concerned not only with your tax position in the state where you are buying the property but also the tax position in the country where you live.

The whole process of obtaining a mortgage and the documentation you will need in order to do so will be different from what you're used to at home. Those differences can be frustrating for both you and the bank. You may find difficulty in producing certain documents requested from you (though that is not usually the case if you deal with a bank accustomed to working with foreigners) and the bank will find it frustrating when you do not send in the documents that they need in order to make a decision. It is worth taking a little time to establish absolutely clearly what is required and then send it all off in one package.

See the table below for the types of mortgage offers that are likely to be available and the evidence that you're likely to need to produce. Do remember that this varies from bank to bank and week to week.

Type of Mortgage	Loan to Value	Interest Rate	Maximum Length or age at repayment
Interest Only	Not currently	n/a	n/a
Variable interest rate repayment mortgage (capital and interest)	35%	4.5%	30 years
Fixed interest rate repayment mortgage (capital and interest)	35%	5%	30 years

Type of Applicant	Evidence Required
Employed	
Self Employed	
Unemployed	Not usually available
Retired	

It is worth remembering that you are under a legal responsibility to make full disclosure of your circumstances to any bank to which you are applying for a mortgage.

This is particularly important if you are thinking of moving to the country. You may have a very good job at the moment, but you may well become unemployed (even if only temporarily) if you move. The bank would be unlikely to grant a mortgage to someone who was unemployed and it might be reluctant to grant a mortgage to someone who had only been in their current job for a matter of a few weeks. In these cases, it can be difficult to obtain mortgage finance. If you find yourself in this position, it is important to approach the most appropriate bank - if you choose the wrong bank and your application is declined, the mere fact that you have made that application may damage your chances of success in any later application to another bank. Seek advice from the estate agent you are dealing with who may well have contacts in local banks and who may, therefore, be able to help you out of this difficulty.

An alternative approach, of dubious legality but adopted very often, is the Alzheimer approach. When you make your mortgage application as a person who has been in secure long-term employment for many years, you forget that you are thinking of moving to live in the property, changing your job and your whole lifestyle. In other words, you take a mortgage on a holiday home. Then, weeks or months later, you decide to move. By this stage, of course, you have the money and the loan is a fait accompli. Apart from the dubious legality of this approach, it can have other consequences which may be damaging to you. Seek professional advice if you find yourself in this position.

If you want to borrow money to finance your purchase, it is better to get clearance *before* you start looking at property. If you can't do that, at least make sure there is a condition in the contract making it subject to your getting a mortgage offer. In other words, if you don't get an offer, the contract will be cancelled and you will get your money back.

On Another Property

Some people may have other properties upon which they can secure mortgage finance. These could be properties that he bought a number of years ago and in which there is no substantial equity. This is a great position to be in. It means that you can choose the cheapest finance and also balance interest rates and currencies in a very sophisticated way.

In these cases, there are three golden principles.

1. The first, and most important, is that you should not mortgage your own home in order to buy an investment. Your home should be a secure refuge.

2. The second is that, unless you have a thorough understanding of the various markets concerned, it is well worth talking to a suitable qualified financial adviser about the merits of the various choices open to you. These are complicated markets and some complicated products are available. Choosing the right option can save you a lot of money. Once again, you need to remember that you are concerned about the impact of your decision not just in the country where you're buying the property, but also in any other countries where you own property and the country in which you live. Accordingly, you need an adviser who specialises in such international transactions.

3. The third factor to take into account is taxation. The choice of where you take your mortgage can have tax implications in various places.

The Exchange Rate Risk

If the funds to repay the mortgage are coming (say) from your £ sterling earnings, then the amount you have to pay will be affected by fluctuations in exchange rates between the £ sterling and the dollar. Do not underestimate these variations. Over the last 15 years – a typical period for a mortgage – the dollar has been as high as $0.7124 = £1 and as low as $0.4124 = £1. This means that sometimes the £ sterling you would have had to send to the US to pay the mortgage would have been almost double the amount at other times. This is less of a worry if you have income in dollars, for example from renting out the property.

Foreign Currency Mortgages

It is possible to mortgage your home in the US, but to borrow not in dollars but Swiss Francs, Japanese Yen or, for all I know, Afghanis.

There may be some attractions in borrowing in £ Sterling if you are repaying out of £ Sterling income. The debt will be fixed in the currency being used to repay it.

Borrowing in other currencies is a very high risk affair. Just Google "Swiss franc mortgage problems" The exchange rate, which once looked so enticing, can turn against you - and turn against you savagely - in a short period of time.

These are only for the very brave.

The use of a Mortgage Broker

Generally, we recommend that, if you want mortgage finance, you should use the services of a mortgage broker familiar with dealing with buyers from your country. This will save you a lot of wasted time and make sure that you get the type of mortgage most suited to your requirements.

Team Feltrim does not give mortgage advice, but we can introduce you to highly experienced mortgage brokers who have given good service to our clients.

Saving Money on your Mortgage Repayments

Your mortgage will usually be paid directly from your US bank account. Unless you have lots of rental or other dollar income going into that account, you will need to send money from your bank account back home in order to meet the payments.

Every time you send a payment to the US you will face two costs. The first is the price of the dollars. This, of course, depends on the exchange rate used to convert your currency. The second cost is the charges that will be made by your home and US banks to transfer the funds – which can be substantial.

There are steps that you can take to control both of these charges.

As far as the exchange rate is concerned you should be receiving the so-called "commercial rate", not the tourist rate published in the papers. The good news is that it is a much better rate. The bad news is that rates vary from second to second, so it is difficult to get alternative quotes. By the time you phone the second company the first has changed! In any case, you will probably want to set up a standing order for payment and not shop around every month.

There are various organisations that can convert your currency. Your bank is unlikely to give you the best exchange rate. Specialist currency dealers will normally better the bank's rate, perhaps significantly. If you decide to deal with a currency dealer, you must deal with one that is reputable. They will be handling your money and, if they go bust with it in their possession, you could lose it. Ask your estate agent for a recommendation.

Another possibility for saving money arises if you "forward buy" the dollars that you are going to need for the year. It is possible to agree with a currency dealer that you will buy all of your dollars for the next twelve months at a price that is, essentially, today's price. You normally pay 10% down and the balance on delivery. If the dollar rises in value you will gain, perhaps substantially. If the dollar falls in value – tough! The main attraction of forward buying is not so much the possibility for gaining on the exchange rate, but the certainty that the deal gives you. Only enter into these agreements with a reputable and, if possible, bonded broker.

Bearing in mind the cost of conversion and transmission of currency, it is better to make fewer rather than more payments. You will have to work out whether, taking into account loss of interest on the funds transferred against bank charges saved, you are best sending money monthly, quarterly or every 6 months.

Fractional or Shared Ownership

If you can't afford to pay the whole price of the property in cash and you can't get a mortgage, why not share the property with somebody else? This could be your brother, your neighbour, somebody you work with or a complete stranger.

Arrangements where you buy with somebody else, who is a friend, or known to you, are usually called co-ownership deals. They are very simple and involve very little, if any, cost over and above the cost that you would incur any way when buying a property.

This does not mean that there are no extra things that you need to think about. It is worth having a lawyer draw up a simple agreement making it quite clear that you are each going to be responsible for paying a certain percentage of the outgoings related to the property, that you are each going to be entitled to use the property for certain periods of the year and that you are each going to be entitled to a certain percentage of the increase (or suffer a certain percentage of the decrease) in the value of the property when you sell it. It is also worth including a clause dealing with when the property is to be sold (e.g. in five years' time or when you both decide it is going to be sold) and a clause requiring each owner to offer their share to the other owner before selling it to a third party. If two people are buying the property and paying equally towards it, then you would expect this percentage to be 50% but, of course, you could have a situation where one brother puts in 50% of the price, another 30% and two neighbours 10% each. In this case the percentages would be adjusted accordingly.

Owning a property in this way can be extremely beneficial for all concerned. I'm surprised it's not done more often.

If you're buying a holiday home and do not intend to occupy it all year round, but wish to let it to reduce your expenses of running the property, then this sort of arrangement works perfectly. You do not need to go to the time, trouble and expense of finding and managing tenants. There are no income tax issues to worry about. You don't need to worry about damage.

If you're buying an investment property, this gives you the opportunity to diversify your investments. You do not need to have so much money tied up in one project. You could use the rest to buy another property somewhere else in the world or, indeed, whatever other type of investment catches your fancy. Of course, if you are buying the property as an investment, you have to deal with the question of whether you are going to permit any of the owners to have any personal use of the property and the related question of how the income generated is to be split between you.

Whether you are buying as an investment or for your own personal use, a great attraction of this type of ownership is that the annual administrative overheads are very low indeed. In many cases, they'll be nil.

This sort of arrangement can also be made by sharing a property with perfect strangers. In this case it is known as fractional ownership.

The main difference between this and doing it with friends is that, of course, the companies that set up and sell fractional ownership programmes are doing so to make a profit. You can therefore expect to pay more for the property than you would for a similar unit sold by way of conventional ownership to a single buyer. One of the key factors determining whether a factual ownership property is a good or bad buy is the size of that mark-up. How much of a mark-up should you expect to pay? It will vary a bit depending upon the cost of the property. Less expensive properties are, inevitably, subject to a bigger mark-up than expensive ones. Think twice if you are asked to pay a mark-up of more than 25%.

The second factor when considering fractional ownership is the annual cost of administering and servicing the property. This, of course, will vary vastly depending on the facilities offered by the property. A luxury property brim full of expensive facilities, or in a resort sharing such amenities, will have a much higher management charge than a more modest, self-contained, apartment. When thinking about management charges there are two key points to consider. Is the seller giving you a solid estimate of the likely charges for the next year, preferably based on the charges for previous years? Is the system of calculating the charges transparent? In other words, are you only being asked to pay the cost of running the project and not some charge inflated by hefty and hidden management expenses?

You will not be able to obtain mortgage finance to buy a fractional interest in a property, although if you are creating an informal fractional – for example, by you, your brother, your best friend and your next door neighbour buying a property together and sharing the use of it, then you should be able to obtain mortgage finance provided that you are not buying a condominium.

Other Methods?

Many clever ways of financing property purchase have been devised and, surprisingly, are still being devised. Treat them with caution.

Financing Stage Payments

If you are buying a property under construction, you may be required to make some stage payments as the build proceeds. This is not usual in the Orlando area. You will normally make a down payment and pay the rest on closing, which happens on delivery of the property.

It is currently difficult to fund such payments. If you want to do this then it will need to be agreed at an early stage.

Useful Names & Addresses

National Association of Home /inspectors – www.nahi.org

National Academy of Building Inspection Engineers - www.nabie.org.

Smart Currency: http://www.smartcurrencyexchange.com

The Legal Process

I am not a lawyer and so I am very grateful to the very well-known and highly experienced Orlando attorney Martha A Hartley of Baker Donelson Bearman, Caldwell & Berkowitz, PC (www.bakerdonelson.com) for her help in the writing of this chapter. The knowledge is hers; the errors are mine.

The general procedure when buying a property in the US seems, at first glance, similar to the purchase of a property in the UK or Ireland, but very different from the process in, say, France or Spain. You sign a contract. You do some checks. You sign a Deed of Sale.

This is deceptive. The procedure is very different and even the use of the familiar English vocabulary to describe the very different steps in the US can produce an undesirable sense of familiarity with the procedure. This can lead to assumptions that things that have not been discussed will work in much the same way as they would in your own country. This would be a wrong and dangerous assumption. **Work on the basis that the system is totally different**.

Caution: Terminology

Words in legal contracts, mortgages and title documents are often technical legal terms. They sometimes have meanings that are very different from the meaning of the same word in everyday language.

This is another reason why you should make sure that your buyer's agent and, if you decide to use one, your lawyer, explain the contract to you very thoroughly, preferably in writing.

Make sure that you understand exactly what you are buying and your on-going obligations after the purchase.

"Let the Buyer Beware"

Caveat Emptor or "buyer beware" is a long-standing principle of law that puts responsibility on the buyer to learn of any defects in the home, even if such defects render the home unfit.

Make sure you understand exactly what you are buying as early as possible in the process, whilst you still have time to pull out. If you wait until after closing, it is too late.

Many jurisdictions do require of sellers a minimum standard of quality, but this can be very hard to enforce.

The only exception to this doctrine is if the seller intentionally tried to conceal the defects.

Caveat emptor applies only to homeowner-buyer transactions, and not builder-buyer transactions. These are governed by different rules that give the buyer some more protection.

Check out that what you are buying meets your needs.

Implied Warranty of Fitness:

This doctrine applies to builder-buyer transactions and places responsibility on the builder/ seller to ensure that the property is fit for habitation.

Once again, you should not accept this at face value. Even if you have rights, taking enforcement action can be slow and costly.

Do you need a lawyer?

No and Yes.

Strictly speaking, you do not need to use a lawyer. As we have already said, many local people do not use one. However, they are local people and know what they are doing. You, probably, do not.

As I explained earlier, real estate agents in Florida are all professionally qualified and licensed. The agency itself is both licensed and closely regulated. So are the individual sales people working in it.

Add to this the fact that the process of transferring ownership is overseen and guaranteed by a title insurance company (see below) and it is easy to understand why most people do not use a lawyer to deal with ordinary property transactions.

Others recommend that you use a lawyer when buying a property overseas, in much the same way that you use a plumber to install a new bathroom, a mechanic to fix the gearbox in your car or a dentist to extract your teeth. Yes, you can do these things yourself but it is not necessarily a good idea. Not only does it give you peace of mind, but also it gives you someone to sue if it goes wrong!

The choice is yours. If you are going to use a lawyer, engage him early – at the time you decide to buy a home and keep him working until the actual closing.

The Role of the Notary

In the United States they do have notaries. However, a US notary is totally different from a notary in most other countries.

In large parts of the world – those that use the Civil Law system, such as France and Spain - the notary has an absolutely essential role in every property transfer. He is responsible for preparing the deed of sale, confirming that the parties have read and understood it and then witnessing their signatures to the document. He is then responsible for the safe custody of the document and has a role in the collection of the taxes due to the government in relation to the transfer of ownership and the presentation of the deed of sale for registration at the local Land Registry.

The notary is, in these countries, a qualified lawyer who has then passed further stringent tests before being licensed to practice in this highly respected and important role.

In the US, the notary does not have either these qualifications or any of these responsibilities.

Is the US, the notary is authorized by the state in which he lives to perform certain very limited tasks. Basically, in the context of the purchase of a property, he will witness the signature of certain documents or produce certified copies of certain documents. That is all. The notary cannot give you legal advice.

I have had documents witnessed by a notary in Florida whose main occupation was that of a hairdresser.

Needless to say, this vastly different role can create some confusion for those who are used to buying property in the French way.

The Price

This can be freely agreed between the parties. Depending on the economic climate, there may be ample or very little room for negotiating a reduction in the asking price. In 2011 and 2012 the scope was substantial. At the moment, at least in Central Florida, there is much less opportunity for this as most prices are realistic and there is more demand than supply.

However, there are still some overpriced properties and there are always some people who desperately need to sell. Your buyer's agent will be able to advise you whether it is worth putting in a lower offer in any particular case.

How much of the price should be declared in the contract of sale?

All of it. This is not Spain, Italy or Mexico where, for many years, there was a tradition of under- declaring the price actually paid for a property when signing the deed of sale. Even in these countries, the days of major under- declarations have now largely gone.

Do not even think of under declaring the price. It is illegal and doing so will come back to bite you in any number of ways.

Where is the money paid?

The price, together with the taxes and fees payable, is usually paid by the buyer to the escrow agent (closing agent) who has been appointed to deal with this transaction. The escrow agent will usually be either the person appointed by your title insurance company (see below) or your lawyer. If you have decided to use the services of a lawyer, try to make sure that your own lawyer is appointed as the escrow agent.

The escrow agent then holds the money until the 'closing' – the official completion of the purchase and sale and the moment when the keys are exchanged for the cash. He will then divide up the money, using some to pay off any mortgage on the property, some to pay the seller, some to pay fees and taxes etc.

The escrow agent will need the money in good time before the closing.

Getting the money to the US

The first thing you are going to need is a US bank account – although the money for the closing will be sent to the closing agent.

Since 9/11 and the rise of organised crime, opening a bank account anywhere in the world is much more complicated than it used to be. This is understandable, but it can be frustrating. Some banks make the process much more difficult than others and so, if you don't already have a US bank account, the choice of which bank to use can be quite important. Team Feltrim can recommend good banks to you.

You will need to transfer that money to the escrow agent by international bank transfer. These days, few are prepared to accept bank certified cheques. None will accept personal cheques. None will accept cash.

Make sure that the escrow agent has the money several days before the closing. Remember that it can take, no matter what your bank might tell you, several days for the money to be transferred from the bank in the country where you live to your escrow agent's bank account. Strangely, the larger the amount the longer it often takes. When sending funds, err on the side of caution.

Similarly, when sending funds, err on the side of caution when it comes to the amount that you send. Your bank, any intermediate banks and the receiving bank are all likely to take some fees from the money transferred. These can amount to quite a lot of money. Depending on when the money is being converted from your currency into US dollars, the amount of money you need to buy those dollars can also change. The rate changes by the second. We always suggest that you add 1 or 2% to the amount of money requested to cover these risks.

Rest assured that any money that is not required will swiftly be transferred by the closing agent into your designated US bank account.

Talking about exchange rates, it is almost always better – often far, far better – to transfer the funds via a reputable foreign exchange (FX) dealer rather than via your bank. The FX dealer will usually give you a much better exchange rate. This is not permitted in all countries.

It is also worth bearing in mind that, in addition to the money needed to buy the property, you will almost always need further money in the US. You may want to buy furniture for the house, you might want to buy a car. You will need money for living expenses. If you are appointing a management company to run the property for you, they will probably want $500 or $1,000 in their account to pay for bills or repairs on your behalf. It is usually cheaper and you will usually get a better exchange rate if you transfer these funds at the same time you transfer the main chunk of money needed to buy the property.

The Basic Process

Making an offer/Reserving the property

Before making an offer there are a few things to check out.

Are you happy with what you are buying? In particular, are you happy with its general condition? Although you can make your offer and the contract of sale subject to conditions (contingencies) e.g. that it passes an inspection – if you are in any doubt, get it checked before you make an offer.

How much does the seller still owe on the home for sale? If this amount is higher than the asking price, it is likely you are facing a short sale. If it is not a short sale, then the seller will need to bring cash to the closing. If neither of these is going to happen, you will waste a lot of time and money and get nowhere.

Once you are happy, your estate agent will make the offer. The reply is usually fast, though it may be a precursor to some negotiations.

The making and acceptance of the offer, in writing, is what creates the contract of sale, but the contract is usually evidenced by a signed document setting out what has been agreed. Real estate agents will usually suggest the use of a standard form that contains the required information for a home sale contract. The use of standard forms helps ensure that the specific requirements for a home sale contract are met, but it can still be a good idea to have a real estate contract reviewed by an experienced attorney before signing on the dotted line. This is particularly important if there are any special conditions associated with the deal.

Just because the contract you are offered is presented to you in a fancy printed form does not mean that your lawyer or realtor will not be able to negotiate highly beneficial changes to it.

An alternative to the standard offer is a 'binder'. This is similar to what, in Europe, we would usually call an option contract.

A binder is a preliminary agreement between a buyer and seller as an offer to purchase real estate. It is secured by the payment of earnest money, a non-binding preliminary deposit otherwise known as a goodwill deposit. A binder secures the right to purchase real estate upon agreed terms for a limited period of time. If the buyer changes his mind, or is unable to purchase, the earnest money is forfeited unless the binder expressly provides that it is to be refunded.

The contract

The purchase agreement is the single most important document in the transaction. Although standard printed forms are useful, a realtor (or your lawyer if you are using one) is helpful in fully explaining the form and making changes and additions to reflect the buyer's and the seller's desires. There are many issues that may need to be addressed in the purchase agreement; below are some common examples:

- If the property has been altered or there has been an addition to the property, was it done lawfully?
- If the buyer has plans to change the property, may what is planned for the property be done lawfully?
- What happens if a buyer has an engineer or architect inspect the property and termites, asbestos, radon, or lead-based paint is found?
- What if the property is found to contain hazardous waste?
- Will the down payment be held safely in escrow in accordance with appropriately worded escrow instructions?
- How is payment to be made?
- Is the closing appropriately conditioned upon the buyer obtaining financing?
- What are the legal consequences if the closing does not take place, and what happens to the down payment?

All of these things mean that the standard contract presented to you may be changed quite a lot. This is true even if the seller's agent tells you that it is not negotiable, though you need to be aware that – in some cases – the seller might not accept major changes. This is especially so where there is a shortage of property and a resulting "sellers' market".

If changes are suggested, they will be for your benefit and if the proposals are not accepted, your Realtor and, if you are using one, your lawyer should explain the impact upon you so that you can decide whether you can live with the situation or whether it is necessary to pull out of the deal and find another home.

The Statute of Frauds is an ancient piece of English common law – nearly 1000 years old – that has been adopted in the United States. In essence, the Statute of Frauds requires certain types of contract to be in writing and contain specific sorts of details about the arrangement. This is to prevent a person from cheating another by claiming a breach of a fraudulent oral contract. Sales of real estate fall under the Statute of Frauds, and so all contracts for the sale of a home must be in writing.

Not only does the home sale contract have to be in writing, it must also contain certain key elements in order to be enforceable. Specifically, the contract must include:

- The identities of the parties involved in the transaction.
- The description of the property. Usually this involves both the address of the property and its legal description, such as the boundaries of the plot on which it is built.
- The purchase price for the property.
- The signature of (or on behalf of) all the necessary parties to the sale.

In addition to what is required to enforce the contract, there are other elements that a home sale contract should include in order to protect the buyer and seller and ensure that the transaction goes down smoothly, with as few opportunities for disagreement as possible. The additional elements that should appear in the contract include:

- The date agreed for the settlement of the transaction and the date when the buyer can take possession of the property.
- A guarantee that the seller possesses clear title to the property.
- A clause that allows the buyer to make inspections of the property for damage, pest infestations, etc.
- The names of the escrow and closing agents.
- Contingency clauses that address the proper actions if certain situations arise. For example, if the buyer can't obtain financing by a certain date, a contingency clause could allow the seller to back out of the deal. A different contingency clause could also require the seller to pay for certain types of structural damage repair or pest eradication. The drafting of these contingency clauses is one of the most important parts of any negotiations to buy a property.
- A clause that makes it clear that the seller is responsible for paying utilities, fees, taxes, etc. for the property up until the transaction is settled.
- A clause, sometimes referred to as a "liquidated damages clause," that requires the seller to pay the buyer a specified amount of money for each day that the buyer had to delay moving into the house.

Signing the contract

Once you and the seller are both happy with the deal, the contract is signed. This does not require any special formalities.

In theory, you can authorise another person to sign the contract on your behalf if you are not going to be there at the time when it is necessary to do so. These days, there are ways in which contracts can be signed electronically. however, especially if you are taking mortgage finance, this is often not acceptable. Usually the contract will be sent to you by FedEx etc. for you to sign and return. You need to think about the arrangements for the signing of all of the documents in good time as this can take quite a long time – possibly up to two weeks.

See below for more about Powers of Attorney.

Complying with any special conditions – 'contingencies'

As we have said, many buyers finance a substantial portion of the purchase price for a home with a mortgage loan. If this is so in your case, the purchase agreement should contain a carefully worded provision that it is subject to the buyer's obtaining a commitment for financing.

Checking title

After the purchase agreement is signed, it is necessary to establish the state of the seller's title to the buyer's - and any lender's - satisfaction.

Generally, a title search is ordered from an abstract or title insurance company. In some states, title insurance is not used but in most (including Florida) it is. In states where title insurance is not used, an attorney is essential to review the status of title and give a formal legal opinion as to title in lieu of a title policy. In states where it is used, it is still a good idea.

Assuming you are in an area where title insurance is customary (as it is in Florida), your realtor and, if you are using one, your lawyer, can help review the title search and explain the title exceptions (i.e. what is not insured) and determine whether the legal description is correct and whether there are problems with adjoining owners or prior owners.

He or she can also explain the effect of easements and agreements or restrictions imposed by a prior owner, and whether there are any legal restrictions which will impair your ability to sell the property. Remember that, in a few years' time, you are likely to want to sell to someone else who is going to insist on the title passing inspection!

The title search does not tell the buyer or seller anything about existing and prospective zoning restrictions concerning the property. Zoning restrictions limit the way in which you can use the property. For example, a property may be in an area where it is not permitted to rent out on short term lets, or to use the property for certain business purposes. These can be important restrictions. A Realtor can also explain whether zoning prohibits a two-family home, or whether planned improvements violate zoning ordinances.

Title insurance protects lenders or homeowners (there are two separate documents, one protecting each) against the loss of their interest in property due to legal defects in its title. Title insurance may be issued as a "mortgagee's title policy." Insurance benefits will then be paid only to the "named insured" - usually your bank – listed in the title policy, so it is important that an owner purchases an "owner's title policy", if he desires the protection of title insurance. The cost of issuing the extra policy is modest.

The cost of title insurance is, traditionally, paid by the buyer but, as with most of the expenses associated with buying a home, this is freely negotiable and should be specified in your contract.

In Florida, the cost of title insurance is fixed by law. It depends upon the value of the property. For example, for a $300,000 property, the cost will be about $1,500 – of which about one third goes to the title company and the other two thirds to the title agent who carries out the work.

If your own lawyer is appointed as title agent, they will be able to reduce their fees, as much of the work they do will duplicate the work of the title agent. This is the so-called Butler rebate (named after the court case where it was confirmed to be permitted).

From your point of view, the process of title insurance starts with the insurance company sending you an insurance proposal. As with everything else, this should be checked carefully, taking advice from your Realtor or lawyer. Some of the exclusions proposed by the company might be neither appropriate nor acceptable. Once the terms are agreed, the company will issue a title commitment – an agreement to issue insurance when you buy the property and sign the deed of sale. After the purchase, this is followed by the issuing of the full title insurance policy. This is an important document and should be kept safe.

The mortgage arrangements

Arrangements must be made to satisfy all of your bank's requirements so that they will release any mortgage monies needed at closing.

The other financial arrangements

Money must be collected from the buyer to cover the purchase price and all expenses. See above.

The closing

The closing is the most important event in the purchase and sale transaction.

Prior to closing, the deed and other closing papers must be prepared.

In readiness for closing, a financial statement should be prepared indicating the debits and credits to the buyer and seller. This is in a specific format, laid down by law.

Your Realtor is helpful in explaining the nature, amount, and fairness of proposed closing costs.

At closing:

- The buyer pays the balance of the purchase price and receives the keys to the property. Of course, frequently, this balance is paid in part from the proceeds of a mortgage loan. This requires further paperwork.
- The deed and mortgage instruments are explained and signed
- Title passes from seller to buyer.
- Title insurance is confirmed

The closing process can be confusing and complex – though interesting – to both the buyer and seller. If there is a physical closing meeting, those present at the closing often include the buyer and seller, their respective attorneys (if any), the title closer (the representative of the title company), an attorney for any lending bank and the real estate brokers involved in the transaction. However, in most simple cases, these days closing takes place electronically, following certain agreed protocols.

There may be last minute disputes or issues to sort out about delivering possession and personal property, or the adjustment of various costs, such as fuel and taxes.

The Payment of Fees & Taxes

On the closing of your purchase, you will be responsible for payment of the various fees and taxes associated with the purchase. These will be paid by the closing agent from the funds that you have sent.

Barring agreement to the contrary, the seller pays his estate agent's fees. If you have employed a buyer's agent then, again barring agreement between you and the agent to the contrary, he will share the seller's agent's commission and so cost you nothing.

See the next chapter for a breakdown of the costs associated with buying a property.

Registration of your legal title

Almost all states require that a title deed be notarized and filed. Some states require that it also be witnessed.

First, the transferring party should go to a notary, who will notarize and witness the signature.

Next, the transferring party should record the deed by filing it with the land records office in the county where the property is located (also commonly called a county recorder, land registry or register of deeds).

The office will keep a copy and return the original to the transferring party.

Note that, unlike in many countries in the world, the duty of the record office is merely to preserve the document. They will carry out one or two elementary checks (for example, to make sure it has been signed!) but take no role in advising or protecting the buyer or seller.

Powers of Attorney

In many cases the person buying a house and the person selling a house will both be present in the area where the property is located and so they will both be able to sign the contract and deed of sale in person. If this can be arranged, it is by far the best way forward. There are many reasons why it is a good idea to be present at the closing of the purchase of your property

However, very often it will not be convenient for you t to go to the US to sign the deed of sale in person. Sometimes there may also be other things that, in the normal course of events, would require your personal intervention, but where it would be inconvenient for you to have to deal with them yourself.

Just as often, you will not know whether you will be available to sign in person. Closing dates can move and so you could plan to be there, but suffer a last minute delay to the signing that makes it impossible.

The solution to this problem is the Power of Attorney. This document authorises the person appointed (the *attorney*) to do whatever the document authorises, on behalf of the person granting the Power (the *grantor*).

Give the Power to someone you trust.

The most sensible type of Power to use will be the US style of Power that is appropriate to the situation. The power will be signed in front of a notary, either in the country where you live or whilst you are in the US. The way of dealing with a Power of Attorney signed overseas varies from country to country. Usually, if it is signed in front of a notary, it has to be ratified by a government body for use overseas. In some cases the Power can, instead, be signed at the local US Consulate.

If signed in some other country outside the US and not in front of the US Consul, it must be ratified by the body in that country nominated under the Hague Convention, which is the international agreement governing the use and acceptance of such documents internationally. This sounds very grand, but is actually quick and simple.

The type of Power of Attorney that you will need depends on what you want to use it for. Your lawyer can discuss your requirements with you and prepare the necessary document. Typically, when buying a house, the Power of Attorney will be limited, authorising the attorney (for example) only to take the steps needed to buy 1120 Florida Boulevard and to sign a mortgage in respect of the purchase. The power might also be limited as to time – for example, it might expire after six months.

In theory, a Power of Attorney drafted in the style of the country where it is signed should also be sufficient, but in practice, it is easier to use one prepared in the US format.

Even if you intend to go to the US to sign, it is sensible to think about granting a Power "just in case". It is not something that can be done at the last moment. From decision to getting the document to the US will take at least seven and more likely 10 or 14 days. If you are able to go, the Power will not be used.

Note that the use of Powers of Attorney will probably not be permitted if you are buying using a mortgage. In this case, any documents that you need to sign will be mailed to you and you will have to sign them in front of a notary (or, in some cases, the US Consul - who by law has the power to act as a notary) in your own country. Once again, I must stress that this can all take quite a lot of time.

Even if you have granted a Power of Attorney, if you get the opportunity to go to the US at the time of the signing it is worth doing so. It is quite interesting – there is something slightly weird about seeing someone hand over $2 million of your money – but, more importantly, you will be able to check the house to make sure that everything is in order before the deed of sale is signed.

Ways to get the money to the US

There are a number of ways of getting the money to the US.

Electronic Transfer

The most practical is to have it sent electronically by international SWIFT transfer from a bank in your country directly to the recipient's bank in the US. This costs about $40, depending on the country and your bank. Even if you are told this is a "same day transfer" service, it is safer to allow two or three days for the money to arrive – especially if it is going to a rural bank. This is despite everyone's protestations that it will be there the same day. To be really prudent, allow a week – if you do this, it will likely arrive in a couple of hours!

Europe has introduced unique account numbers for all bank accounts. These incorporate a code for the identity of the bank and branch involved, as well as the account number of the individual customer. These are known as IBAN numbers. They should be quoted, if possible, on all international currency transfers. However, IBAN numbers are still not used in the US and so you will be asked to quote your bank's 'old' SWIFT number and the full account details of the recipient.

Be careful when asking for these details. Often the money will have to pass through an intermediary US bank – the handling agent for the bank to which you are sending the funds. Getting the codes wrong can lead to significant delay or, in the worst case, the funds being returned to you as undeliverable. You then have to pay two sets of bank charges and take a double hit on currency conversion costs!

You can send the money from your own bank or via a specialist currency dealer.

For the sums you are likely to be sending, you should receive an exchange rate much better than the "tourist rate" you see in the press. There is no such thing as a fixed exchange rate in these transactions. The bank's official interbank rate changes by the second and the job of the bank's currency dealers is to make a profit by selling to you at the lowest rate they can get away with! Thus, if you do a lot of business with a bank and they know you are "on the ball", you are likely to be offered a better rate than a one-off customer.

For this reason it can be better to send the money via your local lawyers in the country where you live, who will be dealing with large numbers of such transactions. This also has the advantage that their bank, which deals with international payments all the time, is less likely to make a mistake causing delay to the payment than the local branch of your bank, for which such a payment might be a rarity.

However, better still, use a specialist currency dealer. This is what I recommend.

Such dealers almost always give a much better exchange rate than an ordinary bank. Sometimes the difference can be significant, especially compared to your local branch of a high street bank. I recently carried out a spot check on a transfer from the UK to the US. We, anonymously, asked a major high street bank to convert £50,000 ($80,000) into dollars and send it to the US. There was a saving of £575 – about $920 – by using the currency dealer. In other countries the savings can be greater.

Although these dealers use major banks actually to transfer the funds, you need to make sure that the dealer you are dealing with is reputable. Your money is paid to them, not to the major bank, as so could be at risk if the dealer was not bonded or otherwise protected.

Your Realtor will be able to recommend a currency broker: often, one they deal with regularly.

However you make the payment, make sure you understand whether you or the recipient is going to pick up the receiving banks charges. If you need a clear amount in the US, you will have to make allowances for these, usually by sending a bit extra or, less satisfactorily, by asking your local bank to pay all the charges – which doesn't always work.

The bank in the US will make a charge – which can be substantial – for receiving your money into your account. Make sure you send enough money to cover it. Better too much than too little.

Certified Bank Cheques/Bankers Drafts

You can arrange for your bank in the US or in your own country to issue you with a banker's draft (bank certified cheque) which you can take to the US and pay into your bank account.

These are very rarely used these days. They are highly unlikely to be accepted. Try to avoid them. If you must use one, make sure that the bank knows that the draft is to be used overseas and issues you with an international draft. Also make sure that the escrow agent or your local US bank will accept one and allow you to draw funds on it immediately.

Generally this is not a good way to transfer the money. It can take a considerable time – sometimes weeks or even months – for the funds deposited to be made available for your use. The recipient bank's charges can be surprisingly high. The exchange rate offered against a foreign certified bank cheque may be uncompetitive as you are a captive customer.

But, most importantly, I repeat that the certified bank cheque in not likely to be accepted. If you turn up at closing with no usable money, you will be in breach of contract and liable to penalties.

You have been warned.

Cash

This is not recommended. You will need to declare the money on departure from your own country and on arrival in the US. You must by law do this if the sum involved is over €10000. You are well advised to do so for smaller amounts. Even then, if you declare $200,000 or so, they will think you are a terrorist or drugs dealer! That suspicion can have far reaching consequences in terms of listings in police "dodgy people" files and even surveillance. To add insult to injury, the exchange rate you will be offered for cash (whether you take cash in foreign currency and convert it in the US or buy the dollars in your own country) is usually very uncompetitive.

Don't do it.

Bringing the money back

When you sell your property you will be able to bring the money back to your own country if you wish to do so. Once again, this is best done electronically.

The Title Insurance

We have already talked about title insurance but, as it is so badly misunderstood by non-Americans, it is worth mentioning it again. This misunderstanding is, mainly, because non-Americans seldom use it. Yet, in the US, it is (in most states including Florida) a central part of the process of buying and selling homes.

Title Insurance is a form of indemnity insurance which insures against financial loss from defects in title to real property – land and buildings – and from the invalidity or unenforceability of mortgages.

Title insurance was developed in the United States as a result of deficiencies in the U.S. land records laws and procedures. It has been around since 1853.

It is meant to protect an owner's or a lender's financial interest in real property against loss due to title defects, liens or other matters. For example, it will defend against a lawsuit attacking the insured title, or reimburse the insured for the actual monetary loss incurred, up to the dollar amount of insurance provided by the policy.

Typically, the real property interests insured are for simple ownership (freehold or absolute ownership) or a mortgage. However, title insurance can be purchased to insure any interest in real property, including an easement, lease or life estate.

There are two types of policies - owner and loan. Just as lenders require fire insurance and other types of insurance coverage to protect their investment, nearly all institutional and other mortgage lenders (banks and private individuals) also require title insurance [a loan policy] to protect their interest in the loans secured against real estate.

Buyers purchasing properties for cash or partly funded by a mortgage lender often want title insurance [an owner policy] as well. A loan policy provides no coverage or benefit for the buyer/owner and so the decision to purchase an owner policy is independent of the lender's decision to require a loan policy. Taking out the additional cover does not involve paying the whole premium a second time. It could cost as little as $200 extra.

There are substantial difference in practice and requirements from state to state.

See www.stewart.com/docs/2-2009-NTS-0912-05-8_StateLaws&CustomsBroch.pdf.

The Timescale

The time lag between seeing a property and closing on the deal varies dramatically.

Much will depend upon:

- the number of contingences (special conditions) in the contract and how much time they give you to do things. For example, the contract could allow 30, 60 or 90 days (usually 30) to complete your due diligence
- whether you are taking a mortgage
- how organised you are when it comes to getting all your paperwork together

It is not likely to be less than three months.

The Condominium/Cooperative

In the US, if you buy a property which shares facilities with other properties, you will probably either own part of a condominium (condo) or the complex will be a cooperative (coop).

In Florida, the coop is rarely, if ever, used.

Sharing facilities could be something as simple as four houses being built around a shared pool and garden area, or it could be something much more akin to a traditional apartment arrangement where the facilities shared might include the roof, the corridors, the elevators, the parking areas, the gardens and even the walls of the building.

The owner of a condominium unit owns 100% of his own unit and owns all of the common areas and facilities jointly with the owners of the other units in the condo. He also has the right, along with other unit owners, to use the common areas and the facilities. Condominium laws vary greatly from state to state, but typically include an association that maintains the building, pays taxes and insurance, and maintains the reserves for improvements.

In a cooperative, a corporation or association owns title to the real estate. A resident purchases stock in the corporation. As a result, he or she indirectly owns a part of the building.

The nature of the stock entitles them to the exclusive right to occupy a unit in the building or property owned by the cooperative – usually, their apartment – and gives them the right to share in the use of the other areas that are not subject to the exclusive use of some other person – e.g. the gardens or parking areas. While the resident does not own his unit, he has an absolute right to occupy his unit for as long as he owns the stock.

The end result is more or less the same, but the way they are managed varies significantly.

The Condo

Colloquially, the term condo is often used to refer to the unit itself in place of the word "apartment". A condominium may be simply defined as an "apartment" that the resident owns as opposed to rents.

It is similar in concept to the Spanish *copropriedad* or the French *copropriété*.

The condo is run by an elected board. They may, in turn, appoint a managing agent.

Expenses are shared, usually per capita or pro rata to the size of your property.

The exact way in which the ownership rights in a condo are defined and the terms on which owners enjoy the right to use the common areas will vary from condo to condo. In most apartment type condos, the individual owners' rights to a particular part of a property stretch no further than from the inside paintwork of one of their outer walls to the inside paintwork of the others. In other words, the whole of the structure of the building, including the walls of their own apartment, is part of the common areas. This means that, if there is any problem or if any repairs need to be undertaken, these are the collective responsibility of all of the condo owners. This makes a lot of sense. If the walls of the ground floor apartment are not kept in good repair, this will have a direct impact on the owner of the upper floor.

In some condos, where the units are basically individual houses sharing common facilities, such as a pool, tennis courts and gardens, the entire structure of the houses could be the responsibility of the owner of each individual house, leaving only the shared facilities to be maintained collectively by the owners.

Clearly, the condo fees – the fees that have to be paid each month or each year to maintain the property and deal with its administration – will be much higher in the first condo than they will in the second.

It follows that, if you are looking to buy a unit in a condo, you need to be clear about which parts you will have to maintain and which parts will be maintained centrally (in which you will not be able to alter without permission). You also need to ask the size of the monthly condo fee. This will be disclosed to you.

For a 2 bedroom condo in Central Florida, condo fees could vary from several thousand dollars per year down to just a few hundred.

When looking at condo properties, bear in mind that the more extensive the facilities enjoyed, the more the fees are likely to be. Look out, in particular, for large pools and lifts (elevators), both of which take a lot of expensive maintenance. Look out also for services such as 24 hour security, which is also expensive to provide.

The Coop

As I have already said, it is rarely (if ever) used in central Florida; however I am including a little information about them in case you find one, or in case you are buying elsewhere.

The coop is (almost always) a non-profit organisation, managed by an elected board. They may, in turn, appoint a managing agent.

It enjoys a number of tax benefits.

One of the major features that differentiates a coop is that the members, through their elected representatives, screen and select who may live in the cooperative.

Expenses are shared, usually per capita or pro rata to the size of your property.

The Home Owner's Association

A home owner's association (HOA) is a corporation formed by a real estate developer for the purpose of marketing, managing, and selling homes and plots in a residential project.

It grants the developer privileged voting rights in governing the association, while allowing the developer to exit financial and legal responsibility of the organization, typically by transferring ownership of the association to the homeowners after selling off a predetermined number of lots.

In some ways, the HOA is similar to a condo. You own your own home and you have certain rights over and certain responsibilities in respect of shared facilities, such as the grass verges, the roads, any landscaping etc.

You will also be required to abide by a set of rules limiting how you can use the property. These are imposed for the benefit of the whole community. For example, you might be required to mow your lawns every 2 weeks or to repaint your house at least every 5 years.

You will also have to contribute your share of the cost of maintaining the common facilities and services – the gardening, the security etc. This is done by the payment of HOA fees. As in the case of condos, these can vary enormously depending upon the level of the facilities provided.

Just to make life a little more complicated, you may find that the development in which your property is located has several different HOAs. For example, if 40 houses were built in 10 clusters of 4, you could find that there were 10 HOAs (1 per cluster) or five HOAs (1 for every two clusters). In these cases, there is also usually a master HOA, the members of which are each of the individual HOAs. The master HOA is responsible for all of the central services such as the maintenance of the roads and the tennis courts and the provision of security. If there were 10 HOAs, each would pay 1/10th of those charges which it would recover from the individual owners as part of their individual HOA fees or dues.

Each individual HOA would then be responsible for the maintenance of its own shared facilities and administrative costs. It would then bill its members for the amount necessary to cover those costs.

If members fail to pay their HOA dues, the law gives the HOA very strong powers to collect payment.

It allows a civil municipality to increase its tax base – by having some communities with much higher levels of facilities than others – but without requiring it to provide equal services to all of its citizens.

Membership in the homeowners association by a residential buyer is, typically, a condition of purchase; a buyer isn't given an option to reject it.

Most homeowner associations are incorporated, and are subject to state statutes that govern non-profit corporations and homeowner associations. State oversight of homeowner associations is minimal, and mainly takes the form of laws which are inconsistent from state to state. Some states, such as Florida and California, have a large body of homeowner association law, and some states, such as Massachusetts, have virtually none.

They are notorious for infighting and long meetings. I should know. I am the appointed manager for quite a number of HOAs in the Orlando area. My wife, Angela, knows to keep my dinner warm in the oven when I go to an HOA meeting!

The HOA is run by an elected board of directors.

Expenses are shared, usually per capita or pro rata to the size of your property.

Some homeowner associations hire and retain property management companies.

Key Points

Key points – property under construction

When buying a new property the key points to look out for are:

- Make sure you understand exactly what you are buying. How big is the property? What will it look like? How will it be finished? What appliances are included? What facilities will it enjoy?
- Think about who should own the property so as to minimise tax and inheritance problems
- Make sure the contract has all of the necessary clauses required to protect your position. See the other chapters in this book.
- Make sure that your money is safe if you are buying "off plan"
- Be clear about the timetable for making payments
- Think about whether you should forward buy currency
- When you take delivery of the property consider carefully whether it is worth incurring the expense of an independent inspection to confirm that all is in order with the construction and to help draft any "snagging list".

Key points – resale properties

When buying a resale property the key points to look out for are:

- Make sure you understand exactly what you are buying. Are the boundaries clear? What furniture or fittings are included?
- Think about whether to have the property inspected, especially if it is a few years old. If you want to take out a mortgage, an inspection will almost certainly be required.
- Think about who should own the property so as to minimise tax and inheritance problems
- Make sure the contract has all of the necessary clauses required to protect your position
- Think about whether you should forward buy currency
- When you take delivery of the property, make sure that everything agreed is present

Special points – old properties

When buying an older property – by which I mean a property built more than, say, 30 years ago, there are one or two additional special points to look out for:

- Are you having an inspection (survey)? Not to do so can be an expensive mistake.
- Are you clear about any restoration costs to be incurred? Do you have estimates for those items?
- Are there any zoning or other problems associated with any alterations or improvements you want to make to the property?

Special points – rural properties

- Such properties have often acquired a number of rights and obligations over the years. Are you clear about any obligations you might be taking on?
- You are probably buying for peace and quiet and the rural idyll. Are you sure that nothing is happening in the vicinity of your property that will be detrimental?
- If you have any plans to change the property or to use it for other purposes, will this be permitted?
- If you intend to build on the site, be very clear about minimum permitted plot sizes and other zoning limitations.

Special points – city properties

- City properties will usually be apartments, concerning which see below.
- Unless you are used to living in a city – and, in particular, a US city – do not underestimate the noise that will be generated nearby. If you are in a busy area (and you are likely to be) this will go on until late at night. How good is the sound insulation?
- Are your neighbouring properties occupied by full time residents, are they weekday only "pieds à terres" or are they vacation homes? Think about security issues.
- If you intend to use a car, where will you park?

Special points – apartments and houses sharing facilities

- Have you thought about an inspection of the property? Will it include the common parts? This can be expensive.
- Make sure you understand the rules of the condo/HOA – see below.
- Make sure you understand the charges that will be raised by the condo/HOA.
- Make contact with its administrator. Ask about any issues affecting the community. Are there any major works approved but not yet carried out? Make sure that the contract is clear about who is responsible for paying for these.
- Make contact with owners. Are they happy with the community and the way it is run? Remember that no one is ever fully happy!
- Understand how the condo/HOA is run. Once you are an owner, try to attend the general meetings of the community and to be a real part of it.

What If It All Goes Wrong?

When we buy a property, whether it is a main, a vacation home or as an investment, we are vaguely aware of the possibility of something going wrong, but we do not expect it to do so.

We are right. Very few sale and purchase transactions go wrong to any significant extent. This does not mean that they are all completed perfectly and with no problems! There is, almost always, some little hiccup. There is seldom a major problem.

If there is a major problem connected with the deal, or that develops later – for example, a dispute with your neighbour or your builder – you are very well placed by buying a property in the US.

The US is, rightly, famous around the world for having an administrative system that works and a legal system that delivers justice. Neither is perfect but they are a lot better than those in many of the countries from which our buyers come.

Title Problems

These are extremely rare – far rarer than you might expect when you see the size of your title insurance premium.

The good news is that, if one occurs, it should be dealt with by your title insurance company – unless it relates to one of the exclusions (such as litigation already in progress) written into the title insurance policy.

Breach of Contract

If you have a dispute with the seller of your home, with any supplier of goods or services or in connection with any other contract, you will find unlimited numbers of lawyers able to deal with it on your behalf. The US has more lawyers than all of the other countries in the world put together! There are nearly 100,000 in Florida.

If you need a lawyer, it is essential to get a recommendation and a good one, rather than just picking the best looking man or woman advertising on the TV.

We hope you never find yourself in this position but, if you do, Team Feltrim can probably recommend a suitable lawyer who has given good service in the field that you need to some of our thousands of clients.

Trying To Solve the Problem

The US is a very litigious place. Central Florida is, probably, even worse than normal. A combination of a lot of retired people with too little to do, lots of sunshine, a fair amount of alcohol and 100,000 lawyers wanting to buy a new Porsche creates quite a bit of activity.

However, before you rush to court, it's worth bearing in mind four key facts:

1. Court cases are long and expensive in any country. If you can avoid them it's generally a good idea to do so.

2. This leads to fact two – well known to all lawyers; even a poor settlement is better than a good court case.

3. Many disputes can be solved quickly, simply and inexpensively if tackled at an early stage. Don't let things drift on and get out of hand. Americans appreciate a direct approach and an attempt to solve a growing problem.

4. If all else fails, think about mediation instead of going to court. There is a growing mediation movement in Florida – see www.floridamediators.org – and mediation is almost always better and hugely less expensive than a court case.

The Court System

A detailed description of the Florida court system is beyond the scope of this book but the basics are the same as in most countries.

There are civil courts and criminal courts.

Each county has a County Court for dealing with civil disputes of up to $15,000.

Beyond that level, cases go to the Circuit Courts – which deal with both criminal and civil cases. There are 20 in Florida.

Appeals from the decisions of the lower courts go to the District Courts of Appeal, of which there are five in Florida. From there, in some cases, you can appeal to the Florida Supreme Court.

The most important thing to understand – especially if you come from a country where the judicial system leaves something to be desired – is that the judicial system in Florida works (albeit more slowly than we would like) and that it is not corrupt. Your rights as a foreigner will be protected with the same level of diligence as the rights of a local person.

Useful Names & Addresses

Baker Donelson Bearman, Caldwell & Berkowitz, PC: www.bakerdonelson.com

Florida Mediators: www.floridamediators.org

State laws and customs: www.stewart.com/docs/2-2009-NTS-0912-05-8_StateLaws&CustomsBroch.pdf.

The Cost of Buying a Property

The cost of buying a property – i.e. the amount you will have to spend over and above the price you have agreed to pay – will vary quite a lot, depending on the cost of the property, whether you are taking out a mortgage, whether you engage a lawyer etc.

These costs include various fees and taxes.

As a very rough rule of thumb, you should allow 2% of the price of the property if you are buying without a mortgage and 4% if you are buying with a mortgage. -

We set out below some typical costs. Please bear in mind these are only illustrations.

Typical Costs

Condo - $150,000 – no mortgage	
Item	**Cost**
Title insurance	$300
HOA estimate	$1000
Misc fees	$200
Total	$1500

House $195,000 –– with mortgage	
Item	**Cost**
Mortgage broker fee	$1300
One-year home insurance	$1000
Title fees	$1050
HOA estimate	$500
Government recording of mortgage	$1887
Lender title insurance	$1000
Appraisal fee	$400
Total	$7137

House $725,000 – no mortgage	
Item	**Cost**
Owner title insurance	$1900

Recording fees	$200
Closing fees	$250
HOA fees estimate	$1200
Taxes estimate	$4500
Total	$8050

House - $285,000 – with mortgage	
Item	**Cost**
Appraisal fee	$600
Mortgage broker fees	$1500
Insurance	$1350
Title insurance	$1500
HOA estimates	$1000
Government recording	$3000
Total	$8950

Moving In

Visas etc.

See chapter on immigration.

Customs

If you wish to bring any goods into the US, you will have to deal with US customs. It is worth pointing out that US Customs, just like US immigration, are much tougher and more thorough than their equivalents in many other countries.

Please be particularly careful about trying to bring plants, seeds or foodstuffs into the US. This is not permitted. Regular searches are carried out. At best, the goods will be confiscated and, at worst, you could be prosecuted. To avoid confusion, this rule does not apply to canned foods, as these do not present a threat to the health of US agriculture.

The way they will deal with you depends upon whether you are a tourist, a person becoming a permanent or temporary resident or a returning resident.

Each person arriving in the US will be given a customs declaration form. You need only make one declaration per family.

You must answer the questions truthfully and fully. Failure to do so can be very expensive.

Note, in particular, the question about money. There is no legal restriction on the amount of cash or other 'monetary instruments' (travellers' cheques, cheques, bankers' drafts etc.) that you can take into the US, but if you are taking in more than $10,000 you need to declare it. Failure to do so will, if you are caught, result in the funds being confiscated or impounded. At best you will then face a lengthy and costly battle to get them back.

If you need to pay duty or import taxes on anything that you are bringing into the country, you will need to do so at the time they are imported. They can be paid in cash, by credit card or by certain cheques drawn on US banks. If you cannot pay, customs will retain your goods.

Visitors

Visitors may import into the US any belongings free of tax and without having to declare them to US customs. They must be brought in for your own use. They cannot be kept in the US for more than six months. You cannot sell them and you must take them with you when you leave the US.

People Wishing to Become Residents

If you are going to become a resident of the US, whether permanent or temporary, you will usually be allowed to import your belongings free of tax and duty – though the precise rules depend upon the country from which you are coming and how long you have owned the goods. You can usually only import goods upon which you have already paid duty in the country where you were living.

If you are sending your furniture and other household goods by a shipper and will not be there when they arrive at customs, you will need a full list of the items that you are shipping, together with the date they were acquired and their value. Most shippers will supply you with a sample list.

Such a list may sound sensible and simple to deal with, but a moment's reflection tells you that it is not. The Americans believe in being thorough and a full list of the contents of your home will be very long indeed. I also suspect that you will have no idea when you bought your cutlery or how much it cost!

You are also permitted to bring with you the tools of your trade or profession.

If you want to bring goods with you as a new resident you need to do so within one year after the date of your arrival.

Once brought into the country, the items may not be sold for one year without customs' authorisation.

Returning Residents

If you have already taken residence in the US and make a trip abroad, you will be treated slightly differently.

You must declare any items purchased abroad, any items purchased duty free and any items that you have taken out of the US but which have been repaired or altered whilst you were out of the country.

You must also tell customs about anything that you are bringing into the country for another person, or any items that you are bringing into the country for the purpose of your business.

Should you wish to bring items into the country, without making a trip abroad, you can do so but, of course, they will have to be declared. This would arise, for example, in the case of an inheritance or items given to you.

When you declare the items to customs, you will have to tell them when the item was acquired and the price paid for it.

It is worth paying particular attention to expensive foreign-made items, such as laptop computers. If you have one in the US and then take it with you overseas, make sure that you have proof that it had previously been brought into the US. Otherwise you may have to pay duty. You can register such articles with US customs before you leave the country and obtain a clearance certificate (Carnet). There is no problem with items that were originally bought in the US.

Registration

The immigration authorities

You must notify the US Citizenship and Immigration Service (USCIS) of your address in the US within 10 days of your arrival and then do so again annually.

When you are issued with a Green Card you will be fingerprinted.

People who are citizens of certain countries, mainly non-European, may have to comply with additional formalities.

See www.uscis.gov for more details.

Your embassy or consulate

Most consulates operate a service under which their citizens travelling or living in another country can register with the consulate.

Registration is not compulsory, but it can be useful. It will help embassy staff contact you if there is a crisis, such as a natural disaster or terrorist attack. Registration is, generally, simple.

Furniture

Should you take your furniture and household goods with you or should you buy replacement items when you arrive?

I strongly recommend that you buy replacement items and take with you only things that are of great sentimental value or items such as antiques, which are expensive and even more expensive in the US.

The climate in Florida – hot and humid with lots of full- on sunshine – can play havoc with any furniture you do decide to bring. A table that has been perfectly happy for 300 years can develop cracks and warping, especially if you do not have the air conditioning on 24/7. Also bear in mind that any wooden furniture you import may need to be treated against insect attack.

Remember that the US operates on a 110-volt electricity supply, so none of your electrical goods will work without adaptors. Even if you buy the adaptors, you will not be able to get spare parts if something goes wrong. Incidentally, you will sometimes see 110 volts expressed as 115 or 120 volts. These are the same thing, measured slightly differently. In the same way the voltage used in other places is sometimes called 220 and sometimes 240 volts. Again, they are the same thing.

As to your general furniture, US houses tend to be much bigger than European houses and so it will probably look out of scale. It will also probably, depending on where you are going to be living, be unsuitable for other reasons. For example, if you are moving to Florida a UK or Irish sofa, upholstered in tweed or velvet, will be too warm.

Moving furniture is expensive, especially if you are going to be living somewhere far from the coast.

If you wish to take your furniture with you, there are a number of very reliable shippers. Some of them operate different levels of service, so that you can either have a container holding just your furniture shipped to your destination, or, if you are prepared to wait, you can have your furniture placed into a container with other people's furniture and shipped when the container is full. The second service is cheaper.

If you are shipping your furniture, always get a quote and make sure that it covers all of the expenses from door to door including, if you wish to take this service, packing and unpacking.

Contracts with Suppliers

Broadly speaking, you will need the same services in the US as you did back home.

TV

Remember that US TVs operate to a completely different standard (NTSC) than European ones, so your old set won't work. Nor will your old videos so convert any precious ones to DVD or other digital format.

Over 50% of people in the US choose to sign up for a cable TV service.

Nationally, the biggest supplier is Comcast (www.comcast.com), with 200+ channels and over 20 million subscribers, followed by Time Warner Cable (www.timewarnercable.com), who have over 12 million subscribers.

In central Florida, the main supplier is Brighthouse Networks, part of the Time Warner group.

Rates start at about $30 per month.

DVD

In an attempt to control piracy, but which probably causes far more inconvenience to ordinary people than it ever does to pirates, the authorities have divided the world up into various zones for the purposes of DVDs. Any DVD you bought in Europe will not work on a DVD player bought in the US and vice versa – unless they are doctored to eliminate this zone restriction. This is probably illegal.

Your European DVDs will still work on your European DVD player. Your Japanese DVDs will still work on your Japanese DVD player. Though, if they operate on mains power, you will have to deal with the voltage issue.

Telephone

For a nation that uses the telephone so much, the US service has always seemed a little primitive.

However, there are now hundreds of telephone companies providing telephone services in the US although the old AT&T companies (now known as the Baby Bells) still tend to have the majority of subscribers. Check out what is available in your area. Look for not just the Baby Bells but companies such as WorldCom, Verizon and Sprint.

Your home in the US will, almost certainly, be wired for a telephone service.

An interesting option used by many Americans living outside the US is to take an internet based service from a company such as Vonage. This will allow you to make calls from a special phone over your broadband connection. It can save you a lot of money, particularly if you make lots of international calls to slightly unusual destinations.

If you wish to contract a telephone service, this is usually very quick, but do note that if you do not have a credit record in the US (and if you have just arrived you are not likely to have one) the company may require you to pay a security deposit amounting to two or three months' anticipated bills. This will be returned to you once you have established a track record with the company. Connecting will usually cost you less than $100.

Then you will just need to go and buy a phone. These are sold by computer stores, electrical retailers and the big supermarkets.

Call charges are usually very low. Most local calls are free.

In an emergency, dial 911. This will connect you to all of the emergency services. There is also likely to be a local emergency number serving the area in which you live. Ask your estate agent for details.

Mobile Phone

In the US, mobile phones are known as cell phones. This is because they work through the cellular network and because Americans started using them much sooner than most other countries and long before they could genuinely be described as truly mobile.

Because Americans started to use phones so early, they started off using an analogue system. They are now in the process of changing to a digital system. If you want to buy a mobile phone that you can also use when you travel back to Europe, then you will have to buy a digital phone and one that works on the European frequencies. Look for a tri-band or a quad-band phone.

As in most countries, you can either take a service contract (typically for two years) or buy a pay-as-you-go phone.

If you do not have a credit history and/or an American credit card, you may have no choice but to take a pay-as-you-go phone.

Internet

Needless to say, the Americans make huge use of the internet and high-speed broadband is available almost everywhere. Seek a recommendation from your estate agent as to which works best in your area. If you are settling in the US and you decide not to take a Vonage phone, don't forget about good old Skype (www.skype.com). This free software allows you to make voice and video calls to any other Skype user anywhere in the world at no cost. Brilliant and a lifesaver!

Electricity

As already mentioned, the voltage is 110 and so electrical equipment bought elsewhere in the world will not work without a 'step up/down' adaptor. This is a unit that plugs into your wall socket next to your appliance, takes the 110-volt electricity supply in your home and converts it to 220/240 volts. The main exception to this is laptop computers, which are usually designed to adjust automatically between 110 and 240 volts, and some other equipment such as hair dryers that you may find to be dual voltage. However that sort of equipment needs to be switched between voltages. It will fry if you get it wrong.

As in other parts of the world, the electricity supply industry is now de-regulated in the US. Check with your estate agent what suppliers are available in your area and ask for a recommendation. There is a gulf between the quality of service offered by the best and the worst.

Generally, meters are read and supplies billed monthly.

You may find you have to pay a deposit as a new customer with no credit history.

Electricity consumption in Florida will be quite high – though prices are lower than many places in the US. This is because you will need to use air conditioning and/or fans for a very large part of the time. It often comes as a shock that you will generally need to leave your air conditioning on even when you are not resident in the property. If you do not, you can come back to a world-class collection of mould.

Although you, therefore, can't completely turn off the electricity supply when you leave the premises, you can and should turn off TVs, microwaves etc.

A typical monthly bill for a two bedroom condo might be $120. A typical bill for a four bedroom house might be $150-$170

Water

Water companies remain public utilities.

You will be billed for water in different ways.

In some areas, your water bill is included in your local property taxes.

In other areas, there is a flat charge for water that is paid separately.

In other areas, water is metered and you are billed in accordance with the amount that you consume.

The most common arrangement is for you to be billed by your HOA or condo, usually as part of a larger bill including charges for sewerage, garbage collection and street lighting.

Water is fairly cheap.

A typical monthly bill for a two bedroom condo might be $50-100. A typical bill for a four bedroom house might be $120.

However, note that, in some condos, the water bills are paid centrally and billed to you as part of your HOA fees. This is more important than might at first appear; if you only use you apartment for a small part of the year and everybody else uses theirs all year round, you will be subsidizing their bills. There is also less incentive to be frugal when you pay in this way –not that Americans in general or Floridians in particular ever do frugal well!

Just like you probably do in your own country, you will typically turn off your water supply when you leave the property for a long period.

Gas

Piped gas is available in most cities, but not necessarily in every area of those cities. It is not generally available outside larger cities.

The gas supplied is natural gas.

If you do not have a gas supply, you will be able to buy bottled gas, but note that the use of such gas is prohibited in some apartments.

If you are in an area supplied with piped gas, you may find that the same utility company can provide both gas and electricity.

Make sure you turn off all gas supplies if you leave the apartment for any lengthy period.

Garbage Collection

Garbage collection is usually the responsibility of your local municipality and will be charged for either through your local property taxes, or by way of a separate levy. In some gated communities, the municipality charges a fee to the community and then the community collects the garbage and delivers it to a central point. In this case, there will be an additional charge raised by the community. This will be part of your dues.

Insurance

Insurance companies in America are, of course, licensed and regulated, as are insurance brokers. It is a huge industry. Shop around.

Some insurance contracts give you the statutory right to cancel within a certain period of time, normally ten days. Read the policy before you sign and then read it again the next day. Cancel if necessary.

Property (Real Estate) Insurance

There are various types of household insurance available. These types of policies can have different names – household insurance, homeowners' insurance, house insurance etc. but they are all basically the same.

The various categories of household insurance have been agreed between the various insurance companies and so you should find that any policy in any given category would provide the same basic cover, though there may be some extras.

The Basic Policy – often called HO-1

This policy covers your home and its contents against what are known as the 'common perils': fire, lightning, windstorm, hail, explosion, riot or civil commotion, aircraft, vehicles, smoke, vandalism or 'malicious mischief', theft, breakage of windows etc. and volcanic activity.

This is not the most common policy in the US but you need only buy a more expensive policy if you really require its extra features.

Broad Policy – often called HO-2

This adds cover for damage by falling objects, weight of ice or snow, sudden tearing apart, sudden damage to your heating, hot water or air conditioning system, water damage from an internal source and certain types of electrical damage.

The All Risk Policy – often called HO-3

Some companies call this the special policy.

This policy, as its name suggests, covers you against everything to do with your property unless it is specifically excluded by the policy, plus the same level of cover for your possessions as is contained in an HO-2 policy. This is the most common type of policy in the US.

Renters' Policy – often called HO-4

As the name suggests, this is designed for tenants. It covers your personal possessions (on the same basis as an HO-2 policy) and any improvements you have made to the property but it does not cover the property itself. This should be covered by the owner of the property.

Comprehensive Policy – often called HO-5

This covers both your building and your personal possessions without limit, except for any exclusions listed in the policy.

Condominium and Co-op Policy – often called HO-6

This, not surprisingly, is designed for people who live in condominiums or co-ops. The co-op or condominium should have an insurance policy which covers the fabric of the building. The HO-6 policy covers your personal possessions and any improvements that you have carried out to your part of the building. In this respect it is similar to a Renters' Policy.

Older Owners' Policy – often called HO-8

Older homes can be extremely expensive to put back into the same condition before any damage was incurred. Insuring them can, therefore, be correspondingly expensive. The HO-8 policy is a simple and lower cost alternative for people living in older homes. It gives the same cover as an HO-1 policy but on the basis that any damage will be made good (i.e. the house will be put back into a condition in which you can live in it) but it will not necessarily be reinstated to the condition in which it was before the damage happened. For example, an ornate plaster ceiling might be replaced by a plain plasterboard ceiling.

If you live in an historic house you may find that you are legally obliged to restore the property to its previous condition, so you may need more all-embracing insurance.

It is worth noting that there are certain items regularly excluded from even the comprehensive or all-risk policies. These include earthquake, flood damage, hurricane damage and damage by war or nuclear accident.

You may wish to seek insurance against these risks but doing so, particularly (for example) if you live in a hurricane zone) can be difficult, expensive or both.

It is also worth noting that personal possessions are, in the US, usually covered to their current value and not on a 'new for old' basis.

You should read the terms of your policy carefully to see exactly what is and is not included in the cover. It may be different from what you are used to.

If you are buying your property with the assistance of a bank mortgage, you will usually be required to take out home insurance.

Insuring the Contents of Your Home

The contents of your home are insured as part of your household insurance policy. Check the position regarding any expensive items (such as jewellery or computers) and check exactly what cover is offered if these items are lost or damaged whilst away from your home.

Legal Liability Insurance

If you have ever watched television, you will realise that Americans are very litigious. Fuelled by no win, no fee lawyers, they will sue anybody for anything at any time. As a result, many perfectly ordinary Americans go to elaborate lengths to protect their assets from attack and they would certainly not dream of being without liability insurance.

This covers you against claims from third parties due to the various categories of loss or injury covered by the policy. For example, if someone injures themselves whist visiting. The big danger here is medical costs. You should therefore insure for a substantial amount. Many experts recommend $300,000 but I would be more comfortable with $1million or even $5million and the extra cost will not be great.

Make sure that your liability insurance covers as wide a range of liabilities as possible.

Medical Insurance

America is very good at medicine, but even the simplest medical treatments can be horrendously expensive. There is of course no free or so-called socialised health service and so you are totally dependent upon good medical insurance.

This can be a big problem if you already have medical problems and as you get older.

Remember that insurance contracts are contracts "of the utmost good faith". In other words, it is your responsibility to declare absolutely everything that is relevant to the insurance company. If you do not, they can just cancel the contract – even after you have made a claim. You should note that the thing that you did not declare need not have anything at all to do with the reason for the claim. You said your wife was 56 instead of 58? If you make a claim on your car insurance relating to an incident that occurred whilst you (and not your wife) was driving, the insurance company can deny liability. They have whole departments examining claims to see whether they can wriggle out of liability on such a technicality. This makes a lot of lawyers very wealthy!

There are three categories of medical insurance that you may need to think about.

Travel Insurance

Many people buying a home in the US will never visit it for long periods and so all that they will require by way of medical insurance is a good and comprehensive travel policy.

With travel insurance there are four main things to bear in mind.

- Does the policy cover the US? Some do not, or charge you extra for such cover, because of the horrific bills that can be incurred. Some will only permit a maximum of 30 days in the US in any one year.
- Does the policy cover you for the likely length of your stay? Some impose limits of 30 days, others 90. A few will allow you to spend 180 days at a stretch in the country, but this is rare and disappearing.
- How many days, in total, will you be away from home during the period covered by your policy? Most travel policies impose a limit of 90 or 180 days per year total exposure to risk.
- What is the cash cover offered by the policy? In the US, if you have a serious accident, you could build up a bill of millions of dollars. Go for the highest cover you can find. $3 million should be your minimum.
- Will you be able to continue to obtain cover as the years go by? Most companies will only insure people up to a certain maximum age.

Remember that a travel policy is designed to provide for emergency medical (and in some cases, dental) treatment. It does not give you the right to travel to the US to be treated for routine conditions. Basically, you will only be covered for something that crops up whilst you are over there.

If you have existing health problems, you may find it difficult to find suitable health insurance. This can become more of a problem as you get older and there has been more time for problems to appear. Most travel insurance policies are annual policies, with no automatic right to renew.

If you can limit your visits to the US to the number of days permitted under a travel policy this is likely to be, by far, the cheapest way of dealing with the medical insurance problem.

Personal Insurance Policy

If you are going to be in America on a permanent basis, or for more than the number of days permitted by your travel insurance policy, you will need to make more substantial arrangements.

You can either arrange cover just for yourself or for your entire family.

Health insurance can be extremely expensive and premiums can vary from company to company by 30, 40 or even 50% for what looks like similar cover. Prices have been rising rapidly. In recent years, there have been increases of 20 or even 30% per year. Some policies will contain deductibles (excesses – the amount you have to pay on any claim before the policy kicks in). Others will limit the maximum pay-out in any given year.

There is a wide range of policies available. Especially if you suffer from pre-existing medical conditions, it is probably a good idea to seek the help of a specialist medical broker to make sure that you get the cover that best suits your needs.

Employers' Insurance for Employees

This is the Holy Grail. If you are going to be working in the US, try to choose a job with comprehensive health care benefits and make sure you understand exactly what those health benefits are.

Sometimes the cover will extend just to you. On other occasions, your whole family could be covered.

You may have to contribute to the cost of your insurance. For example, the company may pay 75% and you 25%.

Comprehensive insurance by your employer is increasingly rare. More and more employers are opting for cheaper solutions, such as cover through Health Maintenance Organisations (HMOs). These will limit the range of medical service suppliers that you can use and usually require that your primary-care doctor (your GP) authorises any higher level of medical interventions that may be needed.

Car Insurance

In order to drive a car, you must have at least third party insurance. You can take more comprehensive insurance. There is a wide range of policies available. Seek the advice of a broker. Make sure that you are adequately insured.

Car insurance costs about the same as in major cities worldwide, unless you have chosen to live in a very rough area – which was probably not a good idea!

Life Assurance

It is a matter for you whether you feel such insurance to be necessary. There are many products available. Once again, consult a broker.

Team Feltrim is not an insurance broker but, once again, we can guide you to brokers who have previously given our clients good service.

You and the HOA/condo/coop

As explained previously, you may well own your property as part of a co-operative, or a condominium. You may live in a development where there is a Home Owners Association (HOA).

It is important that you make contact with the relevant organisation and get to understand how it works. This can be one of your first steps to being integrated into the community.

I recommend that, whenever possible, you take the time to attend the meetings of the organisation. Whilst no-one would pretend that these are always fun, they can help you in many different ways apart from just meeting your neighbours.

You and the Municipality (Town Hall)

Find out where your Town Hall is located and take the trouble to visit them. They will probably be surprised and delighted that you have done so. This could be your first step to being mayor! They will probably have all sorts of helpful materials for you to take away.

Keep abreast of what is going on locally and take the trouble to participate where you can. Remember that the US is a country big on participative democracy. There will be a number of elected boards (school boards etc.) that may be of interest to you.

Find out how the local finances work.

Your bank account

As I have already mentioned, opening a bank account is not as simple as it used to be. You will need to produce proof of identity and address for anti-money laundering purposes. You may have to jump through several other hoops.

As most banks offer pretty much the same level of service – especially when it comes to the fairly basic requirements of the average vacation homeowner or property investor – this means that your choice of bank may well be guided by how easy it is to set up and operate the account.

When it comes to operating the account, make sure your bank offers full internet banking.

If you still cannot decide which bank to use, check out their charges for receiving international payments and look for one that is inexpensive.

If it is still a tie, choose one near to your home and where it is easy to park!

Your Investments

It is well beyond the scope of this book to give you investment advice.

If you are going to move to America, then you will need to review all of your financial affairs, particularly where and how your investments are held.

See the chapter "Investments" on Page 163.

Your Car

Unless you have a vintage Bentley, do not take your car with you to America. Buy another one when you get there. In fact, most people owning vacation homes simply rent a car for the time that they are in the country.

One way or the other, you will need a car if you are living in or visiting Florida. Public transport is rudimentary, but improving.

It is an interesting fact that, at a time when many Americans have been downsizing to smaller (and more reliable) Japanese cars, most foreigners buying a car in the US will buy a big old American car such as a Mustang. This is one of the hidden benefits of the international property industry to the US economy.

Medical

I have already dealt with the question of medical insurance, but there are a number of other medical issues that you will need to think about.

Americans are absolutely obsessive about all things medical. They all think they ought to be immortal. As a nation, they spend well over twice per head what is spent in the UK and Ireland on healthcare.

Your starting point is to appoint a local doctor to be your Primary Medical Advisor (Primary Care Physician). There are many of them and most people would view their relationship with them as a long term relationship. It is a good idea to see your new doctor for a brief health check, as this draws a baseline for any further examinations or action that may be necessary.

In America, it is quite common for a person to have a range of doctors, each taking responsibility for a different aspect of your medical care. For example, a woman might have a Primary Care Physician (who would probably be a Family Practitioner), a Gynaecologist and someone advising on internal medicine.

Fees are high. You will need either to produce evidence of your insurance, or to pay in cash or by credit card at the time of the visit.

Most foreigners going to live in America notice how cautious US doctors have become. If you turn up with a cold, they will want to run a battery of tests costing thousands of dollars. This is not, as many suspect, because they are greedy. It is because they are absolutely petrified of malpractice lawsuits. There have been estimates that litigation adds 30% to the cost of medical treatment in the US.

Before you set out for America, you should ask your current doctor for a copy of your medical records and for a list of all the medicines you are currently taking. It is then worthwhile to pass those to a medical translator, so that the brand names and UK terms can be translated into the American equivalents. This will help you when you are looking for drugs and your doctor when he is prescribing them.

Whilst registering with a doctor, don't forget to register with a dentist and an optician.

A School for Your Child

Taking a child, particularly a young child, and immersing them in a foreign culture and a foreign education system, can give that child enormous opportunities. There are few people in this world who are totally bi-cultural: that is, they are able to move freely and unrecognisably in two societies.

If they can also become bilingual, this is an added bonus. In many parts of the US, it is easy to become bilingual in English and Spanish.

In America there is a much wider range of schooling available than there is in Europe. The public and the private are intermingled. Of course, if you are from the UK, it is useful to remember that a public school is a state funded school.

Depending on where you are going to be living, you may find the choice overwhelming. There are three basic routes that you can adopt.

State Education

These are controlled and funded by the state in which you are living. Well over 80% of Americans attend state schools. In some states they operate to a very high standard. In others, clearly not.

I've seen a big increase in Chinese children attending a school in the area where I live. Around 10% of the school are now Chinese children, who are mainly boarding students

Each State is divided into a number of school districts and each school district is governed by a superintendent and a school board.

If you would like your child to join a school near where you live, you should contact the school district's Board of Education to find out the school to which your child would be allocated and to agree the documentation that would be needed before they could be admitted to the school. You will need to obtain this from the child's old school. Requirements can vary significantly from place to place.

Once accepted by the school, or as a condition of acceptance, your child may need to be immunised or medically examined.

Private Schools

There is a wide range of private schools in most states. These range from the excellent to the freaky, though all schools must be approved before they can operate.

International Schools

In a number of states, including Florida, there is a choice of international schools. An international school, whilst complying with the basic requirements for a school in America, operate largely outside the American system.

They will usually educate students towards a different set of examinations, the most common being the International Baccalaureate. They may educate them wholly, or partly, in a foreign language.

You are most likely to be interested in an international school if your child is only likely to be at the school for a limited amount of time or will be moving on to another international school.

Remember that in most states it is illegal to pass a parked school bus that has its lights flashing.

Finding Help

There are any number of sources of help for those in Florida, whether on vacation or on a more permanent basis.

As with most other things these days, the starting point is usually the internet but you can also find information in the local press.

Look out for community groups, religious groups, groups of people from your own country and – in serious cases – the services of your consulate.

Make a note of all of the emergency numbers in your area.

Police	
Fire & Rescue	
Ambulance	
Doctor	
Dentist	
Vet	
HOA	
Water	
Electricity	
Gas	
Air conditioning	
Electrician	
Plumber	
General repairs	
Etc.	

Making Friends

You will probably already have realised this, but Americans are a pretty friendly bunch. Making friends is not normally an issue, but you do have to create the opportunities to meet your neighbours, co-workers etc. and accept their invitations, which will often come more readily and quickly than you might find at home.

If you have children, this will be a bonus.

Equally, you will have to play your part by reaching out to your neighbours, co-workers etc. and inviting them into your world.

Put down any strange comments to cultural differences or linguistic misunderstandings rather than the wish to cause offence – and bear in mind that you might be creating an equally strange impression in their minds.

Finally, don't ignore the large pool of your own fellow countrymen – or, at least, fellow expats who will be living fairly close to you.

Useful Names & Addresses

British-America Chamber of Commerce for Central Florida (www. britishamericanchamberorlando.com)

Irish-American Chamber of Commerce Florida (http://irishchamberflorida.com/)

Brazilian-American Chamber of Commerce of Florida (http://www.brazilchamber.org/)

Argentine American Chamber of Commerce of Florida (http://www.argentineamerican.org/)

Colombian American Chamber of Commerce USA (http://colombiachamber.com/)

Canadian American Chamber of Commerce of South Florida (http://www.beaconmgmt.com/canam/index.htm)

Letting (renting out) your Property

For the purposes of this section of the book I am using the word "letting" and the phrase "renting out" interchangeably.

Restrictions

You can only rent out your Florida home on a short-term Vacation Rental basis if:

- Your sub-division deed restrictions or homeowners association has no ban on Vacation Rentals, and
- Your city or county has no ban on Vacation Rentals.

Of course, this does not stop you letting the property to long term tenants.

You can always rent your property out for periods longer than 6 months.

The phrase "short term Vacation Rentals" has a specific legal meaning slightly different from what you might expect it to mean in everyday English usage.

Short Term Lettings

These are sometimes referred to as Overnight Rentals.

If your home is to be "rented to guests more than three times in a calendar year for periods of less than 30 days or one calendar month, whichever is less" you must first obtain a hotel license from the Florida Department of Business and Professional Regulation. This is required by Chapter 509 of the Florida Statutes (see note 1 below).

Overseas owners are also required to obtain a US Individual Taxpayer Identification Number (ITIN). If the ITIN cannot be quoted on the hotel license application, you will have to prove that one has been applied for. A temporary hotel license will then be issued until you can supply the office with the ITIN.

Homes are inspected before a license is issued, in order to establish that they are appropriately equipped with things like fire extinguishers, hearing-impaired smoke detectors and battery -backed emergency lighting. Call the department in Tallahassee on 1-800-488-2740 to find your nearest office where you can obtain the forms and details of other requirements.

Most cities or counties that have created Vacation Rental Ordinances use the above definition. Check with your city or county zoning department to obtain a copy of any local ordinance. An ordinance may require you to obtain an occupational license and also re-register your home each year.

General Principles

About 70% of overseas buyers who purchase homes in Florida let them. About half of those people rent out on a "serious" basis. That is to say, they are trying to make money by letting their property and try to find the maximum number of tenants each year. The other half let casually to family, friends and friends of friends: some more aggressively (and successfully) than others. They are looking not so much to make a profit from renting, but to defray some or all of the cost of ownership.

There are fundamental differences in the way these two groups should approach the task.

The first group should put itself in the head of the person they want to rent their property. Which part of the market are they trying to capture? You cannot be all things to all men. The single person or childless couple wanting to enjoy American culture will have very different requirements from the family wanting a cheap and quiet holiday in the countryside. Where would they like to rent? What type of property would they prefer? What features do they require? The serious renters should buy a property, convert it and equip it solely with their prospective tenants in mind.

The second group should make few concessions to their tenants. After all, theirs is - first and foremost - a holiday home for their own use. They will have to make some changes to accommodate visitors, but these should be as few as possible: perhaps slightly darker shades of upholstery, an area where they can lock away their valuables when not in residence and more sets of bedding.

This section relates mainly to the first group. I will make some comments directed specifically at the second and they can pick and choose from the other ideas, depending on how far they are prepared to compromise their wishes to increase letting income.

The right area

The choice of the area in which to buy your rental property is far and away the most important decision that you will make. There are many parts of Florida where it is fairly easy to let your property sufficiently regularly to make it a commercially viable proposition. There are other areas where this is almost impossible.

The factors to take into consideration when deciding upon the area are slightly different from the factors relevant when you're thinking about buying a home for your own personal use. They will also vary, depending upon your target clientele and your preferred way of administering the property.

Letting Agencies?

Strangely, the decision as to how you are going to let your property is one of the first that you are going to have to take. This is because, if you decide to use a professional management or letting agencies, it will alter your target market and therefore the area in which you ought to be buying. See the section on Management below.

If you are going to let your property through a professional management agency then it is worth contacting such agencies *before* you make a final selection of area, to see what they believe they can offer in the way of rental returns. They will also be able to tell you what type of property is likely to be most successful as a letting property in that area.

If you are thinking of finding the tenants yourself then you will have to decide upon your primary market. For example, most British people letting property themselves let it primarily to the British. There are a number of reasons for this. Lack of language skills (when dealing with pesky Europeans) and ease of administration are probably the most common. The rest of this section is targeted mainly at the person wishing to let to a British market.

Climate

Most people going on holiday hope for decent weather. Fortunately, not everybody has the same idea about what this means. The number of people taking summer holidays in Scotland or Ireland shows that a higher than average rainfall is not fatal. Despite this, you are likely to have more success if you are in an area, such as Florida, that is known to be warm – especially if you are letting in the winter months. Being dry also helps. Florida is not always dry and, when it rains, it rains. Fortunately, it seldom rains all day or for days on end. If you prefer not to have the rain you will see from the graphs that the rain is very seasonal and so it can usually be avoided by adjusting the date of your holiday.

It is particularly important that the area has decent weather during the prime US and European holiday season. This is normally July and August. For some, Florida is too hot during this period but (fortunately) others love the heat.

Note that September is very quiet in central Florida, often with the lowest rental potential of the year. This makes it a great time to visit your property without doing much damage to your rental income.

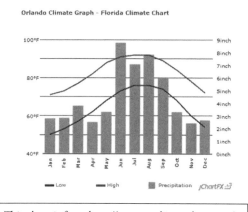

This chart is from http://www.usclimatedata.com/

Apart from this main holiday season, the months of May, June and October offer reasonable letting prospects.

In Florida, of course, the winter climate is well known and this makes it possible to achieve good levels of short winter lets. There is also a relatively good market for longer term winter lets.

One of the great things about renting out a property in Florida is that it has a very long rental season – in effect, all year round. Better still; the rental market is strong for much of the year. Both of these statements are particularly true if the property is within a short distance of the Disney attractions. What is a short distance? 15 to 30 minutes driving time to the main car parks.

In fact, if you are renting out to the Disney vacation market – which, for these purposes, we can take to mean all of the theme park attractions in the Orlando area, about the only times of the year that you will find quiet are the first 2 weeks in October and the first 2 weeks in January.

Study the climate charts in the section on finding a property. Information is also available from your tourist office, in travel publications and on the Internet.

Access

Just as important as the climate is the ability of tenants to get access to your property. This is true at two levels. The area in which the property is located must offer convenient access from the places where the tenants live and the property itself must be easy to find.

For most overseas visitors, convenient access to the area means convenient access from a major local airport. Convenient access is much more difficult to define if you are trying to attract American visitors.

It is worth repeating the results of the research conducted by the travel industry that shows that 25% of all potential visitors will not travel if it involves travelling for more than one hour from a local airport, at either end of their journey. If the travelling time rises to one and a half hours then the number that will choose not travel rises to 50%. This research was undertaken in the context of package holidays, but the principles must also apply to people renting holiday homes. Of course, this does not mean that, if your home is more than one hour's drive from an airport, you will not let it. There are many people who are much more adventurous and those wanting to rent property in rural Florida will often be in that category. Indeed, they will often view the journey as part of the holiday. It is beyond doubt, however, that if you are within easy travelling distance of the major airports, then the number of people renting from you will be increased. In Central Florida the major airports are really the Orlando airports but some fly to Tampa.

Do not underestimate (thank you, George W) the importance of being able to find your property! Navigation in the depths of rural Florida or within a particular development can be trying. There are few people to ask for directions (especially if you don't speak proper American!) and there are few signposts of much help when it comes to locating a rural cottage. The situation is not much better if you are trying to locate a house in Central

Orlando. The closer you are to a main road the better. Giving decent maps and guidance notes is also essential. Nothing is guaranteed to ruin the start of your holiday as much as cruising around for three hours to cover the last 500 yards of your journey – especially if it is 3am after a 12 hour flight. Paying your car hire company $10 a day to hire a Satnav might just save your marriage. It might be worth mentioning this (and the fact that some of the toll roads do not accept cash and so visitors need to buy a pass) in you marketing pack: especially if your property is a little difficult to find.

Tourist attractions

Governments are keen on tourist attractions because they attract tourists! The fact that they are prepared to invest billions of taxpayers' money in encouraging these attractions should persuade you that having one near to you is a "good thing" when it comes to letting your property.

"Tourist attractions" is a term that covers a multitude of things. At one extreme it could be a major theme park, such as Disney or LEGOLAND, attracting millions of visitors each year, all of whom have to find somewhere to sleep. Going slightly down in scale, it could mean being near to a championship golf course or a famous beach or sailing area. At the lowest level, the tourist attraction could be a lady in your town who teaches pottery classes or Native American culture. The point is that there must be something to bring people to your area, so that they will need to use your accommodation. The mere fact that the house is located in the middle of some pretty countryside is not, of itself, enough to attract a significant number of tenants. This is true – though, perhaps, slightly less so if your target audience is the people from Chicago coming to Florida simply to find some winter sun – the so called snow-birders.

Other facilities

Many people going on holiday want to eat out. Even those who will probably end up buying food in their local supermarket and cooking at home think they want to eat out. It will be much easier to let your property if it is within easy distance - preferably walking distance - of one or more restaurants. Of course, in Central Florida being within walking distance of anything, other than the clubhouse in your resort, is unlikely and, with temperatures soaring into the 90s, you probably wouldn't want to walk anyway. So the test is whether there are places within easy driving distance. If you are buying to rent out, the property should also be within a short drive of shops and other facilities.

The right property

The choice of property is almost as important as the choice of area.

Not all properties rent to the same extent. Our experience suggests that properties that the potential client finds attractive will rent up to five times more frequently than properties that do not stand out for any reason. Those other properties are perfectly worthy, perfectly spacious and perfectly comfortable but they just don't have the "wow factor". They just don't leap off the page at you. This is such a significant difference that you ignore it at your peril.

New property is generally cheaper to maintain than older property. Most people going on holiday to Florida are looking for a "typically American" property with or in close proximity to facilities and a pool. Those properties can just as well be new properties.

Can you let the property?

Make sure that there is no restriction on your ability to let your property. – a subject I have dealt with earlier in this book.

Many people ignore these rules. Many people are caught – often reported by their neighbours who want a quiet life and not a succession of strangers living next door to them. Most of those caught will find letting the property has been an expensive mistake.

Stick by the rules.

Pick a pretty home

Most people will decide whether to rent your property after they have seen only a brief description and a photograph. The photograph is by far the more important. Research that we carried out showed that 80% of a group shown 32 potential rental properties picked the same three properties as the places they would like to rent. The common factor in these properties was that they were all pretty. If the person was looking at properties in Florida, then they looked like a 'typical' Floridian house (as they perceive that) and not a boring semi-detached house just like they would find at home. If they were looking for somewhere by the sea, the property had either sand or water within view.

Now, fortunately, there are a lot of very attractive properties. Floridian developers seem to be good at building properties (and resorts) with customer appeal, but a quick drive around any neighbourhood will show that some properties stand out. Buy one of them.

When buying a house for rental purposes make sure you buy one that "takes a pretty picture".

Over the years, I have been to see, literally, thousands of properties. At Team Feltrim, we know the properties that will rent well and, if you are buying with a view to rental, we will guide you in the right direction.

Making it attractive

Make sure the external decoration and garden/pool area are kept in good order. These are what will show up in your photographs and will create the first impression on your guests on arrival.

Where possible, make sure you have a large deck area around the pool. This not only makes it look attractive, but it also saves you money. Your guests will all be able to sit around the pool and so they won't sit with some near the pool and some in the living area – with the doors open and the air-conditioning on.

Equipping and preparing the property

If you advertise the property well, you will get tenants. You will only get repeat tenants and recommendations from existing tenants if the property meets, or exceeds, their expectations in terms of the facilities it offers and its cleanliness.

The facilities required will depend upon the target audience you trying to attract. Think about that audience and think about what you would want if you were part of it. For example, if you are trying to attract an audience of sailors, they will appreciate somewhere to dry their clothes quickly so that they can be ready to get wet again the following day.

The top general tips are:

Welcome

It is much better if someone is present, either at the property or in a nearby house or office, to welcome your guests when they arrive. They can sort out any minor problems or any particular requirements of the guests.

Cleanliness

The property must be spotlessly clean. This applies, in particular, to the kitchen and bathroom. This may require some training for your cleaner, as our expectations when going into rented accommodation are possibly higher than our expectations in an ordinary home. They expect 4 or 5 star hotel standards.

Kitchen

This must be modern, even if traditional in style. Everything should work. You should have a microwave. You should also make sure that there is sufficient cutlery and cooking equipment and that it is all in good condition. A cookbook giving local recipes is a nice touch.

Bathroom

These days, the more bathrooms you have, the better. En-Suite bathrooms for each bedroom are ideal. Make sure that there is soap in the bathrooms. Guests will much prefer it if you provide towels as part of your service.

Laundry

A washing machine and drier are now commonplace.

Bedrooms

The number of bedrooms you choose is very important. Generally, in cities you will get a better return on your investment on properties with fewer (one or two) bedrooms - which will be cheaper to buy - than on larger properties.

In rural areas, or by the seaside, where the majority of your guests may well be families, a three-bedroom property is probably your best compromise.

A five or six bedroom house may look great and seem massive value, but it can be hard to rent profitable. However, there are places – especially near golf clubs – where these properties are a very attractive proposition for groups of sporting friends.

There are even places where there is a market for even bigger properties, to cater for the growing number of multi-generation holidays now taking place. These are holidays where the grandparents invite all of their children and grandchildren to a holiday in a place which offers something for everybody.

When deciding which size property to buy, it is a hard-nosed business decision. Yes, you might be able to rent out your eight bedroom house, but how often would you be able to do so. Would your annual rental generate a better return than you would have got from a three bedroom property?

Of course, if you need (say) a four bedroom property for your own purposes, then you will only worry about the competitive advantages of properties with four bedrooms or more.

This issue of choosing the right size of property for rental purposes is of such importance that it should be at the absolute centre of your plans. You will almost certainly need advice about what would work best in each area.

Check with your Realtor that the situation is in the area where you want to buy. Team Feltrim will be delighted to help.

Bedrooms should have adequate storage space.

Most importantly, bedrooms should have clean and comfortable beds. The only beds that last well in a regularly used rental property, where the people sleeping will be all sorts of different sizes and weights, are high quality beds such as those used in the hotel industry.

These beds can be expensive, but they will save their cost many times over.

Beds should be protected from obvious soiling by the use of removable mattress covers, which should be changed with each change of tenants.

Nothing except dirtiness produces more complaints than uncomfortable beds.

Clients will much prefer it if you supply bedding as part of your service, rather than expecting them to take their own.

You are not running an hotel. Unless you are renting out through a hotel type operation, you will not normally be expected to make beds or change linen. If you are operating an hotel style operation – i.e. where you apartment is being rented out on very short term lettings through a place that looks and feels like an hotel, then the hotel management company will take care of the bedding problem as part of its services.

Living areas

Furniture and upholstery should be in good condition. The style is a matter of personal preference but a "local" style is often attractive.

The furniture must be comfortable, robust, functional and easy to clean. For example, glass coffee tables are not a good idea.

This does not mean the furnishings should be bland or basic. IKEA doesn't work well. If people are paying good money to rent an upmarket property they expect the trappings of luxury.

There should be adequate means of cleaning, including a vacuum cleaner.

Heating

Is heating essential? There are many parts of Florida where it is almost never used. However, there are times when it may be needed and it is a good idea, from a rental point of view, to have a heating system on your tick list. If you are thinking of using the property yourself during the quiet periods, it is even more desirable. Needless to say, it should be effective and cover the whole house.

Air-conditioning

In an ideal world, air-conditioning would probably be best avoided except in the most expensive lettings. It can be very expensive, both to run and maintain. Yet, in Florida, it is so necessary, particularly in the summer months, that it will probably be difficult (or impossible) to let the property without it. These days, it is certainly expected and – in Central Florida – it is routinely built into new houses and apartments.

It is also worth bearing in mind that air conditioning – by extracting the humidity from the air – helps preserve your furnishings and the fabric of the building itself.

Personally, I would not even think of buying a property (or a car) without good air conditioning.

Check your Realtor's recommendation.

Swimming pool

If you are catering to the vacation audience, a swimming pool is highly desirable. It will significantly increase your potential number of tenants.

Even people coming to visit the Disney attractions will rest their weary feet by the pool between visits.

About the only audience for which a pool might not be an attraction is the snow-birder.

A pool should be of reasonable size but need not be heated.

Welcome pack

You should make sure that basic groceries such as bread, milk, coffee, sugar and a bowl of fruit are left in the house to welcome your guests. A bottle of wine goes down well too!

If you are letting your property through a hotel-style operation, such as is available in many resorts, you will find that they will have a policy as to the items to be contained in your welcome pack and that they will provide this automatically (usually at your cost!) to all arriving guests.

Documents

Make sure that all guests are sent a **pre-visit pack**. This should include notes about the area and local attractions (usually available free from your local tourist office), a map showing the immediate vicinity, notes explaining how to get to the property, emergency contact numbers and instructions on what to do if they are for any reason delayed.

Once again, if you are letting through a central letting management agency, they will usually decide upon the content of any preliminary pack and send it out on your behalf.

A **house book** should be available in the property. It should give much more information about local attractions, restaurants etc. and a comprehensive list of contact numbers for use in the case of any conceivable emergency. It can also act as a visitors' book. This will be a useful vehicle for obtaining feedback and a means of making future contact direct with visitors who might have been supplied by an agency.

In your marketing, it is well worth stressing that your property is clean, modern and well-equipped, at the same time showing the traditional outside appearance and pool.

Personal contact

It is a really nice idea – and certainly good for both repeat business and recommendations – if you telephone your guests once during their stay to check that there are no problems. If you are not using a letting agency, this is almost essential. If you are using a letting agency, it is a nice extra touch. The agency should, itself, be in contact with the people, but personal contact from you will make them feel special.

Of course, it also serves the additional purpose of checking to see whether the property is actually let that week. If you speak to somebody, you expect to see some income for that week!

If you find there is a problem you must, of course, fix it promptly and then check back to make sure it is fixed. If you are letting through an agency as part of a hotel style operation, you should report any problems to the agency so that they can deal with them. Take the name of the person you have spoken to at the agency. Give them a sensible amount of time to solve the problem and check back with the tenant that the problem has been solved.

When reporting problems to the agency, do remember that the tenant is (despite what all the books say) not always right and that they might well have given you a far from balanced account of their problem. So, before raising hell with the agency over their poor service, listen to what they have got to say. I can remember one of our owners who phoned our team, very upset that hadn't been supplied with a cot for their baby. Obviously, the first thing we did was supply the cot but – on investigation – it turned out that no cot had been asked for on our booking form and that the tenant had not raised the problem with us after their arrival. They had booked through an agency in their own country and that agency had not, as requested, asked for a cot to be made available. Clearly, this was not the tenant's fault, but nor would it have been right to blame us for the problem. The most important thing is to solve the problem and I am pleased to say that, in this case, we ended up with a happy holidaymaker.

Payment

The delicate question arises as to how – and when – you should be paid for the use of your property.

Letting the property yourself

If you are letting the property yourself, direct to the tenant, the choice is entirely up to you, but common sense says that you need to take a significant deposit at the time the booking is made. Remember, that you can only let this week once and that, if the person cancels at the last minute or simply doesn't turn up, this is a completely lost opportunity. As to how much to take, common practice is a 20% to 30%. Deposit. Some people take 50%. The rest of the rent must be paid either in cash at the time when they take possession of the property, or by credit card or bank transfer several days beforehand. Preferably, the latter.

Some people use the online PayPal service-. Try not to accept cheques:, particularly international cheques, as these can be dishonoured many months after the tenancy has come to an end.

Cash is now very rare for a variety of reasons including the reluctance of the banks to accept large payments without complex anti-money laundering formalities and, in any case, generally not practical if you live thousands of miles away from the property.

Realistically, therefore, this leaves payment of the balance to be made by credit card or bank transfer.

Credit card is easier and more immediate and if you have access to a credit card machine:, the tenant has much less opportunity to change their minds. Unfortunately, many of us do not and whilst there are a number of online credit card payment services, again they tend to be more expensive than regular credit cards. For example, Payatrader (www.payatrader. com) will typically charge you 2.9% of the transaction value if you are a low value trader.

If you are taking payment by bank transfer (national or international), you will need to have an instruction sheet telling the person how to make the transfer. Make sure that you give all of the bank account details, including the IBAN and BICS numbers. You will normally find these on your statement, - if not you can get these from your bank. You should also instruct them to make sure that all bank charges for the transfer are paid by the remitter (the sender) and not by the beneficiary (the receiver).

Letting the property via a letting agent

This could be someone who deals only with the lettings, somebody who rents out the property for you and also provides a welcoming service or somebody who provides both letting management and full property management – i.e. they are also responsible for looking after the fabric of the building and probably filing your accounts and paying your taxes.

Most people are, at first, surprised by the level of the charges raised by letting agencies – especially letting agencies dealing with short term or overnight rentals. In Central Florida, 20% to 35% of the rent received would be normal. Here at Team Feltrim we usually charge 25%.

When thinking about this charge, you need to bear in mind that the letting agent will have to have a sophisticated and expensively marketed website and a substantial administrative system to capture and process these visitors. This costs quite a lot of money. In addition, we will usually have arrangements with travel agents and online marketers (such as Expedia or Hotels.com) for them to introduce tenants to us. We will have to pay them around 15% of the rent received, leaving a fairly small part of our overall charge for us.

Bear in mind, that - on top of this charge – will be the various payments and expenses incurred on your behalf. These should be defined in your contract with the letting agent. Pay close attention to this contract as some contain lots of "extras".

Most owners are equally surprised by the length of time it takes to get paid.

If the property is rented out directly by your letting agents, they should receive the rent before the tenant takes possession (just like you would) and so they should be able to show it in their accounting within a few days. Most letting agents account to their owners either monthly or quarterly.

However, if the property is rented out via a big travel agency or tour operator or online marketing company, it can take up to 90 days (more usually 60) before your rental management company receives the rent – minus, of course, their charges.

Letting extra weeks in a property usually let via a letting agent

I have already said that it is a really good idea to supplement the activities of your letting agents by your own letting activity. If you can, from amongst your family, friends, workmates etc., rent out the property for an extra three or four weeks a year, this will make a big difference to your bottom line.

The question then arises: how should these weeks be paid for?

Different rental management companies adopt different approaches. Some insist that all rentals are paid for via themselves, whereas others (including Team Feltrim) are happy for you to collect money for these casual rentals direct, as long as you pay the appropriate sales tax.

Many owners are uncomfortable talking about and collecting money. In this case, they may prefer to say (even if it is not strictly true) that their contract requires them to pass all rentals on to the company and for the company to deal with the money. If this is what you prefer, you would simply notify the company that you had a potential tenant.

Other owners are quite happy to deal with the money themselves and they might want to offer their family or neighbours a discounted rate. One thing we insist upon is that, if the owner wants to advertise weeks for rent, the advertised price must be similar to that at which we are advertising the same weeks. To do otherwise debases the value of the whole resort, to everyone's disadvantage. There might be minor variations. For example, if the owner lives in the UK, he might want to advertise to a UK audience with UK prices. These will always vary slightly from the dollar prices because of exchange rate variations but, provided the prices are roughly in line and provided that the owner deals with the money, this is not a problem.

If an owner does rent a week themselves, then almost all rental agencies (including Team Feltrim) will charge an administration fee to cover the work they will have had to do: reception, arranging cleaning etc.

Do remember the obvious; you cannot rent out a week that has already been let to somebody else or even block reserved for allocation to someone else, such as a tour operator. Before agreeing a rental with your brother you need to check on availability!

Use of the property yourself

If you are letting the property yourself then, of course, you can simply decide not to rent out some weeks and to use them yourself and you can do this at any stage until the week is rented.

However, if you are renting via a letting agency and, in particular, if you are letting as part of a hotel-style letting operation in a resort, there are likely to be some limitations upon your ability to use the property yourself.

Most hotels require a guaranteed percentage of availability each year. Typically this might be 80%.

With most rental agencies, including hotels, if you want to block out part of the calendar for your own use, you will have to give them notice. This should be specified in your contract but it will, typically, be 90 days. However, most agencies will allow you to use un-let weeks at short notice. If you contact them and find that next week your apartment has not been let, they will not usually have any problem with you using it yourself although, sometimes, they will only agree if they have at least 1 or 2 units still available for last minute rentals.

Clearly, you are more likely to be able to use the property on a casual basis in low season. If you are thinking of booking out time in advance, if you are flexible in your travel requirements it makes sense to use the property in low season when both the weekly rental you are potentially losing is likely to be lower and the likelihood of finding a tenant is likely to be smaller.

Remember that, even if you are using the property yourself, you will have to pay some charges to cover the expenses of the rental managers. These should be stipulated in your contract.

Damage

You will be proud of your new home in Florida and you will want to see it in pristine condition when you next visit. You may have to adjust your sights. Now don't get me wrong. Rental management companies need to maintain the property to very high standards; if they do not do so, they will receive complaints and cancellations when the tenants arrive. However, this does not mean that the property will be kept in perfect condition.

You are choosing to put the property to work. Inevitably, it will suffer the odd knock, scratch and scuff whilst it earns you money. Guests might bang into a door as they are moving their suitcases, spill something on the carpet or put a hand print on the wall.

Our cleaning team is used to dealing with these problems and puts the property back to a very high standard between each visit, but we do not, for example, paint out chips every week.

During the six months since you last visited your two bedroom apartment, over 1,000 might have slept and lived in it (if it was let almost every night to six people on one night stays) – though the figure is more likely to be closer to 400(if we assume weekly occupancy by an average of three people for 75% of the available weeks)! Either way, some wear and tear will be inevitable.

Wear and tear is one thing; damage is another.

If you are renting the property out yourself, you should take a damage deposit. Some people just take a credit card number and get a signed agreement to make a charge in the event of damage, but this does not give nearly as much protection as cash in the bank.

How big a deposit should you take? For a modest two bedroom apartment, most people take about $300 with a clause in the tenancy saying that if more damage is caused the renter will be liable for it. $300 covers most normal accidental damage – surprisingly, people are remarkably careful in other people's apartments – but it does not cover major damage or, of course, someone intentionally trashing the place, which fortunately is extremely rare.

The good news is that, especially if you are renting privately, you are quite likely to find that the renter is so mortified at breaking one of your glasses that they leave you a whole new set.

If you are renting though a management agency they will, of course, deal with the issue of the damage deposit and any deductions that need to be held back when the money is returned. As you might imagine, this can be quite a sensitive issue.

When you receive your financial statement, you might be surprised to see charges for the odd broken glass or broken dinner plate. Why are these there when the tenant paid a damage deposit? This is not laziness or cowardice on the part of the rental management company. There are two good reasons for not holding back money for such small items. The first is that they are, arguably, legally speaking, not damage but wear and tear (not covered by the damage deposit) and the second is that deducting, say, $5 for a broken glass when the renter has paid, say, $1,000 for his stay, seems cheap and is certain to discourage him from booking again and from recommending his friends to book.

Economy

When you look at your financial statement from your letting managers, you will be struck by how much you spend on power. Although Florida has some of the cheapest electricity charges in the United States, we use a lot of power in our homes.

This is, mainly, because of air conditioning. Air conditioning is expensive to run, and, in our climate, it is on most of the time. When looking to economise on air conditioning, your most effective steps are to buy a home with good insulation (particularly doors and windows) and to make sure that the air conditioning is turned down to maintain a temperature of 88 or 89°F (about 32°C) when you are not in the building and for as much of the time as possible when you are.

One thing that I have noticed, after years of living in hot and sticky places, is that everybody seems to play the game of 'my air conditioning is colder than yours'. There is something faintly ridiculous about people turning up the air conditioning to give them a room temperature so cold they need to wear a jacket or a pullover!

You may also be surprised when you find that your air conditioning and your refrigerator are both left on when you have no tenants. I have already dealt with the reasons for leaving the air conditioning on; if you do not leave it on you are likely to generate mould growth and damage to both furnishings and the fabric of the building. As for the refrigerator, there are two reasons why it is left running. Especially if you are letting a property in a resort, it needs to be available for occupation at no notice – and guests expect the refrigerator to be working and ice available as soon as they arrive. If you are not letting a property in a resort, then the costs of sending someone to turn on the refrigerator in preparation for each letting can be more than the cost of the electricity consumed by leaving it on.

The right price

When buying a property as a business, you will be concerned to pay as little as is possible for the property consistent with getting the right level of rental return. If you are only buying the property as a business proposition, then this price/rental balance (or return on investment) together with your judgement of the extent to which the property will rise in value over the years, are the main criteria upon which you will decide which property to buy.

If you are going to use the property not only as a rental property, but also as a holiday home, then there is an additional factor. This is the amount of time that you will be able to use the property yourself consistent with getting a certain level of rental return. For example, if you bought a two-bedroom apartment in Orlando for $300,000, that property might be let for 45 weeks per year and produce you a return, after deduction of all expenses, of, say, 5%. If you bought a three-bedroom apartment in, say, Pensacola for, say, $150,000 and let that for 20 weeks per year, you might also generate 5% on your investment. Both would be performing equally well, but the Pensacola apartment would allow you and your family to use the property for 30 weeks per year, whereas the Orlando apartment would only allow you to use it for five weeks per year. This and the fact that it had one more bedroom could make the Pensacola property the more attractive proposition. I hasten to say that the figures I'm quoting are simply examples to illustrate the point, rather than indications as to what is actually obtainable at any particular moment.

Of course, really everything depends upon whether you prefer Pensacola or Orlando as a vacation destination!

Whatever way we look at it, paying the minimum necessary to buy the property is the key to maximising performance.

Remember the very wise words of advice: - you make money on your property when you buy it, not when you sell it.

One of the great things about the US system of buying and selling property is the existence of the "buyer's agent". This is a Realtor or other real estate agent who is engaged by you to look after your interests and to give you advice but who is paid by sharing the commission of the agent who is selling the property. These agents (including, if I might say so, our award winning team at Team Feltrim) are full of local knowledge and they will be delighted to discuss with you which of the properties on the market are likely to perform best, or will best meet your particular requirements. I cannot recommend strongly enough taking such advice if you are looking to buy an investment property. Whether you take it from us is entirely up to you.

Marketing

Properties do not let themselves.

You can either entrust the letting management to a letting agency (ideally topping up their work with lettings of your own) or you can deal with the problem yourself.

If you want to do the job yourself or even find some additional tenants yourself, you will have to do some marketing. In the early years you will have to do more marketing than in later years because you will have no existing client base. As in any other business, the cheapest type of marketing is catching repeat clients and so some money spent on making sure that the property lives up to or exceeds their expectations (and so secures their return next year) is probably the best spend that you will make.

There seems to be no correlation between the amount spent on marketing and the results achieved. Much money spent appears to be wasted.

What are the key points?

- Choose the method of marketing most appropriate to your property and your circumstances
- Follow-up all leads generated at once. Contact them again after a couple of weeks to see whether they have made their mind up.
- Send them your details again next year at about the same time, as they are likely to be taking another holiday.

Remember that your marketing is only as good as the quality of the response you give to people making inquiries. You will probably do better spending less money on advertising and paying more attention to following up the leads that you have actually generated!

Marketing in your own country

More facilities are available in some countries than in others, largely depending upon the demand for Florida rental property in that country.

Directories

If your property is pretty, then you are likely to get good results from the various directories and magazines focusing on properties to let in Florida. They only work if they are inexpensive, because, for a private owner with only one property to let, you only have one opportunity of letting each week and so a directory that produces, say, 50 enquiries for the first week in September is not particularly helpful.

Advertising

The problems with advertising is its scattergun approach and, in many cases, its cost. You only need a very small number of responses. You cannot afford to pay a large amount in advertising fees for each week's let.

Except for very expensive properties, traditional advertising is too expensive. We have had reports of good results from the specialist American property press - and even better reports from advertising on your local supermarket notice board!

Internet advertising can, however, be very cost effective. See below.

Your own contacts

Your own contacts are, without doubt, the best opportunity you have for marketing your property in Florida. Remember how few people you need to rent it out for, say, 25 weeks per year. Given that many people will take it for two weeks or more, you are probably only looking for 10 to 15 lettings.

The people who find this easiest are those who work for large organisations. If you are lucky enough to work for a major hospital or a large factory, you will almost certainly be able to find enough people to keep your property fully occupied within your working environment. You will have the additional advantage of knowing the people who are going to rent the property. This reduces the risk that they will cause damage, or fail to pay you.

Even without people from work, most owners will be able to find enough friends, neighbours and relatives to rent a nice property in Florida for 10 weeks per year. This will leave only a relatively small number of tenants to be found by advertising or other marketing means.

When renting to family and friends, or indeed close working colleagues, you will have to learn how to raise the delicate issue of payment. I have already referred to this earlier in this chapter. Given that you are not going to be incurring any marketing costs and, probably, very little in the way of property management costs, you should be able to offer them an attractive price and still generate as much income as you would have done by letting through an agency. Do make sure that you address the issue when you accept the booking, as doing so later can be very embarrassing.

American market

Most people who do not live in the US do not understand this market sufficiently well to be able to offer the product on the American market other than through a letting agency.

Other English speaking markets

There are significant English speaking markets in Scandinavia, Germany, the Middle East and elsewhere. They are most successfully addressed via the Internet.

Non English speaking markets

If you speak the appropriate language – particularly Spanish or Portuguese – there are lots of people around the world who want to rent in Central Florida.

Clearly, the cost and complexity of your marketing increases the more such markets you embrace. For most people, with a single home to rent out, the project is not viable and, to capture people from these markets, you will have to rely on the internet. Even then, if the readers do not speak English and have been using Google Translate, then dealing with them could prove a challenge.

Many owners letting the property on their own will not, as a point of principle, deal with renters who do not come from a limited list of countries.

Internet

The Internet offers tremendous opportunities for bringing a specialist niche product to the attention of a vast audience, at very little cost. It also offers the possibility of showing lots of pictures and other information about your property and the area in which it is to be found. As such it is ideal for the person wanting to rent out property.

It is worth having your own little website, designed especially for this purpose. Not only can it be your brochure, it can also act as a way of taking bookings. It is much cheaper to have someone print off a copy of your brochure from their own computer than it is for you to send it by post. You may have the expertise to create your own website. If you do not, it's quite fun learning. If you have not got the time or inclination, a simple but very effective site can be put together for perhaps $250.

As well as having your own website you should consider listing your property on one of the many American property websites currently to be found on the Internet. These listings are either free or low cost. You will soon find the ones that work and the ones that don't.

You will have to decide whether you want to use the site only as a brochure, or whether you are prepared to take electronic bookings. Also decide whether to price your product only in dollars, or perhaps in multiple currencies including £ sterling and euro.

Doing deals

Two particular forms of deal might appeal to you.

If your property is in a rural area, where there is somebody offering a very local tourist service, it can be sensible to make contact with them and try to arrange for the people visiting that facility or attending that course to be introduced to your property. This can significantly increase your lettings, particularly off peak. If you pay the person concerned, say, 20% commission, you will be well ahead.

The second type of deal worth considering is if you know some other people in the area who have properties to let. One of the frustrations of marketing your property is when you find four lots of people who want to rent the property for the same week. Getting together with others in a mutual assistance group will allow you to pass excess lettings to each other.

Management

I have already referred to letting agencies and the importance of selecting a good one. I make no apology for doing so again. The choice of agency can make or break your investment.

Letting agencies - or at least good letting agencies - will have the opportunity to capture clients from the domestic American market as well as from various international markets. They will argue – probably correctly – that the fee that you will pay them will be recovered by extra lettings that they make during the season.

In our experience the people who are most successful, or at least who make the most money from letting their property, are those who attract the clients themselves. This, however, assumes a level of commitment that many people simply cannot afford and a level of skill they do not have. It is simpler to use a Letting Agency. For most people it will also be more profitable.

Even if you use a letting agency, keep on trying to find tenants yourself. The income from an extra five or 10 weeks letting per year is largely profit.

I cannot stress too much that, if you decide to use a letting agency, the choice of agency is critical. There are some excellent agencies in Florida. There are also some crooks. The difference in performance between the two will make the difference between making a profit and a substantial loss. The temptation is clear. If somebody comes into their office on a Friday in August and wants to rent an apartment, yours may be available. Will the agent put the rent - perhaps $1,000 - in your bank account or in his own pocket? Will the agent rent your apartment or the apartment belonging to one of his "special friends"? In the past, too many have thought that you would never find out that they had let the property because you were 3,000 miles away and so have succumbed to temptation.

Selecting an agency

When selecting which letting agency to appoint there are various checks that you should make. Remember these people hold the financial success of your venture in their hands.

- If the agency is an American agency, are they professionally qualified and experienced? Many such services are offered as an adjunct to estate agencies.
- Check their premises. Do they seem welcoming and efficient? Is there evidence of significant letting activity?
- What marketing do they do? If they are reliant upon passing trade then, except in the most exceptional areas, they will not get you good results.
- Ask to see a sample information pack sent to a potential client. You will be able to judge a lot from this. Is it the image you want to give of your property?
- Inspect two or three properties that they are presently managing. If they are dirty or ill cared for, then so will yours be. Then it will not let.
- Ask for references. Preferably they should be from other overseas clients. Take the references up. Preferably speak to the people on the telephone. Ask whether there are happy with the performance and whether the financial projections given to them have been met.
- What contract are they offering you? Unless you are familiar with American law, it is sensible to get this checked before you sign, as some give you far more rights than others. Make sure that the contract gives you an entitlement to full reports, showing when the property was let and for what money. Do not accept an analysis by period. Insist on a breakdown week by week. Also insist on a full breakdown of all expenses incurred in connection with the property. Make sure the contract gives you the right to dismiss them on fairly short notice.
- How many weeks rental do they think you will be able to obtain in this area? How much do they think they would generate for you after deduction of all expenses including the charges?
- What type of property do they think would be the best for letting purposes in this area?

Controlling the agency

Once you have appointed a letting agency, you must control it.

- Check the report you receive from the agency and check that the money you receive corresponds to the amounts shown in the reports.

- Let the agency know, in the nicest possible way, that you and all of your friends in the area check each other's properties every time you are there and compare notes about which are occupied and the performance of your letting agencies. If they believe you, then this is a deterrent to unauthorised lettings.
- Telephone the property every week. If someone answers the phone, make a note of the date and make sure that there is income shown for the week of the phone call.
- From time to time, have a friend pose as a prospective customer and send for an inquiry pack.
- If you get the opportunity, call to see the property without warning to see what state it is in.

All this may sound like hard work. It is, but it will significantly increase the income you receive from your rental property.

Of course, you will not have these worries if you entrust your property to the highly experienced team at Team Feltrim.

We offer the following services:

Property sales

Property rentals (short-term and long-term)

Collection of rental money

Full maintenance division to look after all repair and maintenance issues

Background and credit check on potential tenants

Property inspection every 60 days

For full details, see our website at: http://www.feltriminternational.com/

Furnished or Unfurnished?

From the point of view of the landlord, the safest type of letting is a short holiday letting of furnished property.

If a furnished property is rented as a holiday letting, the tenant's rights to stay on at the end of the period of the tenancy are limited.

If you decide to rent on a longer-term basis then, in Florida, most tenants prefer to rent unfurnished so that they can use their own furniture. This, of course, rather spoils the cunning plan that might have come into your head of using the property for the odd sneaky vacation in the gaps between tenants, or even intentionally delaying a let to a new tenant for a month or so to allow for such a vacation!

The Letting Agreement

A suitably drafted tenancy agreement will take into account all these factors and protect you in the event of a dispute with your tenant and, in particular, in the event that he wishes to stay on at the end of the tenancy.

If your property forms part of a condominium or coop, your tenants will have to agree to abide by the rules of the community and should be supplied with a copy of the rules, or at least of the part of the rules that govern their conduct.

In the rental contract, you should stipulate what things are going to be covered by your insurance and what are not. Typically, the tenant's personal possessions would not be covered under your policy.

Tax Issues

Individual Taxpayer Identification Number for non-residents

Before you do anything else you must obtain a US Tax Identification Number ITIN by completing a form W-7 and sending it to the IRS. The form can be downloaded from http://www.irs.gov/pub/irs-pdf/fw7.pdf.

Better still, get your Realtor or accountant to organise this when you buy the property.

The IRS requires that the taxpayer requests his number when he files his first income tax return. The application is submitted with the return to the ITIN unit.

If a non-resident homeowner sells his home and requests an exemption from the withholding tax, the seller and the buyer must supply their ITIN, social security number or Form W-7 (application for ITIN, for link please see below), with the application.

An exemption to apply early for an ITIN is allowed for those non-residents that need an ITIN for licenses or banks. Proof of the need for an ITIN for the licenses or banks must be attached to the application.

Renting - Form W-8ECI

Before starting to rent, it is essential that overseas owners complete a W-8ECI form and give it to their property manager.

This from officially exempts your property manager from the legal obligation to deduct 30% from any rental income received, before sending you the balance. It also provides you with the right to deduct expenses, mortgage interest and depreciation from the income in arriving at a profit or loss figure for tax purposes.

The form can be downloaded atwww.irs.gov/pub/irs-pdf/fw8eci.pdf

Taxes

Sales and Tourist Taxes

You will also have to register for and pay Sales Tax with the Florida Department of Revenue on all rental monies received. Call the department on 1-800-352-3671 in Florida, or 850-488-9750 from elsewhere, to find your nearest office. Some cities and counties also have a Tourist Tax. This is sometimes payable to the state with the sales tax, but in other cases the city or county handle it themselves. Where this is the case, you will have to register with your city or country tax collector

For a list, see http://floridataxcollectors.com

Tourist tax is also due on rental monies received. Sales and Tourist taxes can be paid online.

Tangible tax

The value of the furnishings and equipment in your vacation home is, because your home is rented. You will again need to register with your city or county Tax Collector. Tangible taxes can be paid online.

Annual Income Tax returns

Overseas owners of vacation homes are required to file a US tax return if you rent your home for more than 14 days in any year. So if you had more than 14 days of rentals between January 1st and December 31st last year you should file a 1040NR return this year.

As far as the US tax authorities are concerned, you must report all income "effectively connected with" your Florida home. Just because you collect some of it overseas does not exclude it from their grasp. As to whether or not you can legitimately claim any part of your travel to Florida, you must lean on your tax return preparer's guidance and your own conscience. One way of coming to a decision is to think how comfortable you will feel having to justify it, if you are across a table from an IRS inspector who is auditing your return!

The deadline for filing a US tax return is June 15th. The US tax year operates on a calendar year basis.

Joint filing for married couples is not allowed and each part owner needs to file a 1040NR to claim their portion of the business deductions.

Incidentally, if you hadn't guessed, the NR in the form number identifies that it is a return by a non-resident. US citizens and US green card holders have to file different returns by even earlier dates.

All IRS forms and completion instructions can be obtained from the IRS web site. See www.irs.gov.

Most overseas owners find the US 1040NR tax return too complicated to complete and use someone to prepare their tax return for them.

General

The good news is that, judging from owner's comments, the US tax rules regarding rental income and expenses are very clear and uniformly applied by the IRS.

Most owners are correctly advised by their tax return preparer that it is in their own interests to declare to the IRS that the rental activity is to be treated as a US business. This is done by completing form W-8ECI (previously called form 4224) each year, and sending it to your property manager, as well as making this election on your tax return. See above for how to deal with this form.

Since the US tax system is a self-declaration system, it is up to you to gather all the information on income and expenses, and in consultation with your tax return preparer, compile the figures for the return. The IRS uses a sophisticated computer system to check all returns, and decide who should have their returns audited in person by an IRS inspector. Since the IRS also has a mass of other information from banks, mortgage companies, property managers, and the sundry people and organisations that provide you with services, it is a dangerous exercise to hope that they will never catch you if you decide that filing a return is too much bother.

As I said before, it is largely a paper exercise. You are unlikely to have to pay any tax.

Apart from the proportion represented by your own occupancy of your Florida home, you can deduct all the running costs and maintenance, the costs you incur getting rentals (such as advertising and mailing details to enquirers) and even your tax preparer's fee. You can also deduct the interest part of your mortgage payments, and any insurance and property taxes that you may have to include with your mortgage payments. Your tax preparer will also compute a depreciation deduction that you are allowed to set against the rentals. The price you paid for your home, less the value of the land, can be depreciated over twenty seven and a half years. Similarly, the furnishings and equipment you put in to make it 'rentable' can also be depreciated. This is usually over a shorter period, such as seven years.

By the time all your deductions are added up, you have to achieve an exceptionally high occupancy level before you become liable for US income tax. And any tax you have to pay in the US can, in any event, be set off against any UK taxes that result from the same rental activity, because most foreign countries have a tax treaty with the USA. So the whole paperwork exercise is not as daunting as it first appears.

Sale of your rental property (non-residents)

Due to depreciation, mortgage interest and other operating deductions, your rental property will probably generate a tax loss while being rented. These losses are accumulated on Form 1040NR and carried forward to reduce future income or gain from the sale of the property.

If a gain on the sale of the property exceeds these losses, the net capital gain is taxed in the US at a maximum rate of 35%, provided the property was held for longer than one year. If not, the gain is taxed as income.

If the property is sold at a loss, fairly obviously no tax liability results.

However, regardless of whether or not you have a taxable gain or any tax is payable, a withholding tax equal to 10% of the gross sales price may be required to be withheld from the seller's funds at closing. When you file your subsequent calendar year's Form 1040NR and report the sale of your property, the withholding tax is reported as a credit. This credit is applied to any tax due from the gain on the sale of your property and any excess will be refunded to you. If you have no gain, all your withheld tax will be refunded to you.

There are certain exceptions to the withholding requirement that may be applicable.

You may submit an application for a withholding certificate, or an application for early refund, to the Internal Revenue Service (IRS) to reduce or eliminate the 10% withholding tax on the sale. In both cases, the basis of the application is that the actual tax liability is less than the amount withheld. An application for a withholding certificate is generally prepared prior to the sale closing. The closing agent will withhold the 10% and retain it in an escrow account until the IRS responds to the application, usually within 90-120 days. Upon receipt of IRS approval of the application, the appropriate amount of tax due (if any) will be paid over to the IRS and the balance of the amount withheld will be returned to you. Thus a withholding certificate, filed before a transfer, notifies the closing agent that a reduced or zero withholding amount is required.

An application for early refund is similar to an application for withholding certificate, except that it is submitted after closing and remittance of the withholding tax to the IRS. If this application is approved, the amount of withholding tax is refunded to you, usually within 120-150 days.

Since this is a complex issue, professional advice should be sought.

Taxes back home

Overseas owners will also have to report the rental income and expenses of their vacation home for tax purposes in the country in which they reside.

If there is a tax treaty between the US and that country, then any tax paid in the USA will probably be deductible against any tax that would be payable in the other country. However, the tax deductions allowed in the US are more generous than in most countries (for example, allowing the deduction of the cost of mortgage interest and an annual allowance of 1/28th of the price of the property), so you may still end up owing tax back home, even if you owed noting in the US.

These taxes are beyond the scope of this book.

Useful Names & Addresses

US Government information: http://www.usa.gov/

IRS- Internal Revenue Service: http://www.irs.gov/How to file US taxes: http://www.usa. gov/Citizen/Topics/Money/Taxes.shtml

Department of Business and Professional Regulation (DBPR) Florida: https://www. myfloridalicense.com/wl11.asp

US tax services PwC: http://www.pwc.com/us/en/tax-services

Investments

I repeat that it is well beyond the scope of this book to give you investment advice.

If you are going to move to America, then you will need to review all of your financial affairs, particularly where and how your investments are held.

US$1 = approximately £0.61, €0.72, ¥6.19 and RUB36.09
€1 = approximately £0.84, $1.38, ¥8.53 and RUB49.75
(Rates correct on 23 March 2014)

An interesting point arises if you are thinking of spending four or five months of each year in Florida. Your home base and tax base will be unchanged, but you might want to think about the mix of your investments.

If you live all year round in (say) Ireland and your income is from Irish sources, such as your salary, a pension and investments, they will all be paid to you in Euro. If (say) 30% of your annual expenditure is going to be in US dollars, it might make sense to look at some investments generating income in dollars. This will help you even out the fluctuations in exchange rates – which can be considerable.

Americans are, by and large, much more savvy than Europeans when it comes to managing their financial affairs and making investment decisions. You will find, in every bookstore, shelves full of books to help you do these things. It is worth reading a few of these. However, as someone who is new to the area and new to this society, you really do need a good financial advisor to help guide you through the mass of options available to you. See the chapter on 'Initial Research' (Page 20) for how to choose an advisor.

The need to do something

Most of us don't like making investment decisions. They make our head hurt. They make us face up to unpleasant things – like taxes and death. We don't really understand what we are doing, what the options are or what is best. We don't know who we should trust to give us advice. We know we ought to do something, but it will wait until next week – or maybe the week after. Until then our present arrangements will have to do.

If you are moving to live overseas you *must* review your investments. Your current arrangements are likely to be financially disastrous – and may even be illegal.

What are you worth?

Most of us are, in financial terms, worth more than we think. When we come to move abroad and have to think about these things it can come as a shock.

Take a piece of paper and list your actual and potential assets:

Asset	Value – $	Value – £/€
Current Assets		
Main home		
Holiday home		
Contents of main home		
Contents of holiday home		
Car		
Boat		
Bank Accounts		
Other Cash type investments		
Bonds Etc.		
Stocks & Shares		
Investment Funds		
Pension Funds		
Other		
Value of your business		
Value of share options		
TOTAL		
Future Assets		
Value of share options		
Personal/Company Pension – likely lump sum		
Potential Inheritances or Other Accretions		
Value of endowment mortgages on maturity		
Other		
TOTAL		
Pensions		
Work Related Pension		
State Pension		
Personal Pension		
Other		
TOTAL		
GRAND TOTAL		

This will give you an idea of the amount you are worth now and, just as importantly, what you are likely to be worth in the future. Your investment plans should take into account both figures.

Who should look after your investments?

You may already have an investment adviser. You may be very happy with their quality and the service you have received. They are unlikely to be able to help you once you have gone to live in the US. They will almost certainly not have the knowledge to do so. They will know about neither the US investments that might be of interest to you or, probably, of many of the "off shore" products that might be of interest to someone no longer resident where you currently live. Even if they have some knowledge of these things, they are likely to be based thousands of miles from where you will be living.

Nor is it a simple question of selecting a new local (US) adviser once you have moved. They will usually know little about the aspects of your case specific to the country where you presently live, or about the tax and inheritance rules in that country that could still have some importance for you.

Choosing an investment adviser competent to deal with you once you are in the US is not easy. By all means seek guidance from your existing adviser. Ask for guidance from others who have already made the move. Do some research. Meet the potential candidates. Are you comfortable with them? Do they share your approach to life? Do they have the necessary experience? Is their performance record good? How are they regulated? What security/bonding/guarantees can they offer you? How will they be paid for their work? Fees or commission? If commission, what will that formula mean they are making from you in "real money" rather than percentages?

Above all, be careful. There are lots of very dubious "Financial Advisers" operating in the popular tourist areas of the US. Some are totally incompetent. Some are crooks, seeking simply to separate you from your money as cleanly as possible.

Fortunately there are also some excellent and highly professional advisers with good track records. Make sure you choose one.

Where should you invest?

For most people the big issue is whether they should keep their current investments.

Most people will have investments that are largely based in their own country and generating income in their own currency. Even if they are, for example, a Far Eastern fund they will probably be denominated in £ Sterling if they live in the UK and Euro if you live in the Eurozone and they will pay out dividends etc. in those currencies.

You will be spending dollars.

As the value of the dollar fluctuates against the value of these currencies, the value of your investments will go up and down. That, of itself, isn't too important, because the value won't crystallise unless you sell. What does matter is that the revenue you generate from those investments (rent, interest, dividends etc.) will also fluctuate in value. Take, for example, an investment that generated you £10,000 per annum. Rock steady. Then think of that income in spending power. In the last few years the dollar has varied in value from £1 = $1.12 to £1 = $2.09. Sometimes, therefore, your income in dollars would have been $20,900 per year and at others it would have been $11,200 per year. The same principle would apply if your investments were in Euro, RMB or any other currency. This is a huge difference in your standard of living BASED SOLELY ON EXCHANGE RATE VARIATIONS.

To my way of thinking, this is unacceptable, particularly as you will inevitably have to accept this problem in so far as your pension is concerned.

In general terms, I therefore prefer investments that pay out in dollars if you live in the US. If you are going to live part of the year in the US you might want to arrange for part of your investments to be dollar based.

Trusts

Trusts are an important weapon in the hands of the person going to live in the US.

Trusts offer the potential benefits of:

1. Allowing you to put part of your assets in the hands of trustees so that they no longer belong to you for wealth tax or inheritance tax purposes

2. Allowing you to receive only the income you need (rather than all the income generated by those assets) so keeping the extra income out of sight for income tax purposes.

3. Allowing a very flexible vehicle for investment purposes.

So how do these little wonders work?

After leaving your own country (and before moving to the US) you reorganise your affairs by giving a large part of your assets to "Trustees". These are normally a professional Trust company located in a low tax regime. The choice of a reliable trustee is critical.

Those trustees hold the asset not for their own benefit but "in trust" for whatever purposes you established when you made the gift. It could, for example, be to benefit a local hospital or school *or it could be to benefit you and your family*. If the trust is set up properly in the light of the requirements of US law, then those assets will no longer be treated as yours for tax purposes.

On your death the assets are not yours to leave to your children (or whoever), and so do not (subject to any local anti-avoidance legislation) carry inheritance tax.

Similarly the income from those assets is not your income. If some of it is given to you, it may be taxed as your income, but the income that is not given to you will not be taxed in the US and, because the trust will be located in a nil/low tax regime, it will not be taxed elsewhere either.

The details of the arrangements are vitally important. They must be set up precisely to comply with US tax law. If you do not do this, they will not work as intended.

Trustees can manage your investments in (virtually) whatever way you stipulate when you set up the trust. You can give the trustees full discretion to do as they please, or you can specify precisely how your money is to be used. There are particular types of trusts and special types of investments that trusts can make that can be especially beneficial in the US.

Trusts can be beneficial even to US resident people of modest means – say $500,000. It is certainly worth investing a little money to see if they can be of use to you, as the tax savings can run to many thousands of dollars. If you are thinking of trusts as an investment vehicle and tax planning measure, you must take advice early – months before you are thinking of moving to the US. Otherwise it will be too late.

It is worth remembering that Trusts can work even if you come from a country where the concept of Trusts is not recognised; indeed, they can sometimes work exceptionally well for people from those countries. It is also worth remembering that they may well not work at all for people from some countries, as the tax office in your own country might simply overturn the arrangements as having no purpose except for to save tax.

None the less, they are worth investigating and these factors make it even more important to do so promptly.

Keeping track of your investments

Whatever you decide to do about investments – put them in a trust, appoint investment managers to manage them in your own name or manage them yourself- you should always keep an up to date list of your assets and investments AND TELL YOUR FAMILY WHERE TO FIND IT. Make a file. By all means have a computer file, but print off a good old-fashioned paper copy. Keep it in an obvious place known to your family. Keep it updated. Keep it with your Will and the deeds to your house. Also keep in it either the originals of bank account books, share certificates etc., or a note of where they are to be found.

Lawyers find it is very frustrating – and expensive for the client – when, after the parents' death, the children come in with a suitcase full of correspondence and old chequebooks. They have to go through it all and write to all these old banks lest there should be

$1,000,000 lurking in a long forgotten account. There never is and it wastes a lot of time and money.

Useful Names & Addresses

Mid Florida Investment Properties: http://www.floridahomeflipping.com/become-an-investor/central-florida-homes/

Smart Currency: http://www.smartcurrencyexchange.com/

Other things to do when you buy a Property

Insure the property and its contents.

See the chapter "Moving In" – Page 120.

Make a full photographic record of the property. This is useful in the event of an insurance claim and for your scrapbook.

Bills

Make arrangements for your bank to pay your bills.

Wills

Make a will in the US form covering your assets in the US or, if your lawyer so advises, a Revocable Trust – which often has the beneficial effect of avoiding the need for an expensive US probate on your death. Either will usually mean also making small changes to your existing will made in your own country.

Lasting (Enduring/Durable) Power of Attorney

A Lasting Power of Attorney is a legal document. It allows you to appoint someone that you trust as an 'attorney' to make decisions on your behalf. Attorneys can make decisions for you when you no longer wish to do so yourself or when you lack the mental capacity to do so.

A Lasting Power of Attorney can help you plan how your health, wellbeing and financial affairs will be looked after. It allows you to plan in advance:

- the decisions you want to be made on your behalf if you lose capacity to make them yourself
- the people you want to make these decisions
- how you want the people to make these decisions

Different requirements apply in different countries and not all countries will accept, or permit, such Lasting Powers. As examples of what is possible, I will look at the rules under US and English law. It is easiest to start with the English rules.

There are two different types of Lasting Power of Attorney under English law:

- health and welfare Lasting Power of Attorney
- property and financial affairs Lasting Power of Attorney

Health and welfare Lasting Power of Attorney

A health and welfare Lasting Power of Attorney allows you to choose one or more people to make decisions for things such as medical treatment. A health and welfare Lasting Power of Attorney can only be used if you lack the ability to make decisions for yourself.

Property and financial Affairs Lasting Power of Attorney

A property and financial affairs Lasting Power of Attorney lets you choose one or more people to make property and financial affairs decisions for you. They do not need to be a lawyer/attorney. They could, for example, be your wife and/or children.

These decisions could include decisions about paying bills, or selling your home. You can appoint someone as an attorney to look after your property and financial affairs at any time. You can also, if you wish, include a condition that means the attorney can only make decisions when you lose the ability to do so yourself.

Similar Powers can be granted in many other countries.

The US equivalent of the Lasting Power of Attorney is the Durable Power of Attorney.

For people coming to the US from other countries, the position is a little more complex but the consensus seems to be that this US Durable Power of Attorney should be useful for them too. This is because, once it is validly created, it can have effect over all the affairs of the person making it. It will have effect over the person's property, wherever that property is located. There is because, it is argued, there is no rule of law that the Power of Attorney has to be made where the person is resident at the time they lose capacity.

Under the common law, as applied in the US, an ordinary power of attorney becomes ineffective if its grantor (the person giving the power) dies or becomes "incapacitated", (meaning unable to grant such a power because of physical injury or mental illness), unless the grantor specifies that the power of attorney will continue to be effective even if he becomes incapacitated.

This type of power of attorney is called "power of attorney with durable provisions" in the United States or "enduring power of attorney" elsewhere. In effect, under a durable power of attorney, the authority of the attorney-in-fact to act and/or make decisions on behalf of the grantor continues until the grantor's death.

In some states, a durable power of attorney can also be a "health care power of attorney", commonly called a "living will". This particular affidavit gives the attorney-in-fact the authority to make health care decisions for the grantor, up to and including terminating care and life support. The grantor, under a living, will can typically modify or restrict the powers of the agent to make end-of-life decisions. In many states a health care power of attorney is also referred to as a "health care proxy" and, as such, the two terms are sometimes used interchangeably.

Make an Advance Health Care Directive ("Living Will")

Related to the lasting power of attorney is a separate document known as an Advance Health Care Directive, also called a "living will". A living will is a written statement of a person's health care and medical wishes but does not appoint another person to make health care decisions.

Depending upon the jurisdiction (the state whose law applies to the case), a durable or health care power of attorney may or may not appear with an advance health care directive in a single, physical document. For example, the California legislature has adopted a standard power of attorney for health care and advance health care directive form that meets all the legal wording requirements for a power of attorney and advance health care directive in California. Compare this to New York State, which enacted a Health Care Proxy law that requires a separate document be prepared appointing one as your health care agent.

Do it!

It might seem morbid to think about things like Wills, Lasting Powers of Attorney and Living Wills at the time when you are buying a holiday home or an investment property, but the truth is that, if you don't do it now, you won't do it at all and your family can then be put to a great deal of emotional distress and costs when you become incapable or die.

Identify People You Might Need

Now is a good time to make a written list, stored on your computer, of the names and contact details of all of the people that you are likely to need in connection with your home in Florida.

It is useful to record not only their contact details but also the hours which their offices will be open and any emergency out- of- hours contact details.

Visas & Immigration

This chapter is complicated, yet only a very basic and over-generalised introduction to the much more complicated topic of immigration to the US.

U.S. immigration laws are meant to provide orderly policies for letting people in (and, in some instances, for keeping immigrants out) of the US. Alternatively, you might think they are some sort of complicated game designed by immigration attorneys to keep other immigration attorneys in business.

US immigration, however, is genuinely complex and, to make matters worse, there is a lot of wrong or confusing information which is provided to intending immigrants from friends, relatives, would-be advisers and even U.S. immigration officials. Taking this into account and taking into account also the manner in which laws and local policies constantly change, it is clear how important it is to have correct and up-to-date information when choosing a visa category and applying for a visa.

For that you will usually need specialist advice.

Types of Visas

Visas are divided into two main categories, non-immigrant and immigrant visas. Whether you wish to seek a temporary (non-immigrant) or permanent (immigrant) visa, your main aim should be to prove that you fit *precisely* into one or other of the rigid visa types defined under each category. The facts of your case may not already meet the requirements of a particular visa type. If so, then it is usually up to you to change your situation so that you do meet the desired visa's requirements. In this case, you would be well advised to seek specialist professional advice before submitting your application. It is much easier to correct problems *before* the papers are submitted.

Whichever visa they apply for, for most intending immigrants it is the "green card" (or lawful permanent residence permit) which is the ultimate goal. There are, again, many different routes to a green card.

Immigrant Visas

Immigrant visa categories are generally based on the personal merits of the applicant (including education, career skills, and financial means), on refugee status, or on immediate family connections.

In some categories a green card (the document regularising your presence in the US on a long term basis and – of course – in this topsy-turvy world no longer green in colour) can be acquired fairly quickly, but in most categories months or even years can elapse because of a quota system.

Once acquired, however, a green card gives the holder the right to live and work in the U.S. permanently.

Non-immigrant visas

Non-immigrant visa categories vary greatly. They are generally issued for specific purposes such as study, holidays, business, employment, investment, or diplomatic representation.

Non-immigrant visas can usually be obtained quite quickly, sometimes even within days of applying, as there are no quotas. However, much depends upon where you are making the application.

These visas generally come with different rights and privileges and different on-going obligations.

The Doctrine of Dual Intent

All people who enter the United States on non-immigrant visas are considered to be there temporarily. If you are there on a temporary non-immigrant visa and you start the permanent resident process, the law generally believes that you have "lost" your intent to stay temporarily because you now wish to immigrate (i.e. stay permanently in the U.S.).

Normally, if you remain inside the United States and do not need to renew your temporary visa, this change of intent is not a problem. However, if you need to travel internationally or you must apply for an extension of your present stay, you could have problems getting back in: you can no longer claim to be (say) a student intending to leave at the end of your course, because you have declared your wish to move permanently to the US.

Having said this, there are a few non-immigrant categories that allow a person to have dual intent: that is, to intend to be here temporarily now but eventually to immigrate. In these categories, international travel and extensions of stay are not a problem. However, these categories have limitations, which mean that you have to do some planning.

Consult a specialist US attorney who is a member of the American Immigration Lawyers Association (AILA), members of which can be found in the UK and USA, to work out your best course of action and help you prepare any necessary paperwork.

Problem Cases

Visa applicants with a criminal record, any disqualifying medical condition, or other visa ineligibility should definitely consult with a US immigration attorney for specialised help before they start the application process.

In some cases, these problems can be circumvented or rectified. It is much easier to do this *before* you make your application.

Visa holders need to be aware that a visa does not in any way *guarantee* entry into the USA. It merely gives the right to present yourself for admission. Without a visa you would automatically be turned back, either at the immigration desk in the US or (more likely) before you got on your plane.

The immigration officials at the port of entry have the authority to consider your application and consent to, or deny, admission. However, in practice, if you have the appropriate visa and you gave accurate information when you obtained it, you will seldom encounter immigration problems when you arrive in the US.

Visiting as a Tourist

Is a Visa Needed?

Possibly. To answer this question, you must first determine whether you are a national of one of the following countries:

Andorra	Hungary	New Zealand
Australia	Iceland	Norway
Austria	Ireland	Portugal
Belgium	Italy	San Marino
Brunei	Japan	Singapore
Czech Republic	Latvia	Slovakia
Denmark	Liechtenstein	Slovenia
Estonia	Lithuania	South Korea
Finland	Luxembourg	Spain
France	Malta	Sweden
Germany	Monaco	Switzerland
Greece	The Netherlands	United Kingdom

If so, then you may be able to use the Visa Waiver Program or "VWP" in order to travel to the United States for tourism or business, for stays of 90 days or less.

The VWP allows you, on certain conditions, to travel without a visa.

These requirements include:

- that you have a valid authorisation through the Electronic System for Travel Authorization (ESTA) prior to travel (For more information see http://london. usembassy.gov/esta-info.html and https://esta.cbp.dhs.gov),

- that you have a machine-readable passport (MRP) which contains a digital photograph or an integrated electronic chip
- that you are travelling on a participating airline (most scheduled airlines from participating countries qualify), do not intend to travel by private aircraft or other non-VWP approved air or sea carriers to the United States, do not have a criminal record or other condition making you ineligible for a visa, have not been refused admission to the United States before, or failed to comply with the conditions of previous VWP admissions (90 days or less stay for tourism or business, etc.), that you do not want to work or study in the United States, you are not travelling as a working foreign media representative, you are not coming to the United States for other purposes not allowed on a visitor visa, and that you do not intend to immigrate to the United States;
- that you hold a return or onward ticket to a country other than Canada,
- that you are screened at the port of entry into the United States,
- that you are enrolled in the Department of Homeland Security's US-VISIT program.

If you wish to visit the USA and are not a national of one of these countries, or you cannot meet these requirements, you will have to apply for a visitor's visa.

The "visitor" visa is a non-immigrant visa for persons desiring to enter the United States temporarily for business (B-1), for pleasure or medical treatment (B-2), or combination of both (B-1/B-2).

Applicants must demonstrate that they are properly classifiable as visitors under U.S. law by:

- possessing evidence which shows the purpose of the trip, intent to depart the United States, and arrangements made to cover the costs of the trip may be provided.
- Possessing evidence, where the applicant does not have sufficient funds to support himself or herself while in the U.S., that an interested person will provide support.
- Possessing evidence substantiating the trip's purpose and specifying the nature of binding obligations, such as family ties or employment, which would compel their return from abroad.

VWP eligible travellers who intend to stay in the US for more than 90 days may apply for a visitor's visa.

The period of time for which the visitors' visa will last is dependent on the equivalent visa duration and fees in your nation. For UK citizens, the maximum visa validity period is 10 years. This does not mean you can stay in the US for 10 years! It means that, at any time during this period, you can present yourself for entry for up to 180 days.

If the purpose of your planned travel is recreational in nature – tourism, vacation (holidays), amusement, visits to friends or relatives, rest, medical treatment, activities "of a fraternal, social, or service nature", and participation as an amateur (who will receive no remuneration) in musical, sports and similar events or contests, then a visitor visa (B-2) would be the appropriate type of visa for your travel.

If you are going to the U.S. primarily for tourism, but want to take a short course of study, which is recreational (and not for credit towards a degree), and the course is less than 18 hours per week, this is permitted on a visitor visa. As an example, if you are taking a vacation to the U.S., and during this vacation you would like to take a two-day cooking class for your enjoyment, and there is no credit earned, then this would be permitted on a visitor visa.

If the purpose for any planned travel is to consult with business associates, travel for a scientific, educational, professional or business convention or conference, settle an estate, or negotiate a contract, then a business visitor visa (B-1) would be appropriate.

If however, you are seeking to *run* a business in the USA, be employed by an organisation within the US, or participate as a professional in entertainment or sporting events, this visa is not appropriate.

How do I get one?

You can apply yourself or through an attorney at your nation's U.S. Embassy or Consulate. An interview at the embassy consular section is required for visa applicants aged from 14 to 79.

Your first step in the visa application process is making your appointment for an interview. The waiting time for an interview appointment for applicants can vary, so early visa application is strongly encouraged. The US embassy website provides further details as to how to schedule an appointment for an interview, pay the application processing fee, review embassy specific instructions, etc.

During the visa application process, usually at the interview, an ink-free, digital fingerprint scan will be taken.

You will need to complete a Form DS-160, which can be done online; provide a valid passport with a validity date at least six months beyond your intended period of stay in the US and provide a photograph taken in accordance with US visa requirements. Some visa applications require further documentation or processing which takes additional time after the visa applicant's interview by a Consular Officer.

What does it cost?

All applicants have to pay an application fee, which is currently $190. Depending on your home nation, there may or may not be an issuance fee. This depends upon whether, or how much, your own nation charges US visitors for such a visa. There is no issuance fee for UK nationals.

How difficult is it to Obtain the Visa

Not generally difficult, unless you are a young, unemployed and single person renting a home and with few family or other ties to your home nation. In this case, the immigration authorities (USCIS) might not believe you are really coming for a holiday.

Visas to Join your Husband/Wife

Is a Visa Needed?

Yes.

How do I get one?

The most common way of acquiring the right to permanent residence in the US is immigration through links to a family member who is a US citizen or permanent resident.

Not every family relationship will meet the standards required for permanent residence. For example, special preferential treatment is given to "immediate relatives" and other close family members of US citizens, such treatment not being given to relatives of permanent residents. This preferential treatment means there is no waiting period for immediate relatives other than the time it takes the USCIS to process the visa petition, and there is no limit or cap on the number of visas allowed per year for those classed as "immediate relatives". Immediate relatives includes spouses of US citizens, unmarried minor children of US citizens, and parents of US citizens age 21 or older.

For spouses of U.S. Citizens where the marriage is less than two years in duration, the immigrating spouse will be granted conditional residence for two years. Then, the couple must apply for removal of this condition.

"Derivative Status" may in some instances allow the visa holder's family to get visas without their own separate petition. For example, where the spouse abroad has a minor child of an earlier marriage, such child will qualify as a stepchild.

The Process

There are two separate stages in applying for the spousal visa. This is the filing of the petition and thereafter applying for the visa once the petition is approved.

The documents generally required in a spousal visa should include:

- I-130 Petition for Alien Relative;
- G-28 Notice of Entry of Attorney

- G-325A Biographical Information for the Petitioner
- G-325A Biographical Information for the alien Beneficiary;
- Marriage certificate for spousal applications;
- Birth certificates for child/parents applications;
- Evidence of U.S. Citizenship or lawful permanent residence;
- Birth or baptismal certificates for both the sponsor and the foreign relative if they are brother and sister with the same parents;
- Divorce papers if there was a preceding marriage for either applicant or immigrant relative
- Two photographs of the applicant and immigrant relative;

Petition Phase

- Petition I-130 is filed.
- Petition is processed/payment is made
- Notice of petition approval should be received
- The matter is transferred to the Embassy/Consular Immigrant Visa Unit

Visa Application Phase

- Notice should be received that the Embassy/Consular Immigrant Visa Unit has the case
- Instructions should be received as to documents to be collected
- Visa application DS-230 to be filed
- Applicant needs to schedule and take medical exam
- 'Ready to Interview' checklist should be returned by applicant
- Interview date set by Consulate
- Interview held

The main USCIS form that is used in all family cases is the I-130 Petition for Alien Relative. The US citizen petitioning relative must complete this form. The application must include documentation of the qualifying family relationship, and of the petitioner's status as a citizen or permanent resident. This I-130 form is basically seeking a determination that someone is eligible to immigrate in the specific category and that he or she can reserve a place in any relevant queue for that particular category.

The I-130 petition which may be filed in either the USA or at certain US consulates abroad. The USCIS London Field Office has jurisdiction for adjudicating I-130 petitions from U.S. citizens who have permission to reside AND who do principally reside in the United Kingdom. US citizens who reside in the USA must file their petition with the appropriate USCIS Service Center there.

Once USCIS approves your application, then the I-130 Petition approval is sent to the petitioner. Then, the documentation is transferred to the National Visa Center (NVC) to process the affidavit of support and Form DS-230. The Department of State's National Visa Center (NVC) retains the approved petition until the case is ready for adjudication by a consular officer abroad. Petitions may remain at NVC for several months or for many years, depending on the visa category and country of birth of the visa applicant. Once the immigrant visa is available on a spousal petition however, the beneficiary is contacted by the U.S. Embassy here in the UK to schedule an interview.

When the US citizen spouse is in the USA, an "application for adjustment of status" may be filed at the same time as the petition. Such application is the actual process where someone converts their status to permanent resident.

As a condition of admission In order to immigrate, the foreign spouse must obtain a legally binding affidavit of support. Sponsors signing the affidavit must be at least 18 years old, domiciled in the United States, and able to support both the sponsor's and the immigrant's families at an annual income level equal to at least 125 per cent of the federal poverty guideline, such guideline for 2012 being set out below:

2012 HHS Poverty Guidelines			
Persons in Family	48 Contiguous States and D.C.	Alaska	Hawaii
1	$11,170	$13,970	$12,860
2	15,130	18,920	17,410
3	19,090	23,870	21,960
4	23,050	28,820	26,510
5	27,010	33,770	31,060
6	30,970	38,720	35,610
7	34,930	43,670	40,160
8	38,890	48,620	44,710
For each additional person, add	3,960	4,950	4,550

SOURCE: *Federal Register*, Vol. 77, No. 17, January 26, 2012, pp. 4034-4035

It is an absolute legal requirement that the US citizen petitioner be domiciled in the US in order to use the spousal visa. If the US citizen petitioner is able to meet the income requirement, but does not qualify as a sponsor because he or she is not domiciled in the United States, a joint sponsor may not be used to overcome this problem. If the petitioner cannot qualify as a sponsor, the beneficiary will not be permitted to immigrate.

Many intending petitioners live outside the US with their foreign spouses. It is fine, normally, where you have two residences, but your domicile must be in the US. If the intending petitioner has abandoned his or her US domicile, he or she may need to go back to the US and re-establish US domicile, and get the following documents with your intended US residential address; a current US driver's license, a current US voter registration certificate, and copies of recent utility and telephone bills with petitioner's name. If the petitioner owns property in the USA, get a copy of the title deed as well as photos etc. Legal advice may need to be taken in relation to domicile.

If the petition is in order and shows the qualifying relationship, the spouse can apply for an immigrant visa at a US consulate. The foreign spouse not filing within the USA will have to prepare for the interview in the U.S. Consulate or Embassy in his or her country and complete the package provided by the same consulate. The following documentation will be required for the interview:

- Passport;
- Birth certificate;
- Photographs of the applicant;
- A copy of the petitioned application;
- Marriage Certificate; and
- Divorce Decrees from prior marriages.

What does it cost?

Filling fee in the amount of $420 USD (subject to changes by USCIS) in the form of cashier's check or money order payable to USCIS.

How difficult is it to Obtain the Visa

Not too difficult, but there may be a lot of documentation. USCIS may issue Requests for Evidence (or RFE's) and Notices of Intent to Deny (NOID's) which must be responded to within the time allotted.

Visas for Children to Join Parents

Is a Visa Needed?

Yes.

Who is eligible?

To obtain a family based green card, you must have a close relative who is a U.S. citizen or permanent resident. Family-based immigrants to the United States are divided into two categories:

1. Immediate Relatives

Those who may obtain permanent residence status without numerical limitation (the spouse, widow(er) and minor unmarried children of a United States citizen, the parents of a United States citizen who is 21 or older, and

2. *Those subject to an annual limitation.*

These immigrants are granted visas on a preference basis, meaning that there is a waiting period; First Preference: Unmarried sons and daughters of U.S. citizens, and children if any, Second Preference: Spouses, children, and unmarried sons and daughters of lawful permanent resident aliens. Third Preference: Married sons and daughters of U.S. citizens, and their spouses and children, and Fourth Preference: Brothers and sisters of U.S. citizens, and their spouses and children, provided the U.S. citizens are over 20. Lawful permanent residents of the US can only file petitions for spouses and their children and unmarried sons and daughters.

So minor unmarried children of a US citizen parent (not all children of US citizens are US citizens themselves) can apply for lawful permanent residency, only to have to wait the normal processing times. Only a certain number of adult children of US citizens, and of unmarried children of lawful permanent residents may apply each year for permanent residency, but they will be subject to waiting periods determined by the preference group they are in. The filing date of a petition becomes the applicant's "priority date". Immigrant visas cannot be issued until an applicant's priority date is reached. In certain heavily oversubscribed categories, there may be a waiting period of several years before a priority date is reached.

How do I get one?

The same procedure is basically used as for spousal-based petitions described above. The same I-130 form is used, procedures, etc., except that the NVC will not forward the documents to a consular immigrant visa unit until the processing of visas has reached the applicable priority date.

As with the spousal immigrant visa, in order to show that there is adequate means of financial support in the U.S., an Affidavit of Support form is again required. This is the case for most family-based and some employment based immigrants.

What does it cost?

The cost is the same as for the spousal visa.

How difficult is it to Obtain the Visa?

Difficult. If the beneficiary of the visa is a qualifying person, can find a qualifying petitioner willing to submit a reliable affidavit of support, and can wait the required time (which may, for those not classified as "Immediate Relatives", be some years – in some cases well over 10), then the visa can be obtained.

Living in the US during Retirement

There is no retirement visa allowing people to live in the US when they are retired – i.e. no longer economically active.

Those wishing to retire in America, live in America say six months a year and have no children under 21 years of age, should consider an E visa investment. In this case the E visa is more flexible for tax purposes and there's no requirement to come to the US for at least one time every six months.

Despite what you might have been told, the US does not have a retirement visa category. The E visa is as close as it gets.

Living Permanently in the US Without Working

There is no visa to live in the USA permanently without working. Such an intending immigrant would need to be independently wealthy and not need to work, but would still have to qualify on an investment visa or family-based visa.

Working as a Salaried Employee

Is a visa needed?

Yes.

What are the criteria for granting this type of visa?

To obtain an employment-based green card, applicants must be skilled/educated - and have a job offer.

Employmentbased immigration is limited by statute to 140,000 persons per year. The process is generally in three parts:

(a) the employer must normally first obtain a "labor certification" from the U.S. Department of Labor (DOL) (showing that you will fill a position that the U.S. employer cannot fill with a U.S. worker). There are employment categories where labor certification is not required.

(b) the employer applies for immigrant visa classification

(c) you then apply for lawful permanent residency in the United States or consular processing overseas.

When you apply for permanent immigration through employment, you are saying to the government that you intend to work for your employer for the foreseeable future. You are not bound to the company for the rest of your life, nor is the company obliged to provide you with lifetime employment.

The various employment-based permanent residency visas include:

EB1	Priority workers. There are three sub-groups: 1. Foreign nationals with extraordinary ability in sciences, arts, education, business, or athletics OR 2. Foreign nationals that are outstanding professors or researchers with at least three years' experience in teaching or research and who are recognized internationally. OR 3. Foreign nationals that are managers and executives subject to international transfer to the United States.	40,000	currently available
EB2	Professionals holding advanced degrees (Ph.D., master's degree, or at least five years of progressive post-baccalaureate experience) or persons of exceptional ability in sciences, arts, or business	40,000	currently available except for individuals from the People's Republic of China and India (5 years)b
EB3	Skilled workers, professionals, and other workers	40,000	6–9 yearsb
EB4	Certain special immigrants: ministers, religious workers, current or former US government workers, etc.	10,000	currently available
EB5	Investors	10,000	currently available

The L-1 visa is also an option.

An L-1 visa can be issued to a foreign national employee who has worked abroad for at least one continuous year within the three years immediately preceding the U.S. transfer for a qualifying, related business entity (e.g., parent, subsidiary, affiliate) in an executive, managerial or specialized knowledge capacity and who is being transferred to the U.S. to work for the same Employer or a parent, subsidiary or affiliate of the Employer. The Employer must be doing business in the U.S. and at least one other country for the duration of the employee's stay in the U.S. as an L-1 non-immigrant.

Managers and executives may be admitted for up to seven years. Specialized knowledge employees may be admitted for up to five years and if promoted to a managerial or executive position after admission (and if BCIS is properly notified of the promotion) may remain for up to seven years. Also, if you own or control a business in your home country and want to establish a branch office, affiliated company or subsidiary in the USA, you may be able to use the L1A visa. BCIS grants 1 year to start up the US business with a total extension periods of seven years. The biggest advantage of the L1A visa is that it can normally be converted to a green card after doing business in the U.S. for one year.

How do I get one?

This category is so complicated that you should consult a specialist immigration adviser before making your application.

What does it cost?

This varies.

How difficult is it to obtain the visa

Very difficult.

Self Employment in a Business

Is a visa needed?

Yes.

What are the criteria for granting this type of visa?

The E-2 visa, a dual-intent visa which (broadly speaking) will let you stay in the USA if you start a business generating employment for (typically) at least two local people. The visa will remain valid for as long as your business continues to operate and be profitable.

There is no limit as to how long you can remain in the US on an E-2 visa, but you must renew that status about every two years until you apply for a green card.

How do I get one?

For these visas you will need to seek specialist advice.

What does it cost?

This varies considerably.

How difficult is it to Obtain the Visa

Fairly difficult – mainly because there is lots of paperwork that needs to be absolutely correct.

Visas Based on Investment

Is Such a Visa Available?

Yes.

What are the Criteria for Granting this type of Visa?

To obtain an investment based green card, applicants must invest in a new commercial enterprise which will create full-time employment for at least 10 persons other than the investor's spouse and children. The usual minimum investment is US$1 million, but may be US$500,000 if the investment is in a designated rural or high unemployment area. The required amount can be higher if the investment is made in an area of high employment.

A migrant by investment must file a petition with BCIS office in the area where the new commercial enterprise will be principally doing business.

How do I get one?

For these visas you will need to seek specialist advice.

What does it cost?

This varies considerably.

How difficult is it to Obtain the Visa

Fairly difficult – mainly because there is lots of paperwork that needs to be absolutely correct.

Other?

There are, literally, dozens of categories of visa to enter the US. Everything from wives of diplomats to sportspeople.

Amongst them there may well be a category that suits you. The knack is to find it.

For this – and making sure that your application is drafted so that it meets the precise requirements of USCIS (often undisclosed on their website) – you should consider using specialist immigration advisers.

Make sure you choose a good one: one who is properly accredited. Your Realtor will probably be able to recommend one to you.

Choosing Advisers

In most countries, there have been problems with poor quality advisers abusing the trust of immigrants seeking a visa to enter the country. The US is no exception.

A person must be authorised and qualified before he or she is allowed to give immigration advice.

Consult a specialist US attorney who is a member of the American Immigration Lawyers Association (AILA), members of which can be found in the UK and USA. One of my companies, eb5 select (www.eb5select.com) specialises in assisting with immigration needs. It also works closely with various immigration attorneys.

Be very careful when selecting an immigration adviser. They can ruin your future. Always ask for a written estimate of fees and expenses. Make sure that you are comfortable with your advisers and their way of working.

Taxes

All tax systems are complicated. The US system is no exception. Fortunately, most people will only have limited contact with the more intricate parts of the system. For many owners of holiday homes in Florida their contact with the system will be minimal.

It is helpful to have some sort of understanding about the way in which the system works and the taxes that you might face. Be warned: getting even a basic understanding will make your head hurt. You also need to be particularly careful about words and concepts that seem familiar to you, but which have a fundamentally different meaning in the US than they do in your own country. Of course, just to confuse you, the rules change every year.

There are several points in this book where I have said that the contents are only a general introduction to the subject. There is nowhere where this is more true that in this section. Books (and long ones at that) have been written about the subject of US taxation. This general introduction does little more than scratch the surface of an immensely complex subject. It is intended to allow you to have a sensible discussion with your professional advisers and, perhaps, to help you work out the questions that you need to be asking them. It is not intended as a substitute for proper professional advice.

Your situation when you have a foot in two countries - and, in particular, when you are moving permanently from one country to another - involves the consideration of the tax systems in both countries with a view to minimising your tax obligations in both. It is not just a question of paying the lowest amount of tax in, say, the US. The best choice in the US could be very damaging to your position back home. Similarly, the most tax efficient way of dealing with your affairs in your own country could be problematic in Florida. The task of the international adviser and his client is to find a path of compromise which allows you to enjoy the major advantages available in both countries, without incurring any of the worst drawbacks. In other words, there is an issue of compromise. There is no perfect solution to most tax questions. That is not to say that there are not a great many bad solutions into which you can all too easily stumble.

What should guide you when making a decision as to which course to pursue? Each individual will have a different set of priorities. Some are keen to screw the last halfpenny of advantage out of their situation. Others recognise that they will have to pay some tax, but simply wish to moderate their tax bill. For many the main concern is a simple structure which they understand and can continue to manage without further assistance in the years ahead. Just as different clients have different requirements, so different advisers have differing views as to the function of the adviser when dealing with a client's tax affairs. One of your first tasks when speaking to your financial adviser should be to discuss your basic philosophy concerning the payment of tax and management of your affairs, to make sure that you are both operating with the same objective in mind and that you are comfortable with his approach to solving your problems.

The Wisdom of Taking Advice!

It is simple. Taking advice will save you not only money but also grief.

The Basics

If you paid or accrued foreign taxes to a foreign country on foreign source income and are subject to U.S. tax on the same income, you may be able to take either a credit or an itemized deduction for those taxes, the IRS says.

Taken as a deduction, foreign income taxes reduce your U.S. taxable income.

Taken as a credit, foreign income taxes reduce your U.S. tax liability. In most cases, it is to your advantage to take foreign income taxes as a tax credit.

Once you choose to exclude either foreign earned income, or foreign housing costs, you cannot take a foreign tax credit for taxes on income you can exclude. If you do take the credit, one or both of the choices may be considered revoked.

The good news is that Florida is one of only a few states with no income tax, although residents still need to pay federal income taxes.

Your Obligations in the US

The foreign tax credit laws are complex, the IRS states. Fir tips to help understand some of the more complex areas of the law, see: http://www.irs.gov/Individuals/International-Taxpayers/Foreign-Tax-Credit-Compliance-Tips

Foreign buyers and sellers of U.S. real property interests need Taxpayer Identification Numbers (TINs) to request reduced tax withholding when disposing of the property interest, and to pay any required withholding. Individuals who do not qualify for Social Security Numbers (SSN) may obtain Individual Taxpayer Identification Numbers (ITINs) to meet the requirement to supply a TIN.

Two forms are generally used for reporting and paying the tax to the IRS regarding the acquisition of U.S. real property interests.

Form 8288, U.S. Withholding Tax Return for Dispositions by Foreign Persons of U.S. Real Property Interests (PDF) (IRC Section 1445)

Form 8288-A, Statement of Withholding on Dispositions by Foreign Persons of U.S. Real Property Interests (PDF) (IRC Section 1445)

Transferees must use Forms 8288 and 8288-A to report and pay to the IRS any tax withheld on the acquisition of U.S. real property interests. These forms must also be used by corporations, partnerships, estates, and trusts that must withhold tax on distributions and other transactions involving U.S. real property interests. You must include the U.S. TIN of both the transferor and transferee on the forms.

If you receive rental income from renting a dwelling unit, such as a house or an apartment, you may deduct certain expenses. These expenses, which may include mortgage interest, real estate taxes, casualty losses, maintenance, utilities, insurance, and depreciation, will reduce the amount of rental income that is taxed. You will generally report such income and expenses on Form 1040 (PDF) and on Form 1040, Schedule E (PDF). If you are renting to make a profit and do not use the dwelling unit as a personal residence, then your deductible rental expenses may be more than your gross rental income. Your rental losses, however, generally will be limited by the "at-risk" rules and/or the passive activity loss rules. For information on these limits, refer to Publication 925, Taxes When Buying a Property

Property tax for foreign nationals is the same as property tax for residents of the United States. A good place to look up property tax is by visiting the county Tax Appraisers office and looking at tax records. - See more at: http://c21feltrim.com/real-estate-information/#sthash.EzXYxymg.dpuf

In the United States, individuals and corporations pay income tax on the net total of all their capital gains, just as they do on other sorts of income, but the tax rate for individuals is lower on "long-term capital gains", which are gains on assets that had been held for over one year before being sold, according to the Property Tax International website (http://www.ptireturns.com/en/tax_info/us.php)

The tax rate on long-term gains was reduced in 2003 to 15% or to 5% for individuals in the lowest two income tax brackets. Short-term capital gains are taxed at a higher rate: the ordinary income tax rate. The reduced 15% tax rate on eligible dividends and capital gains, previously scheduled to expire in 2008, has been extended through 2010. In 2011 these reduced tax rates will "sunset", or revert to the rates in effect before 2003, which were generally 20%.

When selling a property the buyer retains 10% from the agreed sale price as a withholding tax which is paid over to the IRS to cover the sellers' tax obligations. A balancing statement should be filed to determine if an overpayment has been made and a tax refund due.

Income Tax Treaty

Many foreign countries withhold tax on certain types of income paid from sources within those countries to residents of other countries, says the IRS.

The rate of withholding is set by that country's internal law. An income tax treaty between the United States and a foreign country often reduces the withholding rates (sometimes to zero) for certain types of income paid to residents of the United States. This reduced rate is referred to as the treaty-reduced rate. For more information on reduced rates, see

Tax Treaty Tables in Pub. 515, Withholding of Tax on Non-resident Aliens and Foreign Entities.

Many U.S. treaty partners require the IRS to certify that the person claiming treaty benefits is a resident of the United States for federal tax purposes. The IRS provides this residency certification on Form 6166, a letter of U.S. residency certification. Form 6166 is a computer-generated letter printed on stationary bearing the U.S. Department of Treasury letterhead, and the facsimile signature of the Field Director, Philadelphia Accounts Management Center.

Form 6166 will only certify that, for the certification year (the period for which certification is requested), you were a resident of the United States for purposes of U.S. taxation, or in the case of a fiscally transparent entity, that the entity, when required, filed an information return and its partners/members/owners/beneficiaries filed income tax returns as residents of the United States.

Upon receiving Form 6166 from the IRS, unless otherwise directed, you should send Form 6166 to the foreign withholding agent, or other appropriate person in the foreign country to claim treaty benefits. Some foreign countries will withhold at the treaty-reduced rate at the time of payment, and other foreign countries will initially withhold tax at their statutory rate and will refund the amount that is more than the treaty-reduced rate, on receiving proof of U.S. residency.

Taxes on Income

Like many other countries, tax rates in the United States differ depending on the amount you earn, your allowable expenses and other information. For the fullest and latest details, go to the IRS website at http://www.irs.gov/ and talk to your accountant.

For full details on the whole tax process, go to: http://www.irs.gov/publications/p17/ch01.html

As I mentioned earlier – but it is worth repeating because it is such good news – Florida has no income tax.

Sales Tax

In Florida, there is a minimum 6% sales tax rate collected by the state government. Legislation also allows for a local option sales tax that lets each county set its own local tax that is collected on top of the general state rate, so you are likely to pay a slightly different rate, depending on where you are living.

Taxes on Capital Gains

Almost everything you own and use for personal or investment purposes is a capital asset, says the IRS. Examples include a home, personal-use items like household furnishings, and stocks or bonds held as investments. When a capital asset is sold, the difference between the basis in the asset and the amount it is sold for is a capital gain, or a capital loss. Generally, an asset's basis is its cost; however, if you received the asset as a gift or inheritance, refer to Topic 703 for information about your basis. You have a capital gain if you sell the asset for more than your basis. You have a capital loss if you sell the asset for less than your basis. Losses from the sale of personal-use property, such as your home or car, are not deductible.

Capital gains and losses are classified as long-term or short-term. If you hold the asset for more than one year before you dispose of it, your capital gain or loss is long-term. If you hold it one year or less, your capital gain or loss is short-term. To determine how long you held the asset, count from the day after the day you acquired the asset up to and including the day you disposed of the asset.

Capital gains and deductible capital losses are reported on Form 1040, Schedule D (PDF), Capital Gains and Losses, and on Form 8949 (PDF), Sales and Other Dispositions of Capital Assets. If you have a net capital gain, that gain may be taxed at a lower tax rate than your ordinary income tax rates. The term "net capital gain" means the amount by which your net long-term capital gain for the year is more than your net short-term capital loss for the year. The term "net long-term capital gain" means long-term capital gains reduced by long-term capital losses, including any unused long-term capital loss carried over from previous years. Generally, for most taxpayers, net capital gain is taxed at rates no higher than 15%. Some or all net capital gain may be taxed at 0% if you are in the 10% or 15% ordinary income tax brackets. However, beginning in 2013, a new 20% rate on net capital gain applies to the extent that a taxpayer's taxable income exceeds the thresholds set for the new 39.6% ordinary tax rate, ($400,000 for single; $450,000 for married filing jointly or qualifying widow(er); $425,000 for head of household, and $225,000 for married filing separately). For more information, refer to Publication 505, Tax Withholding and Estimated Tax.

There are a few other exceptions where capital gains may be taxed at rates greater than 15%

For frequently-asked questions see the IRS website at: http://www.irs.gov/Help-&-Resources/Tools-&-FAQs/FAQs-for-Individuals/Frequently-Asked-Tax-Questions-&-Answers/Capital-Gains,-Losses,-Sale-of-Home

Taxes on the Sale of Property

There are also detailed tax regulations about the sale of a property.

These can be found on the IRS website at: http://www.irs.gov/publications/p17/ch14.html

If you are a U.S. citizen who sells property located outside the United States, you must report all gains and losses from the sale of that property on your tax return, unless it is exempt by U.S. law. This is true whether you reside inside or outside the United States and whether or not you receive a Form 1099 from the payer.

Taxes on Death

For commonly asked questions about estate taxes, see the IRS website at: http://www.irs.gov/Businesses/Small-Businesses-&-Self-Employed/ Frequently-Asked-Questions-on-Estate-Taxes.

You may also need to ask your accountant about Estate Tax. The Estate Tax is a tax on your right to transfer property at your death. It consists of an accounting of everything you own, or have certain interests in, at the date of death (Refer to Form 706 (PDF)). The fair market value of these items is used, not necessarily what you paid for them or what their values were when you acquired them. The total of all of these items is your "Gross Estate." The includible property may consist of cash and securities, real estate, insurance, trusts, annuities, business interests and other assets.

Once you have accounted for the Gross Estate, certain deductions (and in special circumstances, reductions to value) are allowed in arriving at your "Taxable Estate." These deductions may include mortgages and other debts, estate administration expenses, property that passes to surviving spouses and qualified charities. The value of some operating business interests or farms may be reduced for estates that qualify.

After the net amount is computed, the value of lifetime taxable gifts (beginning with gifts made in 1977) is added to this number and the tax is computed. The tax is then reduced by the available unified credit.

Most relatively simple estates (cash, publicly traded securities, small amounts of other easily valued assets, and no special deductions or elections, or jointly held property) do not require the filing of an estate tax return. A filing is required for estates with combined gross assets and prior taxable gifts exceeding $1,500,000 in 2004 - 2005; $2,000,000 in 2006 - 2008; $3,500,000 for decedents dying in 2009; and $5,000,000 or more for decedent's dying in 2010 and 2011 (note: there are special rules for decedents dying in 2010); $5,120,000 in 2012, $5,250,000 in 2013 and $5,340,000 in 2014.

Beginning January 1, 2011, estates of decedents survived by a spouse may elect to pass any of the decedent's unused exemption to the surviving spouse. This election is made on a timely filed estate tax return for the decedent with a surviving spouse. Note that simplified valuation provisions apply for those estates without a filing requirement absent the portability election.

For additional information, refer to Instructions for Form 706.

Taxes on Inheritance

To determine if the sale of inherited property is taxable, you must first determine your basis in the property, the IRS says. The basis of property inherited from a decedent is generally one of the following:

The fair market value (FMV) of the property on the date of the decedent's death.

The FMV of the property on the alternate valuation date if the executor of the estate chooses to use alternate valuation. See the Instructions for Form 706 (PDF), United States Estate (and Generation-Skipping Transfer) Tax Return.

If you or your spouse gave the property to the decedent, within one year before the decedent's death, see Publication 551, Basis of Assets.

Report the sale on Schedule D (Form 1040) (PDF), Capital Gains and Losses, and on Form 8949 (PDF), Sales and other Dispositions of Capital Assets:

If you sell the property for more than your basis, you have a taxable gain.

For information on how to report the sale on Schedule D, see Publication 550, Investment Income and Expenses.

For estates of decedents who died in 2010, basis is generally determined as described above. However, the executor of a decedent who died in 2010 may elect out of the estate tax rules for 2010 and use the modified carryover of basis rules.

Under this special election, the basis of property inherited from a decedent who died during 2010 is generally the lesser of:

The adjusted basis of the decedent, or

The fair market value of the property at the date of the decedent's death.

However, the executor of the decedent's estate may increase the basis of certain property that beneficiaries acquire from a decedent by up to $1.3 million, but the increased basis cannot exceed the fair market value of the property at the date of the decedent's death. The executor may also increase the basis of certain property that the surviving spouse acquires from a decedent by up to $3 million, but the increased basis cannot exceed the fair market value of the property at the date of the decedent's death. The executor of the decedent's estate is required to provide a statement to all heirs, listing the decedent's basis in the property, the fair market value of the property on the date of the decedent's death, and the additional basis allocated to the property. Contact the executor to determine what the basis of the asset is.

Report the sale on Schedule D (Form 1040), Capital Gains and Losses, and on Form 8949, Sales and other Dispositions of Capital Assets, as described above.

Your Obligations 'Back Home'

Even if you fill in a US tax form, depending on the regulations and obligations, you may also need to file a return in your country of origin or another country or countries where you own overseas property. Talk to your accountant for more details or ask for further information from the relevant tax authorities.

Tax planning generally

Do it and do it as soon as possible. Every day you delay will make it more difficult to get the results you are looking for.

There are many possibilities for tax planning for someone moving to the US.

For someone moving from the UK, some points worth considering are:

- Time your departure from UK to get the best out of the UK tax system
- Think, in particular, about when to make any capital gain if you are selling your business or other assets in UK
- Arrange your affairs so that there is a gap between leaving UK (for tax purposes) and becoming resident in the US. That gap can be used to make all sorts of beneficial changes to the structure of your finances
- Think about Trusts. They can be very effective tax planning vehicles.
- Think about giving away some of your assets. You (or your kids) will save tax and your kids will love you!

Conclusion

Buying a home in the US – whether to use as a holiday home, as an investment or to live in permanently – is as safe (or safer) than buying one where you now live.

The rules may appear complicated. Your rules would if you were an American, coming to your country. That apparent complexity is often no more than lack of familiarity.

There are many thousands of foreign people who have bought homes in the US. Most have had no real problems. Most have enjoyed years of holidays over there. Many have seen their property rise substantially in value. Many are now thinking of spending more time in the US when they retire - if they can find a way to get round the immigration rules.

For a trouble-free time, you simply need to keep your head and to seek advice from experts who can help you make the five basic decisions:

- Where and what should I buy
- Who should own the property?
- What am I going to do about inheritance and about controlling my potential tax liabilities?
- What am I going to do about my immigration status?
- If I am going to live in the US, what am I going to do about my investments?

If you don't like lawyers and other experts, remember that they make far more money out of sorting out the problems you get into by not doing these things than by giving you this basic advice!

Enjoy yourself.

Footnotes, Appendices & Further Sources of Information

Appendix 1 – Maps

The United States

Florida

Florida districts

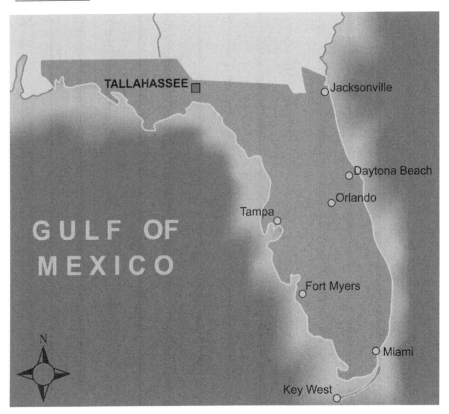

Appendix 2 - Florida Counties

Florida has 67 counties, all of which were established from the first two counties; Escambia and St Johns.

County	2000 Population	Square Miles	County Seat	Created
Alachua County	217,955	874	Gainesville	1824
Baker County	22,259	585	Macclenny	1861
Bay County	148,217	764	Panama City	1913
Bradford County	26,088	293	Starke	1858
Brevard County	476,230	1,018	Titusville	1844
Broward County	1,623,018	1,209	Fort Lauderdale	1915
Calhoun County	13,017	567	Blountstown	1838
Charlotte County	141,627	694	Punta Gorda	1921
Citrus County	118,085	584	Inverness	1887
Clay County	140,814	601	Green Cove Springs	1858
Collier County	251,377	2,026	Naples	1923
Columbia County	56,513	797	Lake City	1832
DeSoto County	32,209	637	Arcadia	1887
Dixie County	13,827	704	Cross City	1921
Duval County/City of Jacksonville	778,879	774	Jacksonville	1822
Escambia County	294,410	664	Pensacola	1822
Flagler County	49,832	485	Bunnell	1917
Franklin County	11,057	534	Apalachicola	1832
Gadsden County	45,087	516	Quincy	1823
Gilchrist County	14,437	349	Trenton	1925
Glades County	10,576	774	Moore Haven	1921
Gulf County	13,332	565	Port Saint Joe	1925
Hamilton County	13,327	515	Jasper	1827
Hardee County	26,938	637	Wauchula	1921
Hendry County	36,210	1,153	La Belle	1923
Hernando County	130,802	478	Brooksville	1843
Highlands County	87,366	1,028	Sebring	1921
Hillsborough County	998,948	1,051	Tampa	1834
Holmes County	18,564	482	Bonifay	1848

County	2000 Population	Square Miles	County Seat	Created
Indian River County	112,947	503	Vero Beach	1925
Jackson County	46,755	916	Marianna	1822
Jefferson County	12,902	598	Monticello	1827
Lafayette County	7,022	543	Mayo	1856
Lake County	210,528	953	Tavares	1887
Lee County	440,888	804	Fort Myers	1887
Leon County	239,452	667	Tallahassee	1824
Levy County	34,450	1,118	Bronson	1845
Liberty County	7,021	836	Bristol	1855
Madison County	18,733	692	Madison	1827
Manatee County	264,002	741	Bradenton	1855
Marion County	258,916	1,579	Ocala	1844
Martin County	126,731	556	Stuart	1925
Miami-Dade County	2,253,362	1,945	Miami	1836
Monroe County	79,589	997	Key West	1823
Nassau County	57,663	652	Fernandina Beach	1824
Okaloosa County	170,498	936	Crestview	1915
Okeechobee County	35,910	774	Okeechobee	1917
Orange County	896,344	908	Orlando	1824
Osceola County	172,493	1,322	Kissimmee	1887
Palm Beach County	1,131,184	2,034	West Palm Beach	1909
Pasco County	344,765	745	Dade City	1887
Pinellas County	921,482	280	Clearwater	1911
Polk County	483,924	1,875	Bartow	1861
Putnam County	70,423	722	Palatka	1849
Santa Rosa County	117,743	1,016	Milton	1842
Sarasota County	325,957	572	Sarasota	1921
Seminole County	365,196	308	Sanford	1913
St. Johns County	123,135	609	Saint Augustine	1822
St. Lucie County	192,695	572	Fort Pierce	1844
Sumter County	53,345	546	Bushnell	1853
Suwannee County	34,844	688	Live Oak	1858
Taylor County	19,256	1,042	Perry	1856

County	2000 Population	Square Miles	County Seat	Created
Union County	13,442	240	Lake Butler	1921
Volusia County	443,343	1,106	De Land	1854
Wakulla County	22,863	607	Crawfordville	1843
Walton County	40,601	1,058	Defuniak Springs	1824
Washington County	20,973	580	Chipley	1825

Source: http://www.e-referencedesk.com/resources/counties/florida/

Appendix 3 - Climate

Climates – a rough Comparison

AVERAGE MONTHLY TEMPERATURES (DAILY MAXIMUM & MINIMUM) AND RAINFALL

Source: USA Today/US Met Office

	Jan	Feb	Mar	Apr	May	Jun	Jul	Aug	Sep	Oct	Nov	Dec
London (UK)												
Max Temperature (C)	7	7	11	13	17	20	22	22	19	14	11	8
Min Temperature (C)	2	2	3	5	8	11	13	13	11	8	4	3
Rainfall (mm)	61	36	51	43	46	46	46	43	43	74	46	58
Dublin (Ireland)												
Max Temperature (C)	8	8	9	11	14	17	19	18	16	13	10	8
Min Temperature (C)	3	3	4	5	7	10	12	12	10	8	5	4
Rainfall (mm)	64	51	51	48	56	56	66	76	64	74	69	69
Malaga (Spain)												
Max Temperature (C)	17	15	18	20	24	27	30	30	28	23	20	17
Min Temperature (C)	11	7	12	11	14	17	20	20	18	16	13	10
Rainfall (Wet Days)	8	8	7	9	6	3	1	1	3	8	9	9
Tenerife (Spain)												
Max Temperature (C)	21	22	23	22	23	24	27	28	27	26	24	22
Min Temperature (C)	16	16	16	16	17	19	21	22	22	21	19	17
Rainfall (Wet Days)	3	3	4	3	2	1	0	1	2	2	5	4
Cannes (France)												

Climates – a rough Comparison

AVERAGE MONTHLY TEMPERATURES (DAILY MAXIMUM & MINIMUM) AND RAINFALL

Source: USA Today/US Met Office

	Jan	Feb	Mar	Apr	May	Jun	Jul	Aug	Sep	Oct	Nov	Dec
Max Temperature (C)	13	12	14	16	20	23	27	27	24	20	16	13
Min Temperature (C)	4	4	7	9	13	17	19	19	16	13	8	6
Rainfall (Wet Days)	7	8	7	9	8	6	3	3	6	9	7	7
Miami (Florida)												
Max Temperature (C)	23	24	24	26	28	31	31	32	31	29	26	24
Min Temperature (C)	16	17	18	21	23	25	26	26	16	24	21	18
Rainfall (Wet Days)	7	6	6	6	10	15	16	18	18	14	8	7

Orlando Temperature	Jan	Feb	Mar	Apr	May	Jun	Jul	Aug	Sep	Oct	Nov	Dec	Year
Avg. Temperature	59.7	61.2	66.7	71.2	76.9	81.1	82.3	82.5	81.0	75.2	68.0	62.1	72.3
Avg. Max Temperature	70.8	72.7	78.0	83.0	87.8	90.5	91.5	91.5	89.7	84.6	78.5	72.9	82.6
Avg. Min Temperature	48.6	49.7	55.2	59.4	65.9	71.8	73.1	73.4	72.4	65.8	57.5	51.3	62.0
Days with Max Temp of 90 F or Higher	0.0	0.0	< 0.5	4.0	12.0	19.0	25.0	25.0	18.0	3.0	0.0	<0.5	107
Days with Min Temp Below Freezing	1.0	<0.5	< 0.5	0.0	0.0	0.0	0.0	0.0	0.0	0.0	< 0.5	1.0	2.0

Orlando Heating and Cooling	Jan	Feb	Mar	Apr	May	Jun	Jul	Aug	Sep	Oct	Nov	Dec	Year
Heating Degree Days	234	164	65.0	5.0	0.0	0.0	0.0	0.0	0.0	0.0	54.0	164	686
Cooling Degree Days	70	58.0	117	191	369	483	536	543	480	316	144	74	3381

Orlando Precipitation	Jan	Feb	Mar	Apr	May	Jun	Jul	Aug	Sep	Oct	Nov	Dec	Year
Precipitation (inches)	2.3	3.0	3.2	1.8	3.5	7.3	7.2	6.8	6.0	2.4	2.3	2.1	48.1
Days with Precipitation over 0.01 inch	6.0	7.0	8.0	6.0	8.0	14.0	17.0	16.0	14.0	9.0	6.0	6.0	116
Monthly Snowfall (inches)	<.05	0.0	<.05	<.05	<.05	0.0	<.05	<.05	0.0	0.0	0.0	0.0	0.0

Other Orlando Weather Indicators	Jan	Feb	Mar	Apr	May	Jun	Jul	Aug	Sep	Oct	Nov	Dec	Year
Average Wind Speed	9.0	9.6	9.9	9.4	8.8	8.0	7.3	7.2	7.6	8.6	8.6	8.5	8.5
Clear Days	9.0	9.0	9.0	10.0	9.0	4.0	3.0	3.0	4.0	9.0	10.0	10.0	89.0
Partly Cloudy Days	10.0	9.0	10.0	11.0	14.0	14.0	17.0	17.0	15.0	11.0	10.0	9.0	147
Cloudy Days	12.0	11.0	12.0	9.0	9.0	12.0	11.0	11.0	12.0	11.0	10.0	12.0	130
Avg. Relative Humidity	61.5	72.5	70.5	69.5	67.5	70.0	74.0	75.5	76.0	75.0	73.5	72.5	73.5

Appendix 4 – Inspection Checklist

Checklist – Do-it-yourself inspection of Property	
Task	✔
Title	
Check the property corresponds with its description in the title	
number of rooms	
plot size	
Plot	
Identify the physical boundaries of the plot	
Is there any dispute with anyone over these boundaries?	
Are there any obvious foreign elements on your plot such as pipes, cables, drainage ditches, water tanks etc?	
Are there any signs of anyone else having rights over the property? Footpaths, access ways, cartridges from hunting etc?	
Garden/Terrace	
Are any plants, ornaments etc. on site not being sold with the property?	
Pool	
Is there a pool? If so:	
What size is it?	
Is it clean and algae free?	
Do the pumps work?	
How old is the machinery?	
Who maintains it?	
What is the annual cost of maintenance?	
Does it appear to be in good condition?	
Walls - Stand back from property and inspect from outside	
Any signs of subsidence?	
Walls vertical?	
Any obvious cracks in walls?	
Are walls well pointed?	
Any obvious damp patches?	
Any new repairs to walls or re-pointing?	
Roof – inspect from outside property	
Does roof sag?	
Are there missing/slipped tiles?	
Do all faces of roof join squarely?	

Checklist – Do-it-yourself inspection of Property	
Task	✓
Lead present and in good order?	
All present?	
Securely attached?	
Any obvious leaks?	
Any recent repairs?	
Enter Property	
Does it smell of damp?	
Does it smell "musty"	
Does it smell of dry rot?	
Any other strange smells?	
Doors	
Signs of rot?	
Close properly – without catching?	
Provide proper seal?	
Locks work?	
Windows	
Signs of rot?	
Close properly – without catching?	
Provide proper seal?	
Locks work?	
Excessive condensation?	
Floor	
Can you see it all?	
Does it appear in good condition?	
Any sign of cracked or rotten boards	
Under floor	
Can you get access under the floor?	
If so, is it ventilated?	
Is there any sign of rot?	
How close are joists?	
Are joist ends in good condition where they go into walls?	
What is maximum unsupported length of joist run?	
Is there any sign of damp or standing water?	
Roof Void	

Checklist – Do-it-yourself inspection of Property	
Task	✓
Is it accessible?	
Is there sign of water entry?	
Can you see daylight through the roof?	
Is there an underlining between the tiles and the void?	
Is there any sign of rot in timbers?	
Horizontal distance between roof timbers	
Size of roof timbers (section)	
Maximum unsupported length of roof timbers	
Is roof insulated – if so, what depth and type of insulation?	
Woodwork	
Any sign of rot?	
Any sign of wood boring insects?	
Is it dry?	
Interior walls	
Any significant cracks?	
Any obvious damp problems?	
Any sign of recent repair/redecoration?	
Electricity	
Check electricity meter.	
How old is it?	
What is its rated capacity?	
Check all visible wiring.	
What type is it?	
Does it appear in good physical condition?	
Check all plugs	
Is there power to plug?	
Does plug tester show good earth and show "OK"	
Are there enough plugs?	
Lighting	
Do all lights work?	
Which light fittings are included in sale?	
Water	
Do all hot and cold taps work?	
Is flow adequate?	

Checklist – Do-it-yourself inspection of Property	✓
Task	
Do taps drip?	
Is there a security cut off on all taps between mains and tap?	
Do they seem in good condition?	
Hot Water	
Is hot water "on"? If so, does it work at all taps, showers etc?	
What type of hot water system is fitted?	
Age?	
Gas	
Is the property fitted with city (piped) gas? If so:	
Age of Meter?	
Does installation appear in good order?	
Is there any smell of gas?	
Is the property fitted with bottled gas? If so:	
Where are bottles stored?	
Is it ventilated to outside of premises?	
Central Heating	
Is the property fitted with central heating? If so:	
Is it "on"?	
Will it turn on?	
What type is it?	
Is there hear at all radiators/outlets?	
Do any thermostats appear to work?	
Are there any signs of leaks?	
Fireplaces	
Is property fitted with any solid fuel heaters? If so:	
Any sign of blow back from chimneys?	
Do chimneys (outside) show stains from leakage?	
Do chimneys seem in good order?	
Air conditioning	
Which rooms are air-conditioned?	
Are units included in the sale?	
Do the units work (deliver cold air)?	
What type of air conditioning is it?	
How old is it?	

Checklist – Do-it-yourself inspection of Property	✓
Task	
Phone	
Does it work?	
Number?	
Satellite TV	
Does it work?	
Is it included in the sale?	
Drainage	
What type of drainage does property have?	
If septic tank, how old?	
Who maintains it?	
When was it last maintained?	
Any smell of drainage problems in bathrooms & toilets?	
Does water drain away rapidly from all sinks, showers and toilets?	
Is there any inspection access through which you can see drainage taking place?	
Is there any sign of plant ingress to drains?	
Do drains appear to be in good condition and well pointed?	
Kitchen	
Do all cupboards open/close properly?	
Any sign of rot?	
Tiling secure and in good order?	
Enough plugs?	
What appliances are included in sale?	
Do they work?	
Age of appliances included?	
Bathroom	
Security and condition of tiling?	
Ventilation?	
Appliances	
What appliances generally are included in sale?	
What is NOT included in sale?	
Furniture	
What furniture is included in sale?	
What is NOT included in sale?	

Checklist – Do-it-yourself inspection of Property	
Task	✓
Repairs/Improvements/Additions	
What repairs have been carried out in last 2 years?	
What improvements have been carried out in last 2 years/10 years?	
What additions have been made to the property in last 2 years/10 years?	
Do they have builder's receipts/guarantees?	
Do they have building consent/planning permission for any additions or alterations?	
Defects	
Is seller aware of any defects in the property?	

Checklist Extra things you may ask your Surveyor/Inspector to do
Task
Electrical condition and continuity check
Drains check, including assessment of drain to point where they join mains sewers or septic tank
Septic tank check
Rot check
Check on cement quality in a property constructed out of cement
Check of under floor areas, where access cannot easily be obtained
Check on heating and air conditioning
Check on pool and all pool related equipment and heating
Wood boring insect check. Roughly half of Florida is infested with termites, so this is important

Appendix 5– Signing a Contract Checklist

Checklist – Signing a contract	
Property in the course of construction	**Existing Property**
Are you clear about what you are buying?	
Have you taken legal advice about who should be the owner of the property?	
Have you taken legal advice about inheritance issues?	
	Are you clear about boundaries?
	Are you clear about access?

Checklist – Signing a contract	
Property in the course of construction	**Existing Property**
	Are you sure you can change property as you want?
	Are you sure you can use property for what you want?
	Connected to water, electricity, gas etc?
	Have you had a survey done?
Have you made all necessary checks OR arranged for them to be made?	
Have you included "get out clauses" for all important checks not yet made?	
Is your mortgage finance arranged OR a Get Out clause inserted in contract?	
Is the seller clearly described?	
If the seller is not signing in person, have you see a Power of Attorney/Mandate to authorise the sale?	
Are you fully described?	
Is the property fully described? Identification? Land Registry details?	
Is the price correct?	
Are any possible circumstances in which the price can be increased or extras described fully?	
Are the stage payments fully described?	Does contract say when possession will be given?
Do stage payments meet the legal restrictions?	Is there a receipt for the deposit paid?
Is the date for completion of the work agreed?	In what capacity is deposit paid?
Is the date for the closing agreed?	
Does contact provide for the sale to be free of charges and debts?	
Does contract provide for vacant possession?	
Is the estate agent's commission dealt with?	
What happens if there is a breach of contract?	
Are all the necessary special "get out" clauses included?	
Mortgage?	Mortgage?
Increase in price?	Survey?
	Planning certificate?
	Other?

Appendix 6 – Checklist – Signing the Deed of Sale

Checklist – Steps to be taken before signing the deed of sale	
Property in the course of construction	**Existing Property**
Prepare Power of Attorney	
Check what documents must be produced on signing *escritura*	
Confirm all outstanding issues have been complied with	
Confirm all other important enquiries are clear	
Confirm arrangements (date, time, place) for completion with your lender if you have a mortgage	
Confirm arrangements (date, time, place) for completion with notary	
Send necessary funds to Florida	
Receive rules of community	
Insurance cover arranged?	
Sign off work or list defects	Proof of payment of community fees
	Proof of payment of other bills

Appendix 7 - Common Legal Terms and their Meanings

Abstract (Of Title)
A summary of the public records relating to the title to a particular piece of land. An attorney or title insurance company reviews an abstract of title to determine whether there are any title defects which must be cleared before a buyer can purchase clear, marketable, and insurable title.

Acceleration Clause
A condition in a mortgage that may require the balance of the loan to become due immediately if regular mortgage payments are not made or for breach of other conditions of the mortgage.

Agreement of Sale
Known by various names, such as contract of purchase, purchase agreement, or sales agreement, according to location or jurisdiction. A contract in which a seller agrees to sell and a buyer agrees to buy, under certain specific terms and conditions, spelled out in writing and signed by both parties.

Amortization
A payment plan which enables the borrower to reduce his debt gradually through monthly payments of principal.

Appraisal
The estimate of value of real property made by an impartial expert, typically including references to sales of comparable properties to estimate the value. A lender will require an appraisal, but it does not take the place of an inspection.

Assessments
Costs charged for public improvements that benefit land. Pending assessments must be addressed in the purchase agreement and at closing.

Assumption of Mortgage
An obligation undertaken by the purchaser of property to be personally liable for payment of an existing mortgage. In an assumption, the purchaser is substituted for the original mortgagor in the mortgage instrument and the original mortgagor is to be released from further liability in the assumption, the mortgagee's consent is usually required.

The original mortgagor should always obtain a written release from further liability if he desires to be fully released under the assumption. Failure to obtain such a release renders the original mortgagor liable, if the person assuming the mortgage fails to make the monthly payments.

An "Assumption of Mortgage" is often confused with "purchasing subject to a mortgage." When one purchases subject to a mortgage, the purchaser agrees to make the monthly mortgage payments on an existing mortgage, but the original mortgagor remains personally liable if the purchaser fails to make the monthly payments. Since the original mortgagor remains liable in the event of default, the mortgagee's consent is not required to a sale subject to a mortgage.

Both "Assumption of Mortgage" and "Purchasing Subject to a Mortgage" are used to finance the sale of property. They may also be used when a mortgagor is in financial difficulty and desires to sell the property to avoid foreclosure.

Binder or "Offer to Purchase"
A preliminary agreement, secured by the payment of earnest money, between a buyer and seller as an offer to purchase real estate. A binder secures the right to purchase real estate, upon agreed terms for a limited period of time. If the buyer changes his mind or is unable to purchase, the earnest money is forfeited unless the binder expressly provides that it is to be refunded.

Broker
See Real Estate Broker

Building Line or Setback
Distances from the ends and/or sides of the lot beyond which construction may not extend. The building line may be established by a filed plan of subdivision, by restrictive covenants in deeds or leases, by building codes, or by zoning ordinances.

Certificate of Title

A certificate issued by a title company, or a written opinion rendered by an attorney, that the seller has good marketable and insurable title to the property which he is offering for sale. A certificate of title offers no protection against any hidden defects in the title which an examination of the records could not reveal. The issuer of a certificate of title is liable only for damages due to negligence. The protection offered a homeowner under a certificate of title is not as great as that offered in a title insurance policy.

Closing

The closing, also known as the settlement, is a meeting at which a transfer of sold property is finalized. At closing, the buyer signs the mortgage documents and pays all closing costs, and the seller signs the deed. Both parties sign the closing statement, which is an accounting of funds credited to the buyer and seller.

Closing Costs

The numerous expenses which buyers and sellers normally incur to complete a transaction in the transfer of ownership of real estate. These costs are in addition to price of the property and are items prepaid at the closing day. This is a typical list:

BUYER'S EXPENSES	SELLER'S EXPENSES
Documentary Stamps on Notes	Cost of Abstract
Recording Deed and Mortgage	Documentary Stamps on Deed
Escrow Fees	Real Estate Commission
Attorney's Fee	Recording Mortgage
Title Insurance	Survey Charge
Appraisal and Inspection	Escrow Fees
Survey Charge	Attorney's Fee

The agreement of sale negotiated previously between the buyer and the seller may state in writing who will pay each of the above costs.

Closing Day

The day on which the formalities of a real estate sale are concluded.

The certificate of title, abstract, and deed are generally prepared for the closing by an attorney and this cost charged to the buyer. The buyer signs the mortgage, and closing costs are paid. The final closing merely confirms the original agreement reached in the agreement of sale.

Cloud (On Title)

An outstanding claim or encumbrance which adversely affects the marketability of title.

Commission

Money paid to a real estate agent or broker by the seller as compensation for finding a buyer and completing the sale. Usually it is a percentage of the sale price. It is, typically, 6 to 7 percent on houses, 10 percent on land.

Condemnation

The taking of private property for public use by a government unit, against the will of the owner, but with payment of just compensation under the government's power of eminent domain. Condemnation may also be a determination by a governmental agency that a particular building is unsafe, or unfit for use.

Condominium

The owner of a condominium unit owns the unit and has the right, along with other unit owners, to use the common areas, which are owned by the condominium association. Condominium laws vary greatly from state to state, but typically include an association that maintains the building, pays taxes and insurance, and maintains the reserves for improvements.

Contract for Deed

A contract for deed is a contract that allows a buyer to take possession of property in exchange for monthly payments, until the balance is paid off, even though the seller maintains legal title to the property until the final payment is made. The parties negotiate the terms of a contract for deed.

Contract of Purchase

See Agreement of Sale

Contractor

In the construction industry, a contractor is one who contracts to erect buildings or portions of them. There are also contractors for each phase of construction: heating, electrical, plumbing, air conditioning, road building, bridge and dam erection, and others.

Conventional Mortgage

A mortgage loan not insured by HUD or guaranteed by the Veterans' Administration. It is subject to conditions established by the lending institution and State statutes. The mortgage rates may vary with different institutions and between States. States have various interest limits.

Cooperative Housing

An apartment building or a group of dwellings owned by a corporation, the stockholders of which are the residents of the dwellings. It is operated for their benefit by their elected board of directors. In a cooperative, the corporation or association owns title to the real estate. A resident purchases stock in the corporation, which entitles him to occupy a unit in the building or property owned by the cooperative. While the resident does not own his unit, he has an absolute right to occupy his unit for as long as he owns the stock.

Deed

A formal written instrument by which title to real property is transferred from one owner to another. The deed should contain an accurate description of the property being conveyed, should be signed and witnessed according to the laws of the State where the property is located, and should be delivered to the purchaser at closing day. There are two parties to a deed: the grantor and the grantee.

See also: Deed of Trust, General Warranty Deed, Quitclaim Deed, and Special Warranty Deed.

Deed of Trust

Like a mortgage, a security instrument whereby real property is given as security for a debt. However, in a deed of trust there are three parties to the instrument: the borrower, the trustee, and the lender, (or beneficiary). In such a transaction, the borrower transfers the legal title for the property to the trustee who holds the property in trust as security for the payment of the debt to the lender or beneficiary. If the borrower pays the debt as agreed, the deed of trust becomes void. If, however, he defaults in the payment of the debt, the trustee may sell the property at a public sale, under the terms of the deed of trust. In most jurisdictions where the deed of trust is in force, the borrower is subject to having his property sold without benefit of legal proceedings. A few States have begun in recent years to treat the deed of trust like a mortgage.

Default

Failure to make mortgage payments as agreed to in a commitment based on the terms and at the designated time set forth in the mortgage or deed of trust. It is the mortgagor's responsibility to remember the due date and send the payment prior to the due date, not after. Generally, thirty days after the due date if payment is not received, the mortgage is in default. In the event of default, the mortgage may give the lender the right to accelerate payments, take possession and receive rents, and start foreclosure. Defaults may also come about by the failure to observe other conditions in the mortgage or deed of trust.

Depreciation

Decline in value of a house due to wear and tear, adverse changes in the neighborhood, or any other reason.

Documentary Stamps

A State tax, in the forms of stamps, required on deeds and mortgages when real estate title passes from one owner to another. The amount of stamps required varies with each State.

Downpayment

The amount of money to be paid by the purchaser to the seller upon the signing of the agreement of sale. The agreement of sale will refer to the downpayment amount and will acknowledge receipt of the downpayment. Downpayment is the difference between the sales price and maximum mortgage amount. The downpayment may not be refundable if the purchaser fails to buy the property without good cause. If the purchaser wants the downpayment to be refundable, he should insert a clause in the agreement of sale specifying the conditions under which the deposit will be refunded, if the agreement does not already contain such clause. If the seller cannot deliver good title, the agreement of sale usually requires the seller to return the downpayment and to pay interest and expenses incurred by the purchaser.

Earnest Money

The deposit money given to the seller or his agent by the potential buyer upon the signing of the agreement of sale, to show that he is serious about buying the house. If the sale goes through, the earnest money is applied against the downpayment. If the sale does not go through, the earnest money will be forfeited or lost unless the binder or offer to purchase expressly provides that it is refundable.

Easement Rights

A right-of-way granted to a person or company authorizing access to or over the owner's land. An electric company obtaining a right-of-way across private property is a common example.

Encroachment

An obstruction, building, or part of a building that intrudes beyond a legal boundary onto neighboring private or public land, or a building extending beyond the building line.

Encumbrance

A legal right or interest in land that affects a good or clear title and diminishes the land's value. It can take numerous forms, such as zoning ordinances, easement rights, claims, mortgages, liens, charges, a pending legal action, unpaid taxes, or restrictive covenants. An encumbrance does not legally prevent transfer of the property to another. A title search is all that is usually done to reveal the existence of such encumbrances, and it is up to the buyer to determine whether he wants to purchase with the encumbrance, or what can be done to remove it.

Equity

The value of a homeowner's unencumbered interest in real estate. Equity is computed by subtracting from the property's fair market value the total of the unpaid mortgage balance and any outstanding liens or other debts against the property. A homeowner's equity increases as he pays off his mortgage or as the property appreciates in value. When the mortgage and all other debts against the property are paid in full, the homeowner has 100% equity in his property.

Escrow

Funds paid by one party to another (the escrow agent) to hold until the occurrence of a specified event, after which the funds are released to a designated individual. In FHA mortgage transactions, an escrow account usually refers to the funds a mortgagor pays the lender at the time of the periodic mortgage payments. The money is held in a trust fund, provided by the lender for the buyer. Such funds should be adequate to cover yearly anticipated expenditures for mortgage insurance premiums, taxes, hazard insurance premiums, and special assessments.

Foreclosure
A legal term applied to any of the various methods of enforcing payment of the debt secured by a mortgage, or deed of trust, by taking and selling the mortgaged property, and depriving the mortgagor of possession. Foreclosure proceedings vary by state, but typically include foreclosure by advertisement, which does not include a court proceeding, and foreclosure by action in court.

General Warranty Deed
A deed which conveys not only all the grantor's interests in and title to the property to the grantee, but also warrants that if the title is defective or has a "cloud" on it (such as mortgage claims, tax liens, title claims, judgments, or mechanic's liens against it) the grantee may hold the grantor liable.

Grantee
That party in the deed who is the buyer or recipient.

Grantor
That party in the deed who is the seller or giver.

Hazard Insurance
Protects against damages caused to property by fire, windstorms, and other common hazards.

HUD
U.S. Department of Housing and Urban Development. Office of Housing/Federal Housing Administration within HUD insures home mortgage loans made by lenders and sets minimum standards for such homes.

Interest
A charge paid for borrowing money. See mortgage note

Lien
A claim by one person on the property of another, as security for money owed. Such claims may include obligations not met or satisfied, judgments, unpaid taxes, materials, or labor. See also special lien.

Marketable Title
A title that is free and clear of objectionable liens, clouds, or other title defects. A title which enables an owner to sell his property freely to others and which others will accept without objection.

Mortgage
A lien or claim against real property given by the buyer to the lender as security for money borrowed. Under government-insured or loan-guarantee provisions, the payments may include escrow amounts covering taxes, hazard insurance, water charges, and special assessments. Mortgages generally run from 10 to 30 years, during which the loan is to be paid off.

Mortgage Commitment
A written notice from the bank or other lending institution saying it will advance mortgage funds in a specified amount to enable a buyer to purchase a house.

Mortgage Insurance Premium
The payment made by a borrower to the lender for transmittal to HUD, to help defray the cost of the FHA mortgage insurance program and to provide a reserve fund to protect lenders against loss in insured mortgage transactions. In FHA insured mortgages this represents an annual rate of one-half of one percent paid by the mortgagor on a monthly basis.

Mortgage Loan
A mortgage loan is a loan that is secured with a lien on real property. Forms of mortgages include fixed rate, adjustable-rate, and balloon mortgages. The functioning, legal effect, and foreclosure of a mortgage vary greatly from state to state.

Mortgage Note
A written agreement to repay a loan. The agreement is secured by a mortgage, serves as proof of an indebtedness, and states the manner in which it shall be paid. The note states the actual amount of the debt that the mortgage secures and renders the mortgagor personally responsible for repayment.

Mortgage (Open-End)
A mortgage with a provision that permits borrowing additional money in the future, without refinancing the loan or paying additional financing charges. Open-end provisions often limit such borrowing to no more than would raise the balance to the original loan figure.

Mortgagee
The lender in a mortgage agreement.

Mortgagor
The borrower in a mortgage agreement.

Plat
A map or chart of a lot, subdivision or community drawn by a surveyor showing boundary lines, buildings, improvements on the land, and easements.

Points

Sometimes called "discount points." A point is one percent of the amount of the mortgage loan. For example, if a loan is for $25,000, one point is $250. Points are charged by a lender to raise the yield on his loan at a time when money is tight, interest rates are high, and there is a legal limit to the interest rate that can be charged on a mortgage. Buyers are prohibited from paying points on HUD or Veterans' Administration guaranteed loans (sellers can pay, however). On a conventional mortgage, points may be paid by either buyer or seller or split between them.

Prepayment

Payment of mortgage loan, or part of it, before due date. Mortgage agreements often restrict the right of prepayment, either by limiting the amount that can be prepaid in any one year, or charging a penalty for prepayment. The Federal Housing Administration does not permit such restrictions in FHA insured mortgages.

Principal

The basic element of the loan as distinguished from interest and mortgage insurance premium. In other words, principal is the amount upon which interest is paid.

Purchase Agreement

See Agreement of Sale.

Quitclaim Deed

A deed which transfers whatever interest the maker of the deed may have in the particular parcel of land. A quitclaim deed is often given to clear the title when the grantor's interest in a property is questionable. By accepting such a deed the buyer assumes all the risks. Such a deed makes no warranties as to the title, but simply transfers to the buyer whatever interest the grantor has. (See Deed.)

Real Estate Broker

A licensed person or entity that represents either the buyer or seller in the purchase or sale of real estate, usually on a commission basis. A "dual" broker represents both parties in the same transaction. The terms of broker agreements are negotiable.

Real Estate Settlement Procedures Act

The Real Estate Settlement Procedures Act (RESPA) requires borrowers to receive disclosures regarding the costs associated with the settlement, the lender servicing and escrow account practices and the business relationships between settlement service providers. RESPA requires a mortgage lender to give the borrower a good faith estimate of the settlement service charges he or she is likely to have to pay.

Refinancing

The process of the same mortgagor paying off one loan with the proceeds from another loan.

Restrictive Covenants

Private restrictions limiting the use of real property. Restrictive covenants are created by deed and may "run with the land," binding all subsequent purchasers of the land, or may be "personal" and binding only between the original seller and buyer. The determination whether a covenant runs with the land, or is personal, is governed by the language of the covenant, the intent of the parties, and the law in the State where the land is situated. Restrictive covenants that run with the land are encumbrances and may affect the value and marketability of title. Restrictive covenants may limit the density of buildings per acre, regulate size, style or price range of buildings to be erected. or prevent particular businesses from operating or minority groups from owning or occupying homes in a given area. (This latter discriminatory covenant is unconstitutional and has been declared unenforceable by the U.S. Supreme Court.)

Sales Agreement

See Agreement of Sale.

Special Assessments

A special tax imposed on property, individual lots or all property in the immediate area, for road construction, sidewalks, sewers, streetlights, etc.

Special Lien

A lien that binds a specified piece of property, unlike a general lien, which is levied against all one's assets. It creates a right to retain something of value belonging to another person as compensation for labor, material, or money expended in that person's behalf. In some localities it is called "particular" lien or "specific" lien. See Lien.

Special Warranty Deed

A deed in which the grantor conveys title to the grantee and agrees to protect the grantee against title defects or claims asserted by the grantor and those persons whose right to assert a claim against the title arose during the period the grantor held title to the property. In a special warranty deed, the grantor guarantees to the grantee that he has done nothing during the time he held title to the property which has, or which might in the future, impair the grantee's title.

State Stamps

See Documentary Stamps.

Survey

A map or plat made by a licensed surveyor, showing the results of measuring the land with its elevations, improvements, boundaries, and its relationship to surrounding tracts of land. A survey is often required by the lender to assure him that a building is actually sited on the land according to its legal description.

Tax

As applied to real estate, an enforced charge imposed on persons, property or income, to be used to support the State. The governing body in turn utilizes the funds in the best interest of the general public.

Title

As generally used, the rights of ownership and possession of particular property. In real estate usage, title may refer to the instruments or documents by which a right of ownership is established (title documents), or it may refer to the ownership interest one has in the real estate.

Title Insurance

Protects lenders or homeowners against loss of their interest in property due to legal defects in title. Title insurance may be issued to a "mortgagee's title policy." Insurance benefits will be paid only to the "named insured" in the title policy, so it is important that an owner purchases an "owner's title policy", if he desires the protection of title insurance.

Title Search or Examination

A check of the title records, generally at the local courthouse, to make sure the buyer is purchasing a house from the legal owner and there are no liens, overdue special assessments, or other claims or outstanding restrictive covenants filed in the record, which would adversely affect the marketability or value of title.

Trustee

A party who is given legal responsibility to hold property in the best interest of, or for the benefit of, another. The trustee is one placed in a position of responsibility for another, a responsibility enforceable in a court of law. See deed of trust.

Zoning Ordinances

The acts of an authorized local government establishing building codes and setting forth regulations for property land usage.

Printed in Great Britain
by Amazon